HARRIS IN HISTORY AND LEGEND

For Chris

HARRIS IN HISTORY AND LEGEND

BILL LAWSON

BIRLINN

First published in 2002 by
John Donald Publishers,
an imprint of
Birlinn Limited
West Newington House
10 Newington Road
Edinburgh
EH9 1QS

Reprinted 2006, 2008

www.birlinn.co.uk

ISBN10: 1 84158 523 8
ISBN13: 978 1 84158 523 9

British Library Cataloguing-in-Publication Data
A catalogue record for this book is available
from the British Library

Typesetting and prepress origination by Brinnoven
Printed and bound by Antony Rowe, Chippenham

CONTENTS

Prologue   vii

Part One – The Machair   I

Part Two – Tarasaigh   38

Part Three – Caol na Hearadh   52

Part Four: An Tairbeart and na Baigh   92

Part Five – The Forest and Scalpaigh   140

Part Six – Hiort (St Kilda)   186

Epilogue   208

Appendix   209

References   211

Picture Credits   216

Maps   220

Index of Persons   222

Index of Main Topics   223

Index of Places   224

PROLOGUE

Clach MhicLeoid (MacLeod's Stone)

On the wild headland of Aird Nisabost, on the west coast of Harris, above a pure white Atlantic shell-beach, stands Clach MhicLeoid – MacLeod's Stone. The name is, of course, a recent one, as the stone is far older than the MacLeods, or their Viking ancestors. It is a relic of Neolithic times, which in Harris were about 5000 years

1. Clach MhicLeoid

ago, one of a set of three still standing along the western side of the island. Clach MhicLeoid stands about 12 feet high and the others, at Sgarasta and on the island of Tarasaigh, about 6 feet, and they were probably erected as calendar stones and as religious sites.

But why is it called MacLeod's stone? The most likely answer to that is that at the time when the MacLeod chiefs owned Harris, most of the people, of the south end at least, lived on the machair and the off-shore islands. When the chief wanted to gather them, for rent payment or for war, the Aird Nisabost stone was used as a central gathering point, visible from all the area around – and that is how it got the name MacLeod's Stone.

The Standing Stone had watched over much of the history of Harris. In its youth – perhaps even before it was hewn out of the rock – the Beaker people were making their homes across on Tarasaigh. That could have been about 5000 years ago, more or less, and still little shards of their pottery appear on the shore there, eroded out from the sand-banks. Then came the Bronze Age and the Iron Age – the age of the duns, or forts, some for refuge and others as watch-towers. Chains of the latter type are found all along the coasts, and speak of settled communities, sufficiently in touch with each other to send word of approaching danger – danger caused by an apparent deterioration in the climate and consequent competition for the best remaining land. The Stone had seen many a fire-message passed from the dun on Tarasaigh to the dun at Na Buirgh, alerting the machair people to a danger approaching from the sea.

Somewhere about 500 AD the stone would have seen the arrival of the first Christian missionaries, making their way up the west coast from bases in Iona and Lismore, only to be wiped out again by the raids of the Vikings in the 800s – wiped out except for the testimony of the place-names given by the Vikings, such as Pabaigh – 'Priest's Island'. The Vikings came first to raid, and then to settle as a ruling class, and the Stone remembered the days when the Norse galleys swept through the Sound of Tarasaigh, and the wrecking of one galley on an off-shore rock, still known as Bo Uspaig – the rock of Uspak, the Viking.

In 1266, the Islands were formally ceded to the Scottish Crown, and a half-Norse, half-Scottish lordship arose there – the

Lordship of the Isles. Here the descendants of Somerled the Viking established for themselves a realm to the west of Scotland, and for many years virtually independent of Scotland. Subject to them were other families with Viking roots, among them the MacLeods – descendants of Leod – who ruled Harris, and had given their name to the Stone. The Lordship had its own court, its own judges, its own bards, and formed a centre of culture independent of, and in many ways in opposition to, that based on the east coast of Scotland. As the Scottish kings developed a better grip on their mainland possessions, so they began to take more account of the Lordship, and when the then Lord of the Isles entered into the Treaty of Ardtornish, by which he and the English king were to partition Scotland between themselves, the struggle between the Lordship and the Scottish Crown reached its final stage, resulting in the downfall and destruction of the Lordship.

In 1494 John, the last Lord of the Isles, submitted to James IV of Scotland, but although the Scots Kings had been able to defeat the Lordship, they were unable to administer it. The various clans, which had been held together in a degree of peaceful government under the Lordship, were left without central control, and the period of inter-clan warfare began, fomented for their own reasons by the Scots Kings. A lasting symbol of the break-up of the power of the Lordship can be seen all over the Islands, as clan chiefs, who had hitherto been buried in Iona, the Lordship's religious centre, now began to assert their independence by building churches for their own family burial, like the MacLeod chiefs with their new Church at Roghadal.

As the clans jostled to fill the power vacuum left by the Lordship, so their raids on each other's lands began. The Stone could remember the great raid on Tarasaigh in 1544, but there had been many others, some now forgotten, and others remembered only in snatches of poetry or in sayings. Gradually the clans had achieved a form of peace and their tenure of lands became fixed. The chiefs, who had relied on their clansmen for support in battle, now began to look to them as a source of income, as they turned to farming in the more settled times.

The Stone remembered some of the great gatherings in the early 1700s, when MacLeod of Harris had gathered all his tenants together to pay their rent and to renew their leases. The settlement pattern then was very different from that of today. The modern centres of An Tairbeart and an t-Ob were merely a few houses on the shores, the rugged east coast, the Bays, was virtually empty, and the population was concentrated on the west machair shore, the off-shore islands, a few sheltered spots among the hills of North Harris, and around the religious centre of Roghadal.

The main centres of population were on the islands – Pabaigh, Bearnaraigh and Tarasaigh – where the land is more fertile than on the mainland, and on the machair strip running from Taobh Tuath to Losgaintir. Each village, in addition to its own town-lands, had a grazing area for airighean, or summer shielings, and these occupied most of the Bays, and large tracts of the North Harris hills, among which were also located the homes of the foresters, or gamekeepers, of MacLeod's deer-forest.

These villages were largely self-supporting, with some trade in small black cattle. In contrast to today, there were only a few sheep, but there was much more growing of small oats and bere. Bearnaraigh, Tarasaigh and Roghadal had good natural harbours, and fishing was a year-round occupation there. But the Atlantic-exposed shores of the machair on either side of the Stone had no harbours, and the people there had to rely on summer fishing in their shieling lands in the Bays.

In 1779 Harris had been sold to Captain Alexander MacLeod of Berneray. He reckoned that the fishings of Harris could be changed from a seasonal activity to a full-scale industry. This could only be done on the Bays side of the island, with its hundreds of little bays facing the Minch, so he constructed a harbour at Roghadal, and set up fishing stations all up and down the Bays. Some of the people of the machair and the islands had moved to these new villages, but many of the new settlers were from Lewis, Uist and Skye, together with masons, boatbuilders etc. brought in from the mainland. Captain MacLeod's experiment worked well for a few years, but after his death, much of the impetus was lost.

But already a new industry had appeared, which provided an unheard-of income for the islands, and in the end ruined their economy. This was the period of the French Wars, and with overseas markets closed to Britain, there was an unprecedented demand for minerals, many of which could be derived from the ash of kelp, or seaweed. The Bays and Islands of Harris were ideally suited for the collection and manufacture of kelp, and the whole economy of the island was changed to one based on the value of the seaweed. More and more people were encouraged to settle on barren shores, where they could not possibly feed themselves from the land – but that did not matter so long as there was employment on the kelp. The landlord had of course got most of the profits, but there had been plenty left over to buy food and to pay the rents, which had been increased to take account of the value of the weed on the shore. Even on the machair, the kelp cast ashore by the Atlantic storms had been gathered and burned, instead of being used for manure on the land – the Stone could remember the choking clouds of acrid smoke coming from the burning kelp.

After the wars came the inevitable crash. The continental markets were open again, and could produce better and cheaper minerals than could be got from kelp-burning. The price for kelp plummeted, and landlords and tenants alike lost their main source of income. Captain MacLeod's son and grandson had become society gentlemen on the strength of the kelp boom, and when it burst, it was reckoned that they lost three-quarters of their income. Unfortunately, like most Highland proprietors, they looked to their estates to replace their lost income. Rents were increased quite beyond the ability of the tenants to pay, despite the fact that they too had lost as great a proportion of their income.

Most of the landlords in the Highlands and Islands left the management of the estates to factors, and on Harris control of the estate was given to Donald Stewart, a sheep-farmer. His idea of a solution to the problem was to evict the crofters from every worthwhile bit of land, and to let it to a sheep-farmer. The Stone remembered the clearance of nearby Horgabost and Nisabost, some of the first villages to be cleared in Harris – it had been strange to have the land around its feet grazed by sheep, where there had once been cultivation, and the noise of people.

After the collapse of the kelp industry, many of the Harris crofters could see only too clearly what the future held. Those on the better lands were conscious of the threat of the expanding sheep-farms, and those on the kelp-shores could see no future but ever-increasing rents, with no income to pay them, and more and more people crowded on to the already insufficient land.

Cape Breton was being laid out for settlement at this time in the 1820s, and hundreds of families decided to emigrate and settle there, mainly around St Anns and Baddeck. When the Clearances began in earnest, the evicted people also went to Cape Breton, but since much of the better land had already been taken up, they tended to settle on the higher, poorer, land behind the coastal settlements, in areas like the North Shore, or at Loch Lomond and Grand River in south-eastern Cape Breton.

By the 1840s, there were no people left on the machair except a few sheep-farmers and their servants. For miles on either side of the Stone where there had been busy villages, there was now the desolation of the sheep farms, many of them run by Stewart and his own relatives.

Matters had become even worse with the advent of potato blight in the 1840s. In most of the Bays, the potato was the only food crop which could be grown on the poor land, and when that failed, there was no choice left but either emigration or destitution. Hundreds of families left from this area too, but by this time the potato blight was in Cape Breton also, so the destination of the emigrants changed to Australia, with the financial assistance of the Highlands and Islands Emigration Society.

The government was eventually forced to pay attention to the distress of the crofters, and the Napier Commission was set up to investigate the causes and possible cures for this distress. The Commission visited Harris in 1882, and the evidence given before them is a valuable record of the history of Harris. The Commission recommended a limited degree of security of tenure for crofters, and after the passing the Crofters Act in 1883, much of the harassment of crofters by factors ceased.

In the early 1900s, the Congested Districts Board supervised the setting-up of new crofting villages at Taobh Tuath and at Borgh in Bearnaraigh, while the Department of Agriculture sponsored a move to Portnalong and Fiskavaig in Skye and to the Loch Portain area of North Uist. After the First World War, the Department acquired the machair farms and resettled them as crofting townships. Once again the Stone could hear the sounds of people working their crofts – and if the sound was that of tractors instead of the horses of the old days, well – that was progress!

But the Stone also knows another story about its own origin – the one the old people told. Long ago, before the time of history, there was a Cailleach in Harris. The Gaelic word Cailleach means an old woman, but in this sense it means specifically a witch – and a fearsome witch she must have been! She was very fond of limpets – and if you have ever tried gathering limpets, you will know how difficult it is to dislodge them from their rocks. So the Cailleach had a stone hammer to knock the limpets off the rocks, and she wandered the shores, gathering her limpets. On Aird Nisabost she saw a particularly large one, and gave it a sideways hit with the hammer. Nothing happened! Another blow, and still nothing happened! Gathering all her strength, the Cailleach gave a third blow to the limpet, which flew off the rock into the sea. But the hammer broke into three pieces with the force of the blow, the smaller parts going flying across the sea, one to land on the island of Tarasaigh and the other along the shore at Sgarasta, and the largest part landing on the hill behind her, where it is still known as the Ord Bhairnich – the Limpet Hammer.

And there you have the two types of story we can tell about Harris. Some are based on historical fact, but others are yarns heard around the fireside. Some are true, and others might not be, but they are all well worth telling!

PART ONE – THE MACHAIR

Losgaintir (Luskentyre)

The village of Losgaintir lies at the end of a side-road from the main Harris road, and the views from that side-road must be among the most beautiful in the whole island – especially on a summer's evening, looking across the sea-pools and the sands against the light of a setting sun. At the end of the road is one of Harris's pure white stretches of shell-sand, with views across to the mountains of North Harris and to the island of Tarasaigh, while the machair itself is a carpet of wild flowers in the summer.

Machair is special to the Atlantic coasts of Scotland and Ireland. In the shallow seas of the Atlantic shelves are great forests of seaweed, and in them great colonies of shellfish. The shells are ground down and washed ashore in the winter storms and blown inland by the gales, giving the land a top dressing of lime-rich shell-sand. It is this wind-blown shell-sand which creates the machair and its lush summer vegetation, but it is a thin soil, liable to sand-blow and needing much feeding with seaweed and byre manure to bring it to its full potential. Many of the wild flowers, too, cannot break

2. Nightfall at Losgaintir

through an established sward of grass, and it is on land which has been ploughed in the last few years that the best range of machair flowers can be found.

The easily worked and fertile soil of the machair has been an attraction to settlers since prehistoric times, and until the late 1700s, the machairs of the west coast and the islands were the main areas of settlement in the Islands.

Robert Heron's *General View of the Hebrides*, published in 1794, gives a description of the various types of land tenure on the machair then.

> The inhabitants . . . consist of several classes, distinguished by gradations of rank and property. Mr MacLeod of Harris, the proprietor of the land of the island, receives, chiefly from tacksmen, to whom it is let out in extensive tracts, £888 sterling of yearly rent. Beside the farms possessed by the tacksmen, here are small tenant farms, possessed each by a number of petty tenants, who live together in a village, hold the farm by one common deed of tack, and have it parcelled out among them in penny and farthing divisions. The tacksmen's tenants differ from those in situation, only by holding from the tacksmen instead of the landlord, having no connection with one another in their tenures, and seldom having formally executed leases. The tacksmen's servants have their wages assigned them, in pasture for a cow, a horse, a breeding mare and any number of sheep; a farthing division of land for corn and potatoes, with a due proportion of sea-ware for manure; a kail-yard; fuel; an allowance of a peck of meal a week; beside a day in the week allotted for the cultivation of their own little possessions . . . The condition of the scallags, or servants, may be deemed hard; not so much because their labours are oppressive, or their wages unreasonably small, as because they are too entirely excluded from the choice of variety of employments, and of such a change of masters, as seems necessary to give the labourer comfortable independence.[1]

At the start of the eighteenth century, Losgaintir was a part of the great tack of Bearnaraigh, held by a cadet family of the MacLeods of Harris. In 1730 William MacLeod of Bearnaraigh gave up the tack of Bearnaraigh itself – for the usual reason of increased rent – and settled at Losgaintir. He died a few years later, in 1738, and is buried in the family caibeal – private burial enclosure – in the churchyard at Roghadal, where his son Alexander erected a tablet to his memory.

> Here lieth William MacLeod, eldest son to Sr. N. McLeod of Berneray by K. McDonald daur. to Sr. J. McDonald of Slate, who dyed upon ye 18th of Febr. 1738 in ye 77th year of his age. He was married to M. McKenzie, eldest daur. to Capt. K. McKenzie of Suddie and by her had sevl. Children, 4 of whom survived him viz. A. his eldest son ... R. McLeod, Wr. to the Signet, his 2nd son married to a daur. of Bannatyne of Keimes of Bute, Margt. married to ye Capt. of Clanranald & Alice to McNeil of Barray. He was good husband, a kind parent & master & a sincere friend, remarkable for Charity, Piety, Integrity of life, which made his death much regretted by all his friends and dependants.
>
> This Chappel was built by ye said A McL and this stone therein by ye said A McL in honour of his father.[2]

The sculptor who inscribed the tablet made a mistake after the words 'his eldest son' and had to erase the next few letters. Local legend has it that a son's name was erased because he disgraced the family, but a careful reading of the text and expansion of the abbreviated words shows that all four of the family are listed. Probably the legend arose from confusion with a kidnapping blamed on a son of a later MacLeod of Bearnaraigh – but that story belongs properly to Fionnsbhagh in the Bays.

Losgaintir passed in the late 1700s to Alexander's daughter Isabella and her doctor husband, William MacLeod of Glendale in Skye. William had a bad reputation for being a petty tyrant to his farm-workers and sub-tenants: John Lane Buchanan has plenty to say about him in his *Travels in the Western Hebrides* from 1782 to 1790.

> Soon after he had acquired possession of the vast tract of country already mentioned, he began, with undaunted courage, to double the rents of the subtenants, either by adding more money to their former rents, or by adding two or more tenants to one bay or town, by taking islands from another, by extorting some tuns of sea-ware for kelp from a third, though their lands should want manure and themselves bread; nay, and to erect new bays in places formerly altogether uninhabited.
>
> ... before he dared to practise those oppressions, he thought it adviseable to fortify himself by a strong matrimonial alliance. This

he did by marrying an old maiden lady; who, in her younger days, would have treated the idea of being united to such a man with the utmost scorn.[3]

John Lane Buchanan is particularly scathing in his comments on MacLeod of Losgaintir, but we do have to remember that he had just been dismissed from his post as missionary on the grounds of immoral behaviour, largely at MacLeod's instance, so his evidence may not be altogether trustworthy.

Mrs MacLeod herself was well enough liked – and a good bard. One of her songs about her own boys going off to the army is still sung in Harris.

Dh'fhalbh na gillean grinn
Fo'n cuid armaibh,
'S ann leam fhin a's boidheach
Thig an cota dearg dhoibh
Dh'fhalbh na gillean grinn.[4]

The bonny boys have left / each with his own gun. / They look so handsome to me / in their red jackets.

(I think I should state here that it is with the greatest trepidation that I have put in rough translations of Gaelic poetry throughout this book. I am only too aware that, except in the hands of another poet, translated poetry is usually doggerel, but it did seem necessary to me to give non-Gaelic readers some idea of the meaning of the words of a poem, even if the music of the words is wholly lost.)

One of the 'gillean grinn' was named Bannatyne after his grandfather's brother's wife, who was one of the Bannatynes of Port Bannatyne in Bute. He got on well with the local people, and one time he gave a golden guinea as a christening present to one of the farm-workers' children across in Seilibost. A golden guinea was well worth having, so all the families in Seilibost called a son 'Bannatyne', and that is why you still find the name here, though it is usually shortened in speech to 'Panny'. If you find a family with the name Panny anywhere in the islands, you can be sure that it traces back to Seilibost.

After a few years, the doctor gave up the lease of Losgaintir and removed to Steornabhagh (Stornoway). James Hogg, the Ettrick Shepherd, thought of taking part of the farm for a time, and a formal lease was even drawn up, which gives an interesting description of the rights of the farmer.

> William MacLeod subsets the grazing of Shelibost marching on the one side with Horguebost and on the other with the river of Laxdale, reserving to himself the sea ware growing on the rocks alongst the shore of Shelibost and liberty to cut his peats as usual on the south side of the river of Laxdale also reserving the whole salmon fishing on the water of the said river, also liberty if required to pluck heather on the hills for ropes to houses. Also subsets the use of the two houses now in Shelibost and the cast sea-ware for manure to the ground, with the whole hill belonging to Shelibost and Luskinter and the pendicle of Laxdale and Bay of Meavac with the liberty of grazing such of the horses of the farm of Luskinter as may be necessary.[5]

The plan fell through and Losgaintir, along with Seilibost, passed eventually to one Donald Stewart, of a mainland family who had been shepherds in the Pairc area of Lewis. The Stewarts had a bad enough reputation there, and the tenants of Bearnaraigh tried to keep him out of Harris by offering a higher rent for Losgaintir themselves, but the estate preferred Stewart – and the clearance of the villages of the machair began.

When the sheep farms began to fail in the face of competition from Australia, all the northern part of the machair and the hills behind it became deer forest, with its main hunting lodge at Losgaintir. After the First World War, Losgaintir was broken into crofts for families who were threatening to raid the farm of Sgarasta Bheag, and it is now firmly on the tourist map, partly for the beauty of the area, and partly because of Donald John and Maureen MacKay, whose specialist patterns of Harris Tweed are justly famous.

Neil MacDonald was one of the raiders on Sgarasta Bheag who later got a croft in Losgaintir, and his song *Oran an Reididh* – Song of the Land-raids – tells the story of the machair.

> Eisdibh rium, a shluaigh nam beannaibh
> Thoiribh aire, ghillean og;
> A h-uile neach a chluinn an duan seo,
> Togail suas e le deagh cheol.

Chaidh ar cairdean chur an fuadach,
Cuid dhiubh dh'fhuarbheannaibh a' cheo
'S a dh'Ameireaga air chuantan
Siud mar chuala sinn na sgeoil.

Thainig saighdearan bhon Bhanrigh
Dhan an aite seo gun choir;
Dh'fhasaich iad an taobh a bh'fhearr dheth
'S dha na Baigh gun deach an corr

Is 'nan aite chuir iad caoraich,
Cuid dhiubh maol, is damh nan croic
'S nuair a thoisich blar na daorsa
Cha robh h-aon dhiubh air an leoin[6]

Listen to me, people of the hills / pay attention, young boys / everyone who hears this song / raise it to a good tune. / Our friends were put to flight – / some of them to the misty mountains / and America across the seas – / so we hear in story. / The soldiers of the Queen came / to this place unjustly. / They cleared the better part of it / And sent the rest to the Bays. / In their place they put sheep – / hornless sheep and antlered deer. / When the fight for freedom began, / none of these were among the wounded.

A trace of the old deer forest still remains on many maps, where Beinn Losgaintir and the surrounding area are shown as the 'South Harris Forest'. Unfortunately the Ordnance Survey, in their new maps with Gaelic place-names, translated this as 'Coille Ceann a Deas na Hearadh', not realising that the proper Gaelic for a deer forest is frith and that coille means trees – there must be many a perplexed visitor hunting in vain for the trees on the slopes of Beinn Losgaintir! To be fair to the Ordnance Survey, they have changed the latest edition of the map to 'Frith'.

The hill of Beinn Losgaintir itself is well worth climbing for the view. From the Losgaintir side it is a steady, though stiff, climb to the top, but on the north side it drops in cliffs and gullies to West Loch Tairbeart. The cliffs on that side are dangerous, and it was there on the Tarcla that Duncan Campbell, the grieve, or farm manager, of Losgaintir fell to his death in 1875.

Seilibost

Seilibost had at one time been a part of the tack of Losgaintir, but in the early 1800s it was divided into crofts. Previously most of the

3. Seilibost and Beinn Losgaintir

townships of Harris had been nuclear villages, with the houses all together in a clachan, and the land held as a single unit, divided annually in rotation between the joint tenants, according to their needs and abilities. Crofting, on the other hand, gave each tenant his own strip of land, for the rent of which he was wholly responsible. The nuclear village had the disadvantage that the tenant could have a different piece of land each year, and so would have little incentive to improve it, whereas in the croft, his landholding was fixed, and so worth improving. The drawback to crofts was that in the nuclear village a family who had fallen on hard times could take a smaller share of the township land and of the liability for rent, whereas in a croft, the tenant was liable for the whole rent, and if he could not pay, risked eviction and the loss of everything.

The purpose of the introduction of the crofting system was to get as many people on to the land as possible. This was the period of the boom in the kelp trade, and the landlords wanted as large an employment pool as possible on their estates. Crofts were intentionally made too small to maintain a family by agriculture alone, so that the tenants would have to take work on the kelp in order to supplement their income. Crofting was never intended to be a full-time occupation, and crofters relied on ancillary employment also, and it is the loss of this employment – mainly weaving and fishing – which has created such problems for the crofting communities today.

The crofting of Seilibost and the other machair villages was successful so long as the kelp trade prospered, but when that began to fail, in the 1820s, arrears of rent began to mount, and the estates began to look for alternative sources of income. Large-scale sheep farming looked to be a preferable source of income, and the days of crofting on the machair were numbered.

It was a bad day for Harris when Donald Stewart came to Losgaintir as a sheep-farmer. When he became MacLeod's factor nothing would do for him but that he would turn the whole of the machair side of Harris into sheep-farms, and send the people away to Canada. Sgarasta had already been cleared, but Stewart cleared na Buirgh, and in 1838 evicted the last of the people from Seilibost.

Not content with clearing the living, he had to clear the dead out as well, for he took over the graveyard that the Seilibost people had at Cnoc na h-Iodhlainn, and ploughed it up. Alexander Carmichael, commenting on the encroachment of the sea on the coast of Tarasaigh while visiting there in 1877, remarks:

> The tide being as ruthless as Stewart who had Loscintir and who ploughed the *cladh* [burial ground] the people had at Seilibost, the oldest in Harris, till skulls and thigh bones etc. were rolling about on the surface of the ground like stones in a stony field, the ground being literally covered with them. The crops were so heavy that the place had to be kept from manure for many years. That is when they made the graveyard at Losgaintir itself. These Stewarts were the greatest curse that ever came upon Harris.[7]

But the Stewarts lost in the end, for Seilibost was turned back into crofts again a hundred years later, after the First World War, and the big rock, where Stewart poured out the pails of milk when Norman MacKenzie was evicted from his house became the cornerstone of the new house his great-grandson built.

If you were cleared out of your house in those days, you might be able to find a site in the Bays; there was plenty of stone there to build a house, and heather for a roof, but where were you going to find timber for roof-timbers? In the old houses, timbers had been gathered from the shores – and in one house on the island of Scarp, whalebone had been used. That is why it was so final when the factor burned the houses: without the roof-timbers you couldn't build another house. So after the first burning of the houses, when people were threatened with clearance, they dismantled the roof themselves and took the timbers with them; and there are many stories of families going through the moors to the Bays of the east coast, the women and children carrying what furnishings they could, and the men carrying the old roof-timbers.

It is sometimes assumed that if the Clearances had not happened, life in the islands would have continued in an idyllic form. Of course this would not have been so, and even in pre-Clearance times, there were major problems. The Revd John MacLeod, writing about Harris in the *Statistical Account* of 1792, described the methods of agriculture whereby the land, after being manured, would yield one year's crop of potatoes, then two of small oats, then three or four of grass, before being cultivated again. He added:

> The grass is the main object for which the farmer labours. It is not for the best returns yielded by his crop of corn that he is at the toil and trouble above described, but chiefly to lay in a store of winter provender for his cattle, and to improve their summer pasture, by meliorating the natural barrenness of the soil as far as circumstances will permit. Could these ends be otherwise obtained, no corn crops ought at all to be raised here, especially on any of the lands unmanageable to the plough; for though no people labour harder, beginning this dreary process so early as the month of November, and continuing it occasionally, as the weather permits, as the cast of the sea-ware may chance to come, and as the necessary attention to their cattle and to the other branches of husbandry allows them, till the month of June; yet the whole produce of the three crops, barley, potatoes and oats, may be fairly estimated at little more than 2000 bolls, Linlithgow measure, even in the best of years; and in bad years the crops fail so miserably as to yield little more than the seed requisite for the next sowing . . . All the bread is generally consumed before the month of June; and such as cannot then afford to purchase imported meal, subsist chiefly on the milk of their cows and sheep, with what fish they may chance to catch, till their wants are relieved by the first fruits of their potatoe crop early in harvest.[8]

It can be argued that MacLeod gives a pessimistic view of the agricultural economy because he himself was of the tacksman class, but 1792 is well before the beginning of any move towards clearance, so he had little reason to show bias in his report.

It is clear then that the agricultural economy of Harris was on a balance of profitability – a good year could give a profit, but a bad one meant scarcity.

With the advent of the kelp industry, much of the sea-ware that had been used for manuring the soil was diverted to burning for kelp-ash. The land suffered, as did the crops, and what had been a borderline economy became even more difficult. Many families emigrated, especially to the newly available lands in Cape Breton – facing the difficulties of life in a new land seemed preferable to remaining in the deepening economic depression of the old one. Despite this, population numbers rose in Harris, putting further pressure on the economy. It would be an exaggeration to say that the Clearances merely removed those families who had not already been able to remove themselves, but like most exaggerations, there is quite a lot of truth in it.

In the Dunvegan Estate Papers, we find cases of tenants being granted 'rests' – years free of rent – because of their poor circumstances, but when the relationship between landlord and tenant became more commercial after the Battle of Culloden in 1746, there was less sympathy for the tenant in a bad year. Still, there was no great danger of dispossession, for what other prospective tenant was any better off? Once the sheep-farmers turned their eyes to Harris, however, there was an alternative tenant for the land, with capital to carry him over a bad year, and the days of the crofter on the machair were numbered. Taobh Tuath and Horgabost were cleared first, then Sgarasta and na Buirgh. Part of Seilibost was cleared in 1829 and the remainder in 1838, and not a single crofter was then left on the machair, only a few cottars and farm-workers, allowed to remain because their labour was necessary to the new farmers.

At the moor end of Seilibost, at the end of the present-day causeway, is a little hill called Cleit na Duthca, with the ruins of two houses at the shore. One of these belonged to Neil Morrison – Niall Choinnich Neill – who spent several years shepherding on the island of Pabaigh and is better known as Am Bard Pabach – the Pabaigh Bard. In the other house was a widow with her son Donald – Domhnall Bessa – who went to Pabaigh along with the Bard. He was not very bright, for Neil refers to him as

'Domhnall gorach, le seacaid bhan air' – 'Foolish Donald, in his white jacket.'[9]

When Seilibost was cleared only one house was left, for the dairymaid Oighric Mhor. Every day she had to cross the bay to Losgaintir Farm, and that could be dangerous, for Seilibost Bay itself is a huge expanse of white sand at low tide, but the tide comes in quickly, and there is quicksand behind the mouth of the river. That is where John MacKenzie – Iain Thormoid Ruairidh – was drowned in 1865, when his horse stumbled in the quicksand and he was thrown into the river, and it was under the surface of the sand that they found their bodies.

To make sure that not a scrap of grazing was lost, Oighric Mhor's house was built right on the shore of Seilibost Bay at a spot called Luib a' Speuradair – the Stargazer's Corner. Who knows who was the man who watched the stars, but Oighric certainly watched the sea, for they had to build a turf barricade outside the door, to keep the high tide out.

Seilibost became part of the deer forest, and the corner of the hill to the east of Luib a' Speuradair is still called Creag Royal, after a 'royal' – a stag with fourteen points to its antlers – which was shot there.

Seilibost east of Creag Royal is reckoned as a separate entity, under the name of Crago, and it is here that the old 'coffin-road' from the Bays reaches the west coast. A new causeway cuts across the head of the bay here, with its salt-flats of thrift or sea-pink – a haze of pink above the water in the summer.

I remember camping once on a little green patch of flat ground, beside the bridge where the old road crosses Allt Gil an Tailleir – the stream of the tailor's gully. As it got dark, I realised that there were eyes watching me from the stonework of the bridge! I wish I had known then the opening verses of Bard Pabach's 'Oran an Rodain':

'S dh'aithnichinn rodain Bho na Ghille
'S iad bu ghile na cuid Chrago[10]

You can tell the rats of Bun na Gill – / they are whiter than those in Crago

I did not wait there long enough to check on their colour!

Horgabost

The very name of Horgabost is full of history, for it is the name
the Vikings gave to the place over a thousand years ago '-bost' for
a village and 'Horgr' for a grave – and not just any grave. Here, at
the corner of the village road, are the remains of a chambered cairn,
which could be 5000 years old and more. So today we are calling
the village by the name the Norsemen gave to it, because of the
ancient grave they found! And not just the one grave – the whole
headland between here and MacLeod's Stone is a mass of burials,
underground houses and the like; it must have been an important
settlement in prehistoric times.

The chambered cairn is now known as Coire na Feinne, the
Cauldron of the Feinne – the followers of the Gaelic folk-hero Fionn
mac Cumhail – but of course it is far, far older than the Feinne.
There are seven stones in a circle – Na Seachd Sagairtean, the seven
priests, they were called locally – and a great flat stone on the top.
Captain Otter of the Naval Survey took a huge skull out of the cairn
and it is still in a museum in Edinburgh.

Horgabost is now the home of Donald MacDonald – Domhnall
Sham – one of the best traditional singers on Harris today.
Domhnall's parents were among the settlers who came back to the
machair after the First World War, and brought its land back into
cultivation, after years of sheep monoculture, followed by more
years of neglect as a part of the deer forest. Even today, with the
turn-down in the crofting economy, there are still cattle kept in
Horgabost, and a different area of machair is ploughed each year as
a communal potato plot.

As well as a singer, Domhnall is a bard in his own right.

Nuair bhios mi san Aird
aig Ord Bhairneach Mhic Leoid
Chan eil sealladh cho alainn
an cearn san Roinn-Eorp

A' ghrian 's i gam fhagail
's i dearrsadh mar or,
Dol sios air Aird Mhanais
's air Gaisgeir nan ron

When I am on the headland / at MacLeod's limpet-stone. / There
is not such a beautiful place / in this quarter of Europe. / The

4. Horgabost

departing sun / gleaming like gold / going down over Aird Mhanais / and Gaisgeir of the seals.

Horgabost was among the first townships in Harris to be cleared for sheep, as early as 1810, and the first farmer here was an Alexander Torrie from Argyll. You can still see the ruins of Faing an Thorraidh – Torrie's sheep-pens – on the hill above the village, and until the village was re-settled in 1935, the people round about and on Tarasaigh island always called it Torraidh.

Horgabost and Tarasaigh are linked by one of the classical stories of Harris. There was a battle on Tarasaigh in 1544 – part of the troubles in the downfall of the Lordship of the Isles. The Morrisons of Ness in Lewis were the brieves or judges of the Lordship, and they had invaded Harris, led by Eoghann, or Hugh, the son and heir of the brieve. First they raided Huisinis, where only one man escaped and took word of the raid to MacLeod of Bearnaraigh. The Morrisons had in the meantime raided Tarasaigh, and it was there that MacLeod found them, feasting after victory. Mac-Iain, writing in the *Celtic Magazine* in 1879, tells the rest of the story.

Arriving at the village of Tarnsay, MacLeod found the Morrisons regaling themselves after having massacred every soul on the island, and listening for a moment at the window of the house in which the Morrisons were feasting, MacLeod heard one of them remark that something very wonderful was wrong with him; 'For,' he said 'although I can chew my food as well as ever, I cannot swallow anything.' 'And that is a great pity,' said Berneray loud enough to be heard by the revellers, 'for soon you will neither be able to chew or swallow!' In a second the speaker inside was a corpse by Berneray's well-directed arrow. This was the signal for a general attack . . . Finding that their case was desperate, the Morrisons retreated, shouting at the top of their voices 'Gu sgeir, gu sgeir, a bhallachaibh Leodhais' – to the rock, to the rock, ye lads of Lewis. The rock was a small one in the vicinity of the place where the fight took place, and although it can be reached dry-shod at low water, the sea surrounded it at full flood. The rock received that day the name of the Sgeir Bhuailte, or smitten-rock, which it bears to the present time, and when any great disturbance of the sand takes place by the storm, large numbers of men's bones may yet be seen around the smitten-rock.

The solitary Morrison who escaped with his life was Eoghann himself – which he did by jumping into the sea, and swimming across the sound to the mainland of Harris. He landed on a rock on Traigh Thorgobost, which rock has been called Sgeir Eoghainn, or Ewen's rock, ever since.[11]

The version of the story current in Horgabost today adds that as Ewen came ashore he remarked 'Faodaidh mi nis' an da shaigheid a tha na mo thoin a shlaodadh a mach!' – I have time now to remove the two arrows stuck in my back-side![12]

Na Buirgh (The Borves)

There were three villages here at one time: Borgh Mhor, Borgh Mheadhanach and Borgh Bheag – Big, Middle and Little Borves – but they were all cleared out to make room for a sheep-farm in 1839. Donald Stewart of Losgaintir had the farms on either side, and he refused to renew his lease unless he got Na Buirgh as well. Stewart was too good a tenant to lose, so the crofters had to go. But they proved unwilling, and the estate took fright. According to the factor's report 'a conspiracy for resisting the law existed in all this quarter of the West Highlands, which, if not at once checked, would lead to consequences no lover of order would care to think about'.[13] So the army was sent for, as reported in the *Inverness Courier* of July 1839.

On Saturday, Lieutenant M'Neill with his party of soldiers returned to Glasgow from the Island of Harris, after an absence of nine days. He has been successful in the object of his mission, and, we are glad to learn, without violence. They reached Harris at 7 o'clock on the morning of Tuesday last, the 23rd, and were enabled to leave it at 6 the same evening. All the cottars or small farmers implicated in the deforcement were requested to assemble at the village, and from the body five men, who had been most active in the illegal proceedings, were selected and carried prisoners to Portree. The visit of the military excited the deepest alarm among the poor islanders, who were heard to express in Gaelic their terror that the scene of Glencoe was about to be acted over again.[14]

'Thus', according to the factor 'terminated an outbreak which, but for the prompt measures of the Government in sending in the military, would have thrown the whole of the West Highlands into confusion for many years'[15] – so severe an outbreak that it could be dealt with by calling the people to a meeting and selecting five of them to take to jail!

Alec Mor in Direcleit used to hear about the 'battle' from his neighbour Ceit Ruadh (Red Kate) up in Cadha. Her father was Donald Urquhart, who had come to Harris as a shepherd from Gairloch, and was working at the time in Sgarasta, which had already been cleared for sheep. Ceit was only eight years old at the time, but she had come along with her father to see what was happening, and the captain of the soldiers had asked her to hold his horse while he spoke to the Borgh people; what a magnificent horse it was, not like the carthorses she was used to – and she got a halfpenny for holding its reins! All the rest of her family went off to Australia, but Ceit married in Harris and stayed here till she died – and even as an old woman she would still tell the story of the halfpenny she got for holding the war-horse at Borgh.

Many of the Borgh people went across to Cape Breton in Canada, and there is a story still told there about one of them, Iain Choinnich Iomhair (John MacLeod.) He had ended up at Cape North in Cape Breton, and even by Cape Breton standards, that was remote – away up in the north of the island and cut off by snow every winter. Iain had been married twice, and as it happened they had one of their very rare visits from a minister at the time that his second wife died, so they had a formal funeral service. On the way home from the funeral, Iain met the sister of one of his neighbours. 'How are you going to look after the children,' she asked, 'with you away at the fishing so much?' 'Well, I suppose I'll just have to get married again.' 'Well, if you asked me, I would take you,' she said. So he did – and she did! 'Right,' said Iain 'let's run back to the church and catch the minister before he leaves.' And so he married his third wife on the afternoon of the funeral of the second – but if they had not taken the chance then, who knows when they would next have seen a minister to marry them.

Murdo Morrison – Murchadh Iain Mhoir – of Caolas Scalpaigh told the Napier Commission of 1883 about some of those cleared.

> I remember, in the time of the wars of Boney [Bonaparte], hearing from my father and my grandfather how soldiers were drafted out of Harris. I remember their telling me of four so drafted from the machair down there which they commenced to clear to make room for sheep – four who fought at the Battle of Waterloo. Three fell on the field, and one of them died in hospital afterwards. Three of the men were James MacLeod, Malcolm Morrison and Angus MacGillespie. Instead of the widows of these men being looked after, they were driven to the wild woods of Canada, and the lands that they possessed were placed under sheep. That was the justice meted out to them.[16]

Strangely enough, Borgh was cleared twice. In 1847 a new factor decided to settle crofters there again, to prove whether crofting could be economically viable, and brought in the most successful crofters from all over the island. But he left, and another factor was appointed who was a sheep-farmer himself, and he made sure that the crofters failed by taking away their cattle as security for the rent. Without stock, they had no income, and so could not pay the rent. By 1853 Borgh had been cleared again, and the prosperous tenants who had been put there were reduced to poverty.

Kenneth MacDonald – Coinneach Sgoilear – the factor of Harris and tenant of Sgarasta Mhor tells the story.

> Three townships were taken from the farm of Luscantire, and the very best and most comfortable tenantry were selected from all parts of Harris to occupy these three townships. They did stock them

fully. In the year 1851 one of these new townships – Borvore – was
ruined, and had to yield. Then Captain Sitwell, who had this idea
in his head, said, 'We will carry on the other two townships.' They
were carried on, but in the year 1853 they had to succumb, and were
left all poor men. They came there quite comfortable and left it poor.
So that even if these parts of Harris were partitioned I should not
be very sanguine of the consequences, seeing by experience what
happened to those three townships which were selected.[17]

John MacLeod (Iain a' Chubair) from Aird Asaig has another side
to the story.

> My father's family was sent to Borve in 1846, and before that he was
> in Pabbay, in good circumstances there. In the first place we went to
> we were allowed to remain three years – that was Big Borve. They
> wanted to add Big Borve to the tack of Scarista-vore. I believe the
> tenants of Big Borve were behind with their rent. The years were
> very bad, and there was no price for cattle. The prices rose the very
> year they left, and never fell to the same point since.
>   Then we were removed to Little Borve, and stayed there two
> years, until we were put out of it. Some of the rent was unpaid.
> When the people were summoned out of this Little Borve, the factor
> told them that if they got security that they would pay £100 at the
> next market, they would not be disturbed that year. The minister
> that was in Scarista at the time offered to become security for the
> required amount, but they would not accept that security. The
> minister said at the time they were sent away that the poorest man
> in the country might become security for them, because they had
> sufficient stock to meet the demands upon them.[18]

As usual when a village was cleared, a few landless cottars were left
living there to provide labour for the farmers. My friend Magaidh
in Sruth Mor used to tell how her own grandmother, Mairead
Dhughaill, was going to be sent to look after her father's cousin
Anna ni'n Aonghais – Ann MacLeod – who lived up in the strath
above Borgh Bheag, where she kept a shebeen and sold illicit
whisky. Magaidh never heard whether Anna distilled the whisky
herself, or whether it was smuggled onto the island, but that
was what she always heard, that Anna kept a shebeen. Whatever
happened, the scheme fell through, and Mairead never went to
Borgh Bheag.

Sgarasta (Scarista)

All the old villages in Harris were on the machair and the off-shore islands, for the machair – the green grasslands along the shores, where the winter winds blew the shell-sand from the beaches to sweeten the land – was the best arable land, unlike the Bays of the east coast, which were nothing but rock. Of all the machair villages, the largest was Sgarasta, with Sgarasta Mhor to the north of the parish church and Sgarasta Bheag to the south. Not that the parish church was always here – at one time it was at the Uidh, out beyond Taobh Tuath, and the minister lived on the island of Easaidh in the Sound of Harris, but the Revd Aulay MacAulay from Lewis moved it to Sgarasta in the early 1700s. There had been a church here long before that: Kilbride, or St Bride's Church. The old rentals refer to the 'kirkpenny' as a part of Sgarasta – the 'pennyland' was an old measure of the value of land – and this would have been the piece of land around the old church.

Some ancient gravestones were discovered recently, hidden under the turf of the graveyard. One of them has the standard sword motif used to designate a warrior, while another is beautifully decorated in a style more suggestive of a woman's grave. It is known that the Campbells of Tarasaigh were buried at Sgarasta, and it would be surprising if there are no stones to commemorate such an important

5. The old farmhouse at Sgarasta Bheag

6. Clach Steineagaidh

tacksman family. On the other hand, we know of other cases where old stones have been re-used – there are examples at Aignis in Lewis and Cille Mhoire in Uist – and it seems quite likely that Kenneth Campbell of the Uidh could have picked up some ancient stones on his travels, and used them for his own family! One of the stones in Sgarasta looks as if it has been abraded by water, and it is interesting in this context that one of the MacKay boys from Losgaintir saw a stone with carving on it in the sea off Traigh Sgaoin on Tarasaigh on the occasion of a very low tide.

There is a standing stone at Sgarasta too – Clach Steineagaidh – and, as with most ancient sites, like the cairn at Horgabost, local tradition ascribes it to the Feinne.

Their cuid anns a' bhaile
(Mas e firinn neo breug e)
Gur clach-cinn i bh'air ceannard
Ann an cogadh na feinne

Ma bhios armachd is eallach
A rithist ag eirigh
Nach e gheibh an damaisd
Tighinn a-mach fo Chlach Steineagaidh![19]

Some in the village say / (Be it true or false) / that it is the headstone
of a chief / from the days of the wars of the Feinne. / If arms and
battle should arise again / wouldn't he cause havoc, / coming out
from Clach Steineagaidh?

So wrote Seonag NicSuain – Joan MacSween – who was born
within sight of it.

They say that the first cleireach or church-officer there was a
MacIver from Uig in Lewis, who was left a legacy by the Revd
MacAulay for showing the place where the great Maighstir
Amhlaidh was buried, at the door of the old church. A later cleireach,
Murdo MacKay, whose ancestor is said to have been shipwrecked
at Gob an Tobha, on the other side of the sands, was an ancestor of
Finlay J. MacDonald, the writer and broadcaster, who told me that
his ancestor had been shipwrecked from the Spanish Armada, but,
as Finlay J. said himself in his book *Crowdie and Cream*,[20] the date
was more than a century out – and Murdo MacKay was one of the
less likely Spanish names!

A rental of 1818 shows fourteen crofts in Sgarasta Bheag and
ten crofts and four half-crofts in Sgarasta Mhor, and no doubt
there would have been plenty of other households not paying rent –
younger brothers and their families, and unmarried uncles and
aunts. But Donald Stewart of Losgaintir was looking out for more
land for his sheep, and in 1828 the factor decided that the people
had to go, in order to leave Sgarasta Mhor for Stewart and Sgarasta
Bheag as a glebe for the minister. Most of the families went to Cape
Breton in Canada, and a hard time of it they had there, before they
cleared the forest and cultivated the land; but at least there they
were their own masters, and needed no longer to fear a factor who
thought that a few more acres for sheep were more important than
a whole community of people.

In 1843 the Church of Scotland broke apart in the Disruption and
the bulk of the people in the Islands joined the new Free Church
of Scotland, apart from the farmers and merchants; it is noticeable
that nearly all the monuments in the nineteenth-century graveyard
in front of the church are for merchants in An Tairbeart.

The minister at Sgarasta then was John MacIver, though he left
very soon after the Disruption. He was asked to provide the section
on Harris for the *New Statistical Account of Scotland* in 1841, though

his article is one of the shortest and least informative in that series. He does however give interesting population figures, which show just how dramatically the population of Harris had risen.

> In the year 1755 the population amounted to 1969 souls; in 1792, to 2536; and at the present period, it is upwards of 4000. By the last census, there were, males, 1863; females, 2037; families, 777; houses inhabited, 759.[21]

He also gives details of the church arrangements on the island then.

> The year in which the parish church (which is now in ruins) was built cannot be accurately ascertained. It is about the centre of the parish, and formerly accommodated 250 sitters. The present incumbent has applied for a new church. [MacIver adds a note that 'a new church was erected last season capable of accommodating 400 sitters.'] The manse was built in 1827, and the value of the glebe is about £16. A Government church was erected in Bernera in 1829. A missionary is supported by the Royal Bounty at Tarbat; a church and manse were granted for his accommodation by the late proprietor, A. N. Macleod.[22]

Later ministers extended the manse, and it is now the world-famous Scarista House Hotel, run by Tim and Patricia Martin.

The Revd MacIver's successor at Sgarasta was Roderick MacDonald from Bhalaigh in North Uist. He was a Gaelic poet of some eminence, one of his earliest poems being a love-song to his intended bride, the daughter of the Revd Roderick MacLean of South Uist.

> 'S ann an Uidhist an eorna
> Tha 'n cailinn boidheach ciuin reidh
> Do 'n d' thug mi 'n gaol falaich
> 'S cha b' aithreach leam e;
>
> Nighean chiallach chiuin socair
> ''S i tosdach 'na beus;
> O 'n is toil leam mo nigh'nag
> 'S toil le m' nigh'nag mi fein.[23]

> In Uist of the barley / is a bonny girl whom I fell in love with – / nor do I have any regrets. / A quiet, sweet, gentle girl / and peaceful in her ways. / O, I love my darling / and my darling loves me.

The Revd Roderick's successor, John Norman MacDonald, also is remembered for a love-song, which opens with a description of the dawn awakening nature.

> Anns a mhaduinn chiuin Cheitein
> 'S a ghrian ag eiridh le dearrsadh
> Tilgeadh lainnir 's na speuraibh
> 'S na neoil a treigsinn nan ardbheann
> 'S aoibhneach glinn agus sleibhtean
> Gach aon creutair ri manran
> 'S nadur ait' dol na h-eideadh
> 'S i sior ghleusaidh a clarsaich.[24]

> On a mild May morning / with the beams of the sunrise / throwing brightness in the skies / the clouds fleeing the mountains / the happy glens and slopes. / Every creature with its own song / joyful Nature clothing herself / and setting her harp in tune.

Those who had joined the new Free Church would have said that the poetry merely showed that the ministers had plenty of time on their hands, with hardly any congregations remaining in the parish church. Even the Revd John Norman's invocation of nature would have brought frowns from some, like the elders who, when they could not dissuade their minister from having a flower garden, suggested that he might at least concentrate on the wee quiet flowers, rather than the big gaudy ones!

Sgarasta had been the early home of Neil Morrison, Bard Pabach, and in his *Oran a Chianalas* – Song of Homesickness – he praises the hill of Bleabhal behind the village.

> Coire Bhlith-bhal is tric air m' inntinn
> Le fhuarain fhior-ghlain bu chubhraidh faileadh
> Biolair uaine a' fas ' a bruachaibh
> Gur mor an suaimhneas do sluagh an aite.
>
> Gach lus is boidhch' air an tulaich chomhnard
> A mach o'n t-sroin 'dhianamh lon us arach
> Do dhaoine breoite 'am bailtibh mora ,
> 'S e chur ri'n sroin 'bheireadh beo o'n bhas iad.[25]

> Bleabhal corrie comes often to my mind / with its pure sweet-smelling springs / and green cresses growing on its slopes, / giving great peace to the people of the place. / Each lovely flower growing

on the smooth hill / to the nose would bring food and strength /
to the weakly folk of the big cities / and would bring the dead back
to life.

Not everyone was put out of Sgarasta in the clearance: the
blacksmith was left, for the farmers could not do without him. In
any case his land was at Stangigearraidh, at the head of the valley
separating the farms of Sgarasta and Taobh Tuath. The Morrisons
had been blacksmiths here for generations, and Gobha Mor
Stangigearraidh – the big smith of Stangigearraidh – was the subject
of many stories, such as one about the party of robbers who raided
the house when the smith was away, and stole a web of cloth that
his wife had been weaving. When the smith came home and heard
about it, he chased the robbers as far as Nisabost, thrashed the lot of
them single-handed and took the web back to Stangigearraidh.

The Sgoilear Ban – Donald Morrison – a cooper in Steornabhagh,
but originally from Harris, collected a book of stories about 180
years ago, and one of these tells how the Morrisons came to be
blacksmiths.[26] Sometime in the 1500s, MacLeod of Harris paid a
visit to Pabaigh and decided to try a wrestling match with Peter
Morrison, the local champion. Morrison was unwilling, as he was
not sure how MacLeod would take a possible defeat, but MacLeod
assured him that he would not object, and so they wrestled, and
Morrison won. MacLeod stayed true to his word, but one of his
henchmen killed Morrison with his sword for daring to beat his
chief. MacLeod had his henchman killed, brought up Peter's only
son in his own family, and eventually made him his secretary.

Young Morrison went along with MacLeod at one time on a visit
to MacLean of Coll, and it was proposed that a daughter of Coll
should marry Morrison. She was willing, but made the condition
that if there were two sons of the marriage, one should be brought
up a blacksmith and the other a minister, and that MacLeod should
give each of them a living. This was agreed, and from a son of this
marriage came the Morrison blacksmiths of Harris.

The traditional pedigree of the Morrison blacksmiths traces them
back to Donald Ban Morrison of Borgh, and suggests his birthdate
as about 1670, which fits in very well with the evidence of estate
rentals of the time. Donald Ban had three sons – John, Donald
and Angus. John was Gobha Mor Stangigearraidh, and Donald's

family removed from Sgarasta to Roghadal, where their descendants included John Morrison – Gobha na Hearadh – the blacksmith and hymn-writer. Angus remained in Sgarasta, and his grandson Norman (Tormod Aonghais Oig) appears as a joint tenant there in 1819. Norman's son Neil was the last member of the family to be connected with the Sgarasta area; he appears in the 1841 census in nearby Nisisith, from where he moved a few years later to Breanais in Uig, Lewis.

Sgarasta has a more recent connection with story-telling through Finlay J. MacDonald, whose books describe his young days in Sgarasta. They are full of marvellous little pictures of the people of the area – not always very well disguised!

Sgarasta was re-settled in 1928, and for a picture of life there at that time there is no equal to Finlay J.'s books. But don't look for his house there today; like all the rest of the new crofters Finlay J.'s father built a temporary hut of corrugated sheeting, and, while the rest eventually built proper houses, Iain never got around to it. What was left of his hut was blown away in the winter gales a few years ago.

Nisisith (Nisishee)

This little village was at the shore on the boundary between the farms of Sgarasta and Taobh Tuath, at the mouth of the stream coming down from Stangigearraidh. Christopher MacRae from Kintail came here after the clearance of the crofters from Sgarasta. Crisgean Saighdear he was called locally, as he was a pensioner from the 78th Regiment. His house was on a little green hillock, Cnoc an t-Saighdeir or the Soldier's Hill, above the present road, where he was the boundary shepherd maintaining the dykes and keeping the flocks from the two farms separate, a job in which he was succeeded by Fionnlaigh Tarsainn – Finlay Campbell – from Molinginish, whose nephew Domhnall Maireid was the last person to live at Nisisith.

Crisgean died in 1868 and was buried in Sgarasta, and it is ironic that the only legible gravestone in this part of Sgarasta cemetery for a person living on the machair is for Crisgean Saighdear, a stranger from Kintail.

Little is left of Nisisith today: the site of Crisgean's house still shows green above the road, while below it the ruins of Domhnall Maireid's house still show a foot or so of stonework. But the strangest looking thing in the area is a few yards south of the village, where an old road branches off from the main road, and disappears into the sea. This dates from the time of the feldspar quarry on Ceapabhal, when there was no road through the village of Taobh Tuath to the quarry, and the lorries went there across the sands. It was on the same beach that the inter-island plane run by Loganair used to land – until they put a bigger plane on the run, and it took three tractors to get it out of the sand.

Taobh Tuath (Northton)

Northton may seem a strange name for a village at the south-west corner of Harris. The Gaelic Taobh Tuath – literally north side – makes more sense, for at one time there were two villages on the shores of the hill of Ceapabhal, one on the north side and one on the south, and when the new village was made here in 1902 it was called Taobh Tuath, even though it is a mile or two away from the original Taobh Tuath.

7. Ceapabhal

The name Ceapabhal is old too, especially in its hybrid form of Chaipaval, for the '-val' stands for the Norse word *fjell*, meaning hill. What it was called before that we have no idea, for the Vikings who raided and settled here in the ninth century gave everywhere new names in their own language, and it is these names in a Gaelic version that we still use today – '-vat' for a loch, '-bost' for a village and '-siadar' for a grazing. When you are coming down from Sgarasta you see Ceapabhal as two rounded tops, side by side, so little wonder that the Norsemen gave it the name of Bow-shaped Hill.

The settlement of the area is far older than the Vikings – like Horgabost it was a settlement for prehistoric people, and there was a dig here by students from Leicester University in the 1960s, when they discovered Bronze Age and Iron Age villages on the shores of Ceapabhal. At the main village, just inside Pairc an Teampaill – Temple Park – they uncovered houses and a child's grave, and just beside it there is a midden or rubbish-tip, full of ashes, the empty shells of shellfish and the occasional piece of pottery. The Iron Age pottery, from between two and three thousand years ago, is rather heavy and crude, but the earlier Bronze Age pottery is much finer and ornamented with fine patterns of lines – straight and diagonal and herring-bone.

Most of the empty shells in the midden are limpets, though there are winkles too, and cockles from the sands. I have chewed limpets myself for bait when fishing for cuddies, but they are tough, and would need some cooking. The pottery they made in those days couldn't be put straight on to the fire; they had to heat stones in the fire and put them into the water in the cooking pots. These 'boiling stones' can still be found, usually round and polished and with the marks of the fire on them still, but it must have taken quite a time before the limpets were ready to eat!

Further out on the south and west side of the hill is Rubh' an Teampaill, the headland of the Temple, which is the word used here for a pre-Reformation church. At the north end of the Teampall you can still see the circular foundation of an Iron Age dun, or fort: a lookout from which to survey the whole of the Atlantic approaches to Harris, as far as St Kilda, almost fifty miles out on the horizon. It is said that there was a worsening of the weather in Iron Age times,

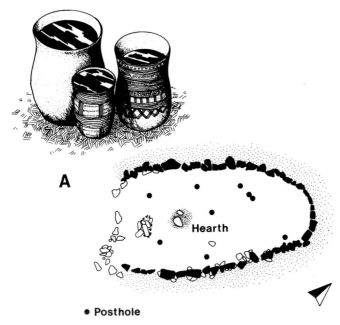

8. Bronze age site and pottery at Taobh Tuath

and people started to fight for the better land. All travel at that time was by sea, and so it was the sea approaches which had to be watched, to give warning of imminent danger. If a threat was seen from the dun, a fire would be lit that could be seen from all around. Another dun on the island of Pabaigh to the south-west would pass on the message, and yet another on Bearnaraigh Island would pick it up, and pass word to the dun at Roghadal, at the southern tip of Harris. Because of the shape of the coast and the hills, the fire at Dun an Teampaill could not be seen from the machair coast, but there was a dun on the island of Tarasaigh, and it could see Bearnaraigh over the Uidh or isthmus at Taobh Tuath, and pass on the message to the dun at Borgh, to alert the machair. There was another dun above Aird Groadnis behind Losgaintir, and although there is little to be seen of it now, you can work out where it had to be to be able to pass on the message clear of Beinn Raa, the mountain on Tarasaigh, to Huisinis and all the shores of North Harris.

The Gaelic name Borgh, or Borve in English, is a version of the

Norse word for a fort, so everywhere you find the name Borgh you can look for an Iron Age fort – and when you talk about the fort at the dun in Borgh, you are talking about the fort at the fort in the fort!

Beside the dun at Rudh' an Teampaill is the Teampall itself. The present building dates from the time of Alasdair Crotach, Chief of the MacLeods, who re-built the Teampall in 1528, the same year as the church of St Clement at Roghadal – one to watch the eastern approaches to the Sound of Harris and the other the western. There was a church long before then, and it would have been the early Christian missionaries in the time of Columba, who set up the first church here, though it was probably followers of St Maelrubha of Applecross who were here, rather than those of Columba himself. The missionaries of those days were in the habit of having a *disertum* – a remote place for solitary meditation – and you can see the ruins of one on Eilean Hopraidh, an isolated rock-stack just inside the point of Gob an Tobha, the furthest point of Ceapabhal.

The early church would have been raided by the Norsemen. They came first in the 800s, and the early churches with their altar vessels and manuscripts were obvious targets, and though the Vikings had no use for writing, the intricately decorated manuscripts and Gospels were of value, if only as ornaments. There is a marginal note in Gaelic written on a Latin grammar preserved in the monastery of St Gall in Switzerland:

> Is acher ingaith innocht fufuasna fairge findfolt
> No agor reimm mora minn dondlaechriad lainn ua lothlind

> Sharp is the wind tonight, and white tresses rise on the ocean / I need not fear the calm sea, bringing the fierce warriors of Norway.[27]

Bad seas were the only defence the churches had against the Viking raiders, who if the weather permitted would have burned the church at the Teampall and looted it of everything of value.

Maybe not everything: the priests would have hidden their most valuable treasures for safety when they saw the danger coming. The old people used to say that there was treasure buried on Ceapabhal, on a spot where you can see the three uidhean, or sand-shores, of Huisinis, Tarasaigh and Taobh Tuath. Old traditions take a long

9. Teampall na h-Uidhe

time to die out altogether, and it could well be that this treasure came from the church. The old folk even knew who was going to find it – Amadan MhicCuthais: a simpleton by the name of MacCuish.

The Teampall as it stands today was rebuilt by Alasdair Crotach in 1528, and I am sure that with the masoned stone of the Iron Age dun lying around, the masons would have used that for building the Teampall. The walls are of stone, mortared and washed inside with the lime-rich shell-sand from the nearby beach, and the roof would have been thatched with reeds from the reed-banks which still surround the little stream below the Teampall. The water supply was a spring on the hillside, still called Tobar an t-Sagairt – the Priest's Well – and the land around is still some of the most fertile in Harris. Today the church is called Teampall na h-Uidhe, the Uidh being the narrow isthmus of sand connecting the hill of Ceapabhal with the present-day village of Taobh Tuath and the rest of Harris. For a time it was the parish church of Harris, easily accessible for the populous islands of Pabaigh and Bearnaraigh in the Sound of Harris, but in the early 1700s the parish church was moved to Sgarasta, where it still appears on old maps as Uig Church, a misprint for 'Uiy', for the Uidh.

Liuiridh

Further out than the Teampall is the cliff face of Liuiridh, and at the side of it an almost inaccessible cave. The story of the cave takes us back to 1746 and the collapse of the Jacobite rebellion after Culloden. The chief of the MacLeods at Dunvegan supported the government – and there is another story about why he did so, but it belongs to Fionnsbhagh – and he sent to his relative Donald MacLeod of the island of Bearnaraigh, in the Sound of Harris, to come with his tenants to fight along with him, as his duty to his chief required. Donald, who was nicknamed 'The Old Trojan', had a mind of his own, and sent a letter to MacLeod:

> I place at your disposal the 20 men of your tribe under my immediate command, and in any other quarrel would not fail to be at their head, but in the present juncture, I must go where a more imperious duty calls me

and went himself to join Prince Charlie. After Culloden Donald had to go into hiding, first in a cave on Sron Ulladal in the forest of North Harris, and then in the cave on the Liuiridh, where he was attended by a young boy, John Martin.

The *Inverness Courier* of 25 March 1846 contains the obituary of this John Martin, at the age of 112, which notes that, 'in youth he was remarkably swift of foot, and up to the age of 60 he could outrun and seize a sheep on the steepest hillside, and was able to walk about till within twenty-four hours of his death'.[28] He must have been quite a character, but so was Donald himself! Donald is buried in the Bearnaraigh caibeal, or private grave enclosure, in the churchyard at Roghadal. According to the inscription there, 'In his 75th year he married his third wife, by whom he had nine children, and died in his ninetieth year.'[29]

Taobh Tuath and Taobh Deas (North Town and South Town)

In time there came to be two townships on Ceapabhal: Taobh Tuath, or north side, on the shore facing Sgarasta and Taobh Deas, or south side, near the Teampall. The old MacLeod rentals of the late 1600s talk about the 'North Town and South Town of Quoppival' – a rather odd attempt at spelling Ceapabhal – but not half so odd as that on a map of 1804,[30] 'Hypervaule'. Taobh Tuath was a farm belonging to the family of MacLeods known as the Albannaich – literally Scotsmen – perhaps because they had been for a time on mainland Scotland. A rental of 1701 shows two brothers at 'North Town', John and Norman MacLeod, sons of Alexander 'Albinich'. Neil MacLeod (Neilidh Thormoid) in An Tairbeart used to claim that he was Niall mac Thormoid mhic Dhomhnaill mhic Choinnich mhic Neill mhic Choinnich mhic Thormoid mhic Alasdair – Neil son of Norman son of Donald son of Kenneth son of Neil son of Kenneth son of Norman son of Alexander – and that would fit in with the rental.

By 1800 'North Town' had passed to an army surgeon, William MacGillivray; he was from mainland Inverness-shire, though his wife was a daughter of MacNeil of Pabaigh. Being a soldier, he left the running of the farm in the hands of his brother Roderick, and when William was killed in the Napoleonic Wars, Roderick took the lease into his own hands. Before he married, William had had an illegitimate son in Aberdeen, where he was a student, and this son, also called William, was sent to 'North Town' to his uncle to be brought up. Young William also went to Aberdeen University, and became the famous ornithologist.

The old Taobh Tuath had been out on the hill, beyond Bun an Ois – the mouth of the river draining Sgarasta beach – but in about 1810 MacGillivray took over the Taobh Deas also. Its people were put further out on to the hill towards Breithasgeir, beyond the Teampall, but the land there was so poor that they soon left, and only the feannagan (lazy-beds) and the ruins of their houses remain to show the hopeless attempt to wrest a living from such poor, storm-lashed land. The land of Taobh Deas, from the old village out to the Teampall, was enclosed with a stone dyke, and became Pairc an Teampaill –Temple Park – part of the farm of 'North Town', while the farmhouse was moved in to a sheltered valley between the two 'towns', where the present-day sheep fanks are.

When John MacKay (Iain Mhurchaidh a' Chleireach – John the son of Murdo the Church-Officer) was giving evidence to a Royal Commission in 1894, he was asked who MacGillivray was, and he had no doubt about his answer: 'S e droch dhuine a bh'ann' – He was a bad man.[31]

William MacGillivray kept a journal of a year's visit to 'North Town' in 1817–18,[32] which gives a very good picture of life in Harris at that time, as long as you remember that he was of the gentry and the life of the tenantry would have been very different. It was about this time too that crofting in its present form began. In the old townships, there had been joint tenancies, with the houses all together in a cluster, and the land being shared out year by year, whereas under crofting each tenant had his own piece of land with his house on it.

MacGillivray brought his own cattlemen to Taobh Tuath with him, the brothers Norman and John MacCuish; at least, MacCuish is what their descendants are called now, but they claim that the family came from Forres in Moray, and you wouldn't find the name MacCuish there. Probably theirs was a name that sounded quite like MacCuish, but the name MacCuish was known in Harris and theirs was not, so MacCuish they became too. The old folk also claimed that the MacCuishes had a different way of cutting peat – they cut the peat-bank round instead of square – which could be consistent with their coming from a drier area, where you did not have to drain the corners of the peat-bank.

John MacCuish was the brother living out at Gob an Tobha and Norman was at Druim a' Phuind, where the village is today. John was known as MacCuthais Mor nam Mogan – Big MacCuish of the Mogans – Mogan being a kind of footless stocking which was his usual wear. One night when he was looking after the cattle he saw an uilebheisd – a sea monster – coming out of the sea, and he got such a fright that he and his family cleared out and went to Norman's house and never returned to the hill. But there is a feeling to the old story that somehow or other MacGillivray was behind the whole scare. Was he afraid that MacCuish was the amadan who was going to find the treasure on the hill?

MacGillivray lost the farms of Taobh Tuath in the 1820s, and they passed to Alexander MacRa from Ardintoul in Lochalsh, called Fear Huisinis after his main farm in the North of Harris. This MacRa was of the gentry in Lochalsh, but his wife Margaret was not, and many of her brothers and uncles got work as shepherds on MacRa's farms, which is how many of the MacRaes came to Harris. From MacRa Taobh Tuath passed to the MacDonalds of Caolas

10. The village of Taobh Tuath

Stiadair, then in 1902 it was taken over by the Board for Congested Districts, and split into forty crofts, running from the Uidh to Druim a' Phuind; the new village was called Taobh Tuath, though is more than three miles away from the original 'North Town'. The crofters did not like the original proposed layout, as it would have left them with crofts liable either to waterlogging at one end of the township, or to burning in a dry summer at the machair end, and in the end the crofts were all grouped together in the village, with half their land around the houses, and the other half on the machair as permanent apportionments.

Crofting in Taobh Tuath was mainly a cattle economy, and the whole of the machair was cultivated with fodder crops for the cattle and for the horses for ploughing. The machair was grazed by the stock in winter, then they were moved out on to the hill, to leave the land ready for cultivation. This alternation of grazing and breaking the surface of the sward is ideal for the encouragement of the machair flowers, and the machair here is an incredible show of colour from May right through to October. For a time in the 1980s and 1990s the cattle vanished from the machair: people in the village got older, and with the availability of milk delivered to the door,

11. Drying tweed and fleece at An Taigh Sgoile, Taobh Tuath

there was no longer the need for milking cattle, but recently there has been a move to keep cattle again, and there is a small herd now, mostly of Highlanders, grazing and feeding the machair in winter.

An Taigh-Sgoile (The School-House)

In common with most crofting townships, Taobh Tuath began to lose its people after the Second World War, and as the availability of local jobs has decreased, the number of young families decreased also. The school, which had opened with eighty-seven children in 1908, closed in 1983 with only five pupils – and one of them was the teacher's nephew, brought by her from the Bays each day.

Like many schools of its day, it was a kit, manufactured by Speirs and Co. of Glasgow; their business making kits for schools and churches supplied the needs created by another of the frequent splits in the churches. It had a heavy timber frame, clad externally with corrugated iron sheeting and internally panelled with timber V-lining. The school and the schoolhouse were under one roof, but with separate access, the school door facing the village street, and the house door facing into the hill – whether to give the schoolmaster privacy from the children or to give the children privacy from the schoolmaster is an arguable point.

The local men had prepared the site and the found, and the kit was brought in by ship to An t-Ob, then made into a raft and floated along the shore to the far-end of Taobh Tuath, with the local fishing boats controlling and directing it with ropes. I am told that there was one boy on the raft, and that at one point the raft was in danger of breaking loose and being carried out into the Atlantic. The boy on the boat grew up to have rather a colourful reputation, and as one of my friends said 'If we had known then what we know now, you wouldn't have had a schoolhouse to live in!'

The Old Schoolhouse became the centre of our genealogy resource for the whole of the Western Isles – and the emigrant areas overseas - based on an amalgam of written records and oral tradition. Written records in the Islands are generally poor, and were often kept by incomers with no knowledge of Gaelic, and even less interest. Oral tradition, on the other hand, comes from within a community and is much more likely to be accurate, even though it does tend to be more localised. Neither by itself is a complete record, but if the two can be amalgamated, a more complete picture emerges, sometimes with surprising results. For example, it was generally accepted that the Bays of the east coast of Harris were first settled by families evicted from the machair, but when we came to gather family histories from the Bays, the picture was very different – most of them had come to the Bays long before the machair clearances, and a lot of them had come from other parts of the Islands and mainland Scotland. Equally, when we tried to trace families evicted from the machair, we found that in many cases their descendants were not in the Bays at all, but in Canada. Certainly, some of the evicted families did manage to find spaces among the people of the Bays, but that certainly was not how the Bays were first settled.

So much of this oral tradition was going to be lost with the old folk, as few of the younger people were listening if only because the educational system had taught them to devalue all things local, and only now is it being realised that the memories of the older people are a vital resource for the history of the Island and their people.

The genealogical business is called *Co Leis Thu?*, which in Gaelic means 'Who do you belong to?' – not 'Who are you, as an individual?' but 'Where do you fit into the community?' – which in itself makes a valuable point about the social structure of the Island communities. The genealogy business has now been transferred to a local trust – Northton Heritage Trust – set up specially to run *Co Leis Thu?* and it is now housed within *Seallam!* Visitor Centre at the corner of the roads into Taobh Tuath, along with exhibitions on

12. *Seallam!* Visitor Centre.

local and natural history – an ideal introduction to the Island for the visitor, and a source of information for the ancestor-hunter!

Publishing the results of research is just as important as the research itself, and this side of the business – Bill Lawson Publications – has been retained in the Old Schoolhouse.

PART TWO – TARASAIGH

Taransay

It is about two miles from the island of Tarasaigh to Traigh Horgaboist, the nearest point for landing on the Harris mainland, though headland to headland it is little more than a mile. There is a nice little natural harbour for small boats on the Tarasaigh side, but the only place to bring a boat ashore on the mainland is through the Atlantic swell on the beach at Horgabost, or by the long journey to An Tairbeart or to Abhainnsuidhe in North Harris. There is a gully at Geo nan Caorach – the Sheep's Gully – on Aird Nisabost where it would be possible to put a person ashore: indeed I have been landed there myself in weather when the beach proved impossible.

I spent many summer weeks on Tarasaigh in the 1970s with the MacRaes, the last family to live there. Eoghann and his son were lobster fishermen; his son was Eoghann as well, so the son was Eoghann Beag and his father Eoghann Mor, even though Eoghann Mor was not much over five feet tall, while wee Ewen was over six feet, and strong as a horse. Lecsaidh, Eoghann Mor's wife, kept house for them. Life on an off-shore island was not easy for them, and they could be cut off for weeks in the wintertime, but the little thatched house was warm, and the welcome inside it even warmer.

At one time Tarasaigh had been home to a flourishing community. Martin Martin, the first travel writer to visit the Hebrides, visited there when gathering information for *A Description of the Western Isles of Scotland*, published in 1703.

> The Isle Taransay is a mile distant from the main Land of Harries, and when the inhabitants go from this Island to Harries with a design to stay for any time, they agree with those that carry them over, on a particular motion of walking upon a certain piece of ground, unknown to every body but themselves, as a Signal to bring 'em back.[33]

What seems to have fascinated him most here are the two little churches, Teampall Tharain and Teampall Che, on either side of the little stream flowing down to the landing place, each with its own little graveyard – Cladh Tharain and Cladh Che – though all of Cladh Tharain has now been washed away by the sea, and the storms open up the part of Cladh Che nearest to the shore, so that skulls and bones appear on the shore. In Cladh Che is a little unroofed building – caibeal or grave-enclosure – called Caibeal nam Fidhleirean, the Chapel of the Fiddlers, named for a family of MacLeods from North Harris who were for a time on Tarasaigh, and had this little burial place for themselves.

> There is an antient tradition among the Natives here, that a Man must not be bury'd in St. Tarran's, nor a woman in St Keith's, because otherwise the Corps would be found above-ground the day after it is interred. I told them this was a most ridiculous Fancy, which they might soon perceive by experience if they would put it to a tryal. Roderick Campbell, who resides there, being of my opinion, resolved to embrace the first opportunity that offer'd in order to undeceive the credulous Vulgar; and accordingly a poor man in the island, who died a Year after, was bury'd in St. Tarran's Chapel contrary to the antient Custom and Tradition of this place, but his Corps is still in the Grave, from whence it is not likely to rise until the general Resurrection.[34]

In Teampall Tharain Alexander Carmichael found a skull 'large and thick with a piece on the left back of it about 4 by 3 inches

13. Cladh Che on Tarasaigh

clearly cut off as if with the sword. The piece is there. The sword cut in the skull is about 4½ or 5 inches long. Forehead rather receding and skull very thick – a large man's skull. Close to this a skeleton whose bones were something awfully large – the end of the femur about 4 inches broad and the rest of the bones equally large.'[35]

Tarasaigh is full of things of interest to the amateur archaeologist. At the Uidh there is a standing stone, matching those at Sgarasta and on Aird Nisabost, and on one face of it is carved a cross. Presumably this dates from the time of the early Christian missionaries to the islands, and the breaking of the religious power of the pagan stone by the physical conversion of the stone itself to Christianity. The stone is now known as Clach an Teampaill (the Stone of the Church) or sometimes Clach an t-Sagairt (the Priest's Stone) so presumably there was a later religious settlement around its base.

Clach an Teampaill is at one end of the Uidh isthmus, and at the other end, facing the Atlantic, the sea has ripped into different levels of a prehistoric midden, full of empty shells, like the midden at Taobh Tuath, but with much larger shards of pottery and great banks of red ash. The Uidh itself has a beautiful beach on either side; that facing the Atlantic reddish-orange in colour and pounded by the full Atlantic swell, and the other facing Loch na h-Uidhe with the finest grains of greyish-white sand.

Across the hill from the Uidh, at the head of the central valley of Tarasaigh, lies Loch an Duin, so called from the dun on an island in the loch. According to Carmichael,[36] there were six or seven feet of the walls still standing in 1877, and he notes 'that the Dun was up and entire within the memory of people living. It was about 16 feet high with a window at each side and the court paved with flags.' The dun is a typical refuge fort, where the people would have gathered in time of trouble, and the only access to it is a staran or causeway of stones from the shore. In the middle of the causeway is a clach ghlutraman or warning stone, so balanced that you cannot stand on it without making it clatter against the stones on either side, and so give warning to the people in the dun.

As well as the shelter dun there was the more common type of watchtower dun – Dun Raa – on the shore between Raa and Paibil.

There had been three villages on Tarasaigh at one time – Raa,

Paibil and the Uidh – and there is still in existence a record of the rent paid by each village in 1724, at a time when rents were paid partly in cash and partly in kind.

> Donald MacDonald in Eye being sworn, deponed that the yearly pay of the Four pennies of Eye possest by him is One hundred and thirty three pounds six shillings eight pennies Scots money rent, Ae marte, Eight pounds cess, Twenty one pound six shillings eight pennies tegnes, Twelve bolls meal, Sixteen stones half butter half cheese and Twelve wedders. As also deponed that the Three penny lands of Raa possest by Kenneth Campbell pay yearly Sixty six pounds thirteen shillings four pennies money rent, Ae marte, Six pounds cess, Sixteen pounds tegnes, Four bolls meall, Twelve stones half butter half cheese and Six wedders and that the said places pay Noo more, which he depones.
>
> Finlay Morrisone in Pabaill being sworn depones that the yearly pay of the said place, being Four pennie lands, is Eighty pounds money rent, Ae marte, Eight pounds cess, Twenty one pounds six shillings eight pennies tegnes, Twelve bolls meall, Sixteen stones half butter half cheese and Twelve wedders, and Noo more.[37]

The division of land into penny lands was the basis of the old method of land taxation – the amount of land liable for one penny in tax – and may date back to the days of the Norse settlement of the islands. A tenant in these days was also liable for government land tax – cess – and for the upkeep of the parish church: tegnes, or teinds. A part of the rent was also paid in kind – wedders, or sheep, and marts, or cattle – and the division of the rent between these and meal and dairy products gives an idea of the type of farming carried on in each area.

We know how the Morrisons lost their money and their lease. Angus Morrison (Aonghas mac Fhionnlaigh), probably a great-grandson of the Finlay of 1724, was sent by his father with cattle to the drobh or the cattle-sales in Steornabhagh, and there he met and fell for a sister of George Morrison, tacksman of Cros in Lewis. So Angus went to Cros, and the money for the cattle went there too, and never came back to Tarasaigh!

A later Kenneth Campbell, a grandson of Kenneth of 1724, was tacksman of the Uidh, and an enterprising merchant as well. Several of his cousins, including Donald Campbell of Scalpaigh, had emigrated to the plantations of the Carolinas, and Kenneth was trading directly with them from Tarasaigh. Cotton and sugar and timber would have been among the goods coming back across the Atlantic, and more exotic items such as tobacco.

I remember Eoghann Mor showing me tobacco plants growing in the garden of the old farmhouse at the Uidh, though of course they did not ripen here, and they used to say that the wild mint that grew behind the house at the Uidh was a special kind, brought in by him as well. Just below the house is Port a' Bhata – the boat harbour – where they used to land the supplies from Campbell's schooner.

West from the Uidh is the headland of Aird Mhanais, joined to Tarasaigh only by the sandy isthmus of the Uidh; in Kenneth Campbell's time, the sea came right through the Uidh and made an island of Aird Mhanais, marooning Malcolm MacKinnon, the shepherd, there for several days.

> Cnoc Togul is Creag Tonus
> An da chnuic sona 's an Aird
> Is maise leam Heiribhal gaolach
> Far 'm bi na daoine tamh
>
> Cnoc Togul and Creag Tonus, / the two fairest peaks of the Aird; / fair to me is dear Herrival / where the people used to live.

So the old people used to say about Aird Mhanais, and they say too that the little sandy beach of Sanndabhaig was the home of families who went to Sanndabhaig outside Steornabhagh in Lewis, and took the name with them, though I think that the name is very old there too.

When Donald Campbell of Scalpaigh went to Carolina, his daughter Peggy went also, with her husband Duncan MacNab from Islay. He was a soldier, and fought on the British side in the War of American Independence in 1776. When the war was lost, Duncan and Peggy had the choice of moving to Canada as United Empire Loyalists, or returning to Scotland. Since Peggy's brother Kenneth had the farm of Scalpaigh himself at this time, she no doubt reckoned on being given a home there, but Kenneth refused – not even a croft on the rocky shores of the mainland part of the farm. Her cousin, Kenneth Campbell of the Uidh, got a croft for them on the machair at Raa, with grazing for two cows, and there Peggy kept a school for the local children while Duncan laboured to clear the croft of stones and make it fully arable.

In due course, after her brother died, Peggy was able to get a croft on the shorelands of Caolas Scalpaigh. According to Carmichael, she was 'tall, straight and stout, with hair of a rich auburn, the colour of all the family'. On Tarasaigh you can still see the ruins of Taigh-Sgoile Raa (the Raa Schoolhouse) and Cnoc an t-Saighdeir (the Soldier's Hillock) piled high with the stones he had gathered off the machair.[38]

Carmichael gives the pedigree of Kenneth Campbell as Coinneach mac Alasdair mhic Choinnich mhic Dhomhnaill mhic Iain Oig – Kenneth son of Alexander son of Kenneth son of Donald son of Young John – and we will see later that this Young John was John son of John son of Kenneth, the warden of Pabbay Castle and the first of the Campbells to come to Harris.

> Captain Kenneth Campbell of Tarasaigh was perhaps one of the most gentlemanly men who ever lived. When he went to Rodel, so great was the veneration for him that the whole 60 families there ran into the houses for fear of giving offence by looking at him! He was the most remarkable fine man and was buried in Scarista with his father, mother and sister. He was so grinn [lordly] that when he went to Ensay, Fear Ensay [the farmer there] folded up the sheets and blankets till he came again, they being too sacred to go over anybody else![39]

Heron's *General View of the Hebrides* in 1794 gives the population of Tarasaigh as 140. By the early 1800s there were farms at Paible and the Uidh, and only Raa was left to crofters, but in 1840s Raa also was cleared, and all that was left was the farms at Paible and the Uidh – and both of them belonged now to the MacDonalds – and a few cottar-fishermen above the shore at Paible.

Allt na Muilne – the Mill-Stream – runs from Loch an Duin through the central valley of Tarasaigh to its mouth, Bun na Muilne, near Paibil. As the name suggests, there were several old watermills on the stream. The one nearest to Loch a' Chromlaich is in the best condition, and the great stone discs of mill-wheels still lie beside it. The stream can be diverted here into a mill-lade, and the mill, built of the usual dry-stone, was built across the lade. On a timber

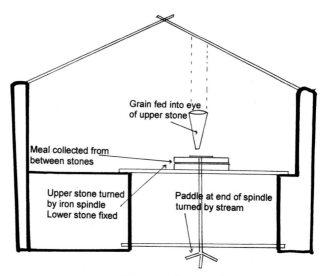

Grain fed into eye
of upper stone

Meal collected from
between stones

Upper stone turned
by iron spindle
Lower stone fixed

Paddle at end of spindle
turned by stream

14. Diagram of corn-mill

platform over the lade sat the two mill-wheels, each about three feet
across. Each had a central hole, and the upper stone also had a cross-
shape cut into its upper face. An iron spindle passed through the
eye of both stones; at its upper end a crosspiece which fitted into the
cross-shape on the upper stone and at its lower end flanges, dipping
into the water of the mill-lade. When the sluice was opened, and
the stream poured down the lade, it struck the flanges, turning the
spindle, which turned the upper stone. A timber hopper suspended
above the stones dribbled grain into the eye of the upper stone, and
it was ground between the stones, and came out around the rim
of the lower stone. It was a primitive way of grinding grain, but it
worked, and any repairs could be done from local materials, the
stones themselves being cut from gneiss near the top of Beinn na
h-Uidhe, where there still is one lying which started to crack when
it was being cut.

Beside the mill is a bounded-off piece of land, with the remains
of two buildings – no doubt the miller's store and his house for the
times when he needed to live there to work the mill. There are at
least three mills on the stream, and it is possible that at one time
each village had its own mill. When the crofters were cleared, a
new mill was made beside the farm at Paibil, and its ruins can still

be seen at Bun na Muilne, at the end of the remains of the old cart-track from there to the farmhouse of Paibil.

In 1883 the government appointed a Royal Commission, usually referred to as the Napier Commission, to enquire into conditions in the Highlands and Islands. Evidence was invited from local representatives, and the stories they tell are our most detailed source of information about Harris. No doubt some of the witnesses were a bit shaky in their dates, but there is little doubt that the general picture they paint was in essence true.

Angus Ferguson (Aonghas mac Neill mhic Raoghaill, Angus son of Neil son of Ranald) gave evidence on behalf of the Tarasaich.

> I wish to speak of the poor condition of the people ever since I first remember them. When I first remember the place my father had a holding there. The third part of the island was under crofts. There were fourteen families upon that portion. These crofts were removed when I was nine years of age and the island was cleared for John MacDonald. The whole fourteen families were removed from the island in all directions. Some went to the south-west of Harris, some to Lewis and others elsewhere. My father was allowed by the tacksman to remain in the place where we were when we had a croft, and that accounts for us being on the island. Ever since we lost that land we have not been able to get a holding of land since. We had nothing but to be cottars under the tacksman, and to be dealt with just as he pleased; and the arrangement between him and us, which subsisted while he was in life, was this – we worked the land for him, and we gave him half the produce. He allowed us to keep a cow and eight sheep.
>
> His son succeeded him, and he made a different arrangement with us. We had not cow or sheep since that time. At that time we had to take to the lobster-fishing and such work as goes on in the place. The tacksman gave us potato ground to the extent of four or five barrels, upon condition that we would give him in return farm service any day of the year he wished us. And now because we were in a very remote corner of the world, where few advantages could be got, we were obliged to accept these conditions, although we felt them hard.
>
> We are not allowed to sow either oats or barley, but only potatoes; and we are obliged to fish the whole year, summer and winter, autumn and spring, in order to enable us to obtain a livelihood, for this amount of potatoes does little to support us. I have been the

head of a family for the last twenty-six years, and during that time I have had neither cow nor sheep, and I did not earn sixpence on Taransay ever since. I have obtained my livelihood by braving many a danger upon the wild shore through the spring and winter months, where a stranger could scarcely expect that a boat would live. Upon certain days we must remain at home from our own fishing – such days as we have to ferry heavy cattle between the shore and the island, and such work as that, that requires people in order to carry it out. We work very irregularly – a bit of a day now and a bit of a day again – but I believe, if they were all strung together, they would make about sixty full days in a year. Perhaps some weeks we might be called once, and others not.

There are a lot of cattle, but we are not allowed to keep a cow or a sheep, by the will of the tacksman. There are seventy-six inhabitants on the island – I do not know the number of children – and we get no milk at all, unless from some of the neighbours when they come ashore from the mainland.[40]

Angus' counting must have been at fault, for the census of 1881 shows only fifty-five people on the island, and that includes visitors as well as MacDonald and his own servants.

Iain Domhnallach – John MacDonald the tacksman – belonged to a family known as na Stalcairean, the Stalkers. Eoghann Mor used to say that they had come from North Uist with a purse of money, and none too good a reputation. 'MacDonalds of the Second Blow' was another name for them, and it was in Uist that they got that name. In the wild times of about 500 years ago Gilleasbuig Dubh of Uist had killed his two brothers to get North Uist for himself, but he had spared their two young sons. Years after, when these sons had grown up, they were out after deer on the hill of Lee with their uncle; one of the boys, later known as Domhnall Gruamach, took the chance when his uncle was unprepared to kill him with his sword. One of the stalkers who was with them suggested that he take the opportunity to kill his cousin as well, so that there would be nobody who could dispute his right to North Uist. Domhnall Gruamach would not take the advice, and the stalker had to flee from Uist and the wrath of the other nephew, but Domhnall Gruamach was not so annoyed at being given the advice to strike the second blow that he didn't give the stalker a good purseful of gold to take with him. It was this money that bought the Stalcairean the lease of the Inn at Roghadal and set the family on their way to becoming tacksmen on Tarasaigh and on the machair.

When John MacDonald was the farmer at the Uidh, he built himself a new house, the Taigh Geal or white house, two storeys high with a Ballachulish slate roof, but it was not successful, and the roof was taken off and sent to An Tairbeart. A few years ago the gables were taken down and the building re-roofed to make a bothy for the Scottish Mountaineering Club; if somewhat spartan, it is on a magnificent site, especially with the summer sun going down across the Uidh. Sadly, the club seems now to have given up maintaining the bothy, and the roof is sorely in need of repair – though even so it is still a welcome shelter in poor weather, and idyllic in good weather.

There is no sign now of the old farmhouse that Coinneach na h-Uidhe had, though there are some signs in the sand-cuts in the machair above Clach an Teampaill to suggest that there may have been a foundation there. On the hill behind the Taigh Geal are the ruins of an even older nuclear village, with the tobhtaichean – foundations – of the old house and byres still visible, a little stream running through the village and a dyke surrounding it, to keep the stock away from the houses and the drinking water.

When the roof of the Taigh Geal started to give way, John MacDonald moved to the old farmhouse at Paibil. In front of the main house was a small building with plastered walls and a chimney, and it is said that this was the house for the governess who looked after the MacDonald children at the Uidh in the summer, after their parents had moved to Paibil.

The ground between Paibil and the Uidh is very broken, and Carmichael reports that Coinneach na h-Uidhe used to say that he could walk the two miles between the two farms without putting his foot except on grass, and back without putting it down except on rock! Midway between the farms is Sorachan a' Ghille-Hiortaich, the St Kilda Boy's Rest, a strangely shaped rock with a ledge for sitting and a higher level for resting a creel – or a rucksack. It is said that the Ghille-Hiortach was employed to carry loads between the two farms, and took his halfway rest here. The Fergusons on Tarasaigh claimed a St Kilda connection, and perhaps the Gille-Hiortach was the first of that family to come to Tarasaigh.

15. Taking the peats home on Tarasaigh

In 1901 John Campbell, who had been tacksman of Borgh on the Isle of Bearnaraigh, took over the lease of Tarasaigh from the Stalcairean, and Raoghall – Ranald – the last of them was left in the old farmhouse, amusing himself with that most Victorian of genteel hobbies, trying to invent a machine for perpetual motion. The Campbells had the reputation for being mean, and they were no better to their cottars than the MacDonalds had been, and when the cottars got the chance to leave, as with Lord Leverhulme's schemes for developing the fishing industry in An t-Ob in the 1920s, most of them took the chance, until eventually only the MacRaes were left.

They say that before Ian Mor Caimbeul (John Campbell) took the lease of the place, he came over for a night, and in the evening he left a penny lying on the machair; he picked it up again in the morning, so that he could judge the amount of growth of grass there had been underneath it. 'Well,' said Eoghann Mor, 'I find that hard to believe. He might have been able to judge the growth of the grass in such a short time, but I can't see him risking losing the penny!'

Ian Mor Caimbeul's son Ruairidh was the last resident farmer on Tarasaigh, and he sold out to Iain Mor MacKay from Horgabost – then changed his mind and wanted his farm back again. The court case ran for years, but Ruairidh lost at every stage, and eventually left Tarasaigh to settle at An t-Ob.

In 1978 the *Reader's Digest* published a story titled 'Stranger in Taransay', taken from a book by the Canadian writer, Farley Mowat. It told the story of an Eskimo who had come to Tarasaigh. At first glance the story was not impossible, as in the days of the whaling station at Steisean nam Muc in North Harris, the whalers did come in behind Tarasaigh, and could possibly have brought an Eskimo with them. But as you started to read the story, it got more and more impossible:

> The few strangers who visit Taransay remember the acrid smell of peat-smoke on the windswept hills, the tang of the dark local ale and the sibilant patter of the Gaelic tongue spoken by the shepherds and fishermen who gather during the long evenings under the smoke-stained ceiling of the Crofter's Dram. Strange objects, delicately carved, hang from the ceiling beams or crown the shelves behind the bar – narwhals, walrus, polar bears snarling defiance and a pack of Arctic wolves.[41]

The Eskimo was supposed to have married a local girl called MacCrimmon – a name unknown on Tarasaigh – and to be buried in the village churchyard on Tarasaigh, with a tomb-stone inscribed in English verse. As my own interest in Tarasaigh was well known, I had a lot of requests for further information about the Eskimo, and found it rather difficult to convince people that it was a good story, but complete fiction.

The tides have always caused destruction to the shores of Tarasaigh, as Carmichael noted. The bay where boats are landed now is called Miosadar, with Rubha na Cruaich, the point of the peat-stacks, to the east and Sgeir Bhuailte, from where Eoghann swam across to Horgabost, to the west. But Miosadar sounds more like a land-name than a sea-name, and it is the bay on the other side of Sgeir Bhuailte – Am Bagh – which has the landing place names: Laimrig an Arbhair, Laimrig an Eorna, the landing of the harvest and of the corn. The old folk used to say that at a very low tide at Miosadar, you could see the roofs of houses under the water, and although that had to be an exaggeration, it was perhaps a memory of the days when the village was in Miosadar, before the sea broke in. I am the more inclined to believe that when I look at Rubha na

Cruaich today. Where we used to wheel barrowloads of peats from the point to the houses, the sea has cut through, leaving a sand cliff of up to twelve feet in height. On the sand face it has revealed a beautiful prehistoric midden, full of empty shells and pottery. But the sea is still eating in, and soon the midden will have gone too, and its contents will be spread along the beaches towards Raa.

Eoghann Beag married June Flower from England, and they settled in the old farmhouse where the Campbells had lived. June was as fond of the open-air life as was Eoghann Beag, and she went out to sea with him, working the lobster creels from which he made his living.

Life there was never easy for the MacRaes, having to take all their provisions across in an open boat – and having to do without, when the weather was against them – and there was ever-increasing fear of illness as they got older. Eoghann Mor died in 1974, and Lecsaidh, Eoghann Beag and June left then, and the island lay empty, apart from occasional visits to tend their stock by the MacKays. Sadly, none of the MacRaes were to live for long in their new house in Seilibost. First June died and then Lecsaidh, then Eoghann Beag was drowned in an accident looking after his boat, and the story of the Tarasaich came to an end.

There was one last chapter to the story, and a farcical one at that. Lion Television decided to mark the year 2000 by basing a *Castaway* programme on Tarasaigh, putting over thirty people from different walks of life on the island, to see how they could survive as a community. The survival aspect was doomed from the start, for someone at an office desk decided that the year would begin on 1st January, instead of starting in the summer to prepare for the following winter. The buildings for their homes were not ready in time, and 'flu struck; most of the 'castaways' spent January and February in the Harris Hotel in An Tairbeart, or in luxury self-catering accommodation! Those who knew Tarasaigh and the difficulties the Tarasaich had had to face could have felt that the whole idea of the programme was a bit of an insult – 'Let us show you how much better we can do' – but as the programme became less and less to do with survival, most of the Harris people began to find it rather funny. There is little survival involved when a helicopter is at hand to take across hundreds of bags of coal!

All the fuss has now died down, the castaways have left, and Tarasaigh can get back to normal once again; though the MacKays have gained from the rebuilding of the old farm steadings and are now offering them as self-catering accommodation. I suspect that in a year or two, all traces of the castaways will have gone from the island, and nothing will remain of the whole concept except a wry smile from the local people when they remember the hype, and the fiasco.

PART THREE – CAOL NA HEARADH

Sound of Harris

It is strange how the concept of travel has changed over the years. Today, people think of the Islands as being on the outside edge of Europe, whereas a hundred years ago they were on the inside edge of the Atlantic. When all travel was by boat, the sea was the link, not the divider. The same applied on a smaller scale to Caol na Hearadh; until the advent of the car ferry *Loch Bhrusda* we had been conditioned to think of Caol na Hearadh as separating Harris and Bearnaraigh, so much so that Bearnaraigh is now Bearnaraigh Uibhist. But our predecessors were in no doubt that Bearnaraigh was Bearnaraigh na Hearadh, and the islands of Caol na Hearadh were an important part of the lands of Harris – and much more accessible to MacLeod's headquarters at Roghadal than, say, Huisinis or even Losgaintir.

I can remember myself the old ferry *Loch Mor* standing off Roghadal, and the launches coming from Bearnaraigh, from Lochportain and from the hotel at Roghadal itself to collect the passengers and freight, and take them ashore. For the Isle of Pabaigh, the main route was from An t-Ob through the tide-race of the narrows of Caolas Sgaraigh, between the islands of Easaidh and Cilleagraigh, both of them farms in their latter days. An t-Ob was also the base for travel to the far-out island of Hiort (St Kilda), and for a time the Hiortach women used to come to An t-Ob to have their children.

Caolas Stiadair

Caolas Stiadair, or Kyles Lodge, is on the shore between Taobh Tuath and An t-Ob. At one time Caolas Stiadair was the ferry point to the islands in the Sound of Harris, for there are references in the old Dunvegan Papers to a salary being paid to the 'Cullishteeder Porter'[42] – the ferryman at Caolas Stiadair. When Anna Caimbeul's boyfriend was drowned, one of the places she would look for his

16. Caol na Hearadh

body would be Caolas Stiadair anns na Hearadh – but that's another story again, and belongs properly to the Isle of Scalpaigh.

Bald's Map of Harris in 1804 shows Caolas Stiadair as a part of the farm of Druim a' Phuind, though the farmhouse itself appears to be at Caolas Stiadair. When the MacGillivrays took over the farm at Taobh Tuath, Caolas Stiadair was a part of their lands, but their successor Alexander MacRa (Fear Huisinis) made Caolas Stiadair his main farmhouse, until his death there in 1874, so maps of this period show Caolas Stiadair as 'Husinish House'. Alexander MacRa was the great exponent of sheep-farming in the Islands, and at their greatest extent his farms included large areas in Lewis and the Uists, as well as Huisinis and Taobh Tuath in Harris.

MacRa's successor in Caolas Stiadair was Roderick MacDonald – Ruairidh Chaluim Ruairidh – a son of the innkeeper in An t-Ob, and one of the Stalcairean MacDonalds whom we met in Tarasaigh. Ruairidh was married to Sarah Grant from Grantown on Spey, and we shall come across some of her correspondence when we come to An t-Ob and Srannda.

In 1902 the Taobh Tuath end of the farm was taken for the new village there, along with the hill grazings, but Kyles Lodge remains as a private house, on a beautiful site above the shore where the old ferry landed.

An t-Ob (Obbe or Leverburgh)

The Gaelic An t-Ob comes from the Norse 'hop' for a tidal bay, so the name An t-Ob strictly applies only to the central part of the village, with Ceann Thuilibhig at the road leading to Taobh Tuath, Sruth at the pier and Creag Stor at the road to Srannda. But at least An t-Ob is better than Leverburgh, the name given to it when Lord Leverhulme tried to make it the centre of his commercial fishery in the 1920s. Leverhulme had bought Lewis and Harris from their proprietors, and he tried to develop Lewis first. After failing there, he came to Harris and devised his schemes for Leverburgh. He claimed that the seas around the islands were far more valuable than any land on them, and so a fishery would be the most sensible basis for the economy. He may have been right, but certainly Leverburgh was no proper site for his main harbour, with all the shoals and reefs of the Sound of Harris to be negotiated.

The Harris people gave him their support, and for one year, 1924–25, all prospered; fish were landed, kippering sheds were built and new houses were made for the workers and management of the new factory, a railroad was built from the pier to the kippering sheds, and there was even talk of extending it through past Loch Langabhat through the moor to Fionnsbhagh and the Minch coast and a better harbour there. But then Leverhulme died, and the accountants took one look at the finances of the project and closed it down, selling the lot for scrap. Many of those who had moved to his new village were left destitute, with neither work nor land.

The sales particulars of 'The Port of Leverburgh' give some idea of the extent of Leverhulme's developments:

> The Fishing Station includes a timber-built pier with about 950 feet of quay space, capable of accommodating 50 drifters, together with the following buildings –
>
> Two large Curing Sheds, built of steel framing, covered with corrugated iron and with concrete floors, each 210ft by 70ft. Kippering house of 12 kilns, 100ft by 65 ft, with extension for curing whale meat, 8 kilns with plant for same.
>
> Two Women's Barracks, each with 20 rooms, accommodating 240 women in all.
>
> Men's Quarters of 6 huts, each 60 ft by 20 ft, accommodating about 180 men in all.

A two-storey net store, 90 ft by 20 ft, with outside verandah
Large garage for 20 cars
Three Huts, 60 ft by 20 ft used as Store Sheds
Offices, Refrigerating Plant and Store Sheds, 2 Smithies and
Workshop
The house property includes 9 houses of stone with corrugated
iron roofs, each containing 3 bedrooms, living room, and scullery,
also the mechanic's house, stone and slated, of 6 rooms, a house near
the Post Office of 4 bedrooms, 2 public rooms, kitchen and servants'
room, as present let to the Post Mistress, and Post Office.
In addition there are 11 pairs of excellent houses under erection
(on which work has been stopped) for Managers and Foremen, of
which 6 are practically completed, 8 are externally completed, and
8 commenced.
These are first rate houses, the best containing Sitting Room,
Living Room, Scullery, 3 Bedrooms and Bathroom with w.c. and
Lavatory Basin, and are built either of stone or concrete blocks with
asbestos composition and slated roofs.[43]

Even the list of premises for sale has a flavour about it of the
desperation to get rid of the whole development as quickly as
possible. Little remains now of his schemes except the name
Leverburgh, which is still used as the postal address and in
timetables, but many think it is time to drop that also, and go back
to the old name of An t-Ob.

Louis MacNiece was even more cutting in a poem on Leverhulme
in his *I Crossed the Minch,* after detailing Leverhulme's difficulties
in Lewis.

To the Island of Harris he turned his eyes
As more adapted to enterprise;
He introduced his commercial cult –
Leverburgh is the sole result.
Leverburgh was meant to be
The hub of the fishing industry;
All that remained at Lever's death
Was a waste of money and a waste of breath.
All that remained of Lever's plans
Were some half-built piers and some empty cans.[44]

One of the oldest schools in Harris was at An t-Ob, or more
accurately, between An t-Ob and Roghadal. In his journal, William

An t-Ob, 's na Herradh. Copyright.

17. The old Smiddy at An t-Ob

MacGillivray mentions that he was at school there, and although the site is now covered by sheep pens, one area at the back is still referred to as the tobhta – the ruins. The teacher then was Armchuil Nicolson from Skye, but he later moved to the Island of Bearnaraigh, and his daughter Isabella married Donald MacKinnon, a boy from St Kilda who was being trained to go back to that island as a teacher. He settled at An t-Ob instead, and became a catechist and teacher there. The ruler that Armchuil had in the school in Bearnaraigh is still in the possession of his great-grandson Tormod Thormoid Seonaid in An t-Ob, a good friend of mine and a great champion of Gaelic.

In the 1850s the estate built a big house at the Roghadal end of An t-Ob for a gardener and a schoolmistress. The gardener was Henry Galbraith from Ireland, and his wife, Mary Henry, took on the job of 'embroidery mistress'. Mrs MacDonald of Caolas Stiadair gave details in an article for *Scottish Home Industries*:

A word must also be said of the embroidery industry for young women and girls, established many years ago by their great benefactress, Lady Dunmore – who sent a competent teacher to the island, paid her salary, and built a house as a work-room and residence. Many of the girls had never seen a thimble before, yet in a very short time, such was their quickness under their clever teacher, the finest of cambrics were embroidered, trimmings for ladies' and children's clothes were made, and many a trousseau and layette was furnished with this beautiful work. For some years this industry has entirely ceased.[45]

The flax for the school was grown at An t-Ob: there is still an area of ground called Leob a' Lin (the Flax Park) and there are still some specimens around of the fine work done in the school, mixtures of linen and wool.

Another big house in An t-Ob was the Coffee House, at the end of the road to Srannda. When Wilson the factor was living there, and his wife had two servant girls from the Bays, they started to hear strange noises in the house. The Wilsons were going away on one occasion, and the girls were scared to stay on their own in the house, so they invited some of the local boys in, to stay downstairs when they went to bed. In the middle of the night, the boys started to hear screaming from upstairs, and went to the girls' room – and they heard it too. It started with a scrabbling noise, which you could have blamed on a rat, but then it changed to a series of knocks, each group louder than the last, until it reached the stage of a real banging on the walls. Then it would stop, and start again from the scratching. The boys decided to say a prayer and that quietened things down, but then it started up again, and so it went on till dawn, when all became peaceful. When the Wilsons came back and heard the story, Mrs Wilson was scared to live there any longer, but one of the girls told her it would be all right – she was leaving, and she said the noises would follow her. Whatever was the cause of it, the noises did stop, but then the house burned down. Even the joiners working to repair the house were very edgy about any strange noises, and the lady who took it over wouldn't sleep a night there on her own.

There was another cailleach there called Catriona Mhartainn (Catherine Martin) living in the Clachan, a group of old houses where An Clachan shop is today. She had been in service in the farms on the machair most of her life, and the farmers' wives had given her a lot of cheap jewellery and trinkets; and she wore all of them all the time. I can remember if anyone turned out over-dressed, the comment would be 'Seallaibh Catriona Mhartainn' – 'Look at Catriona Mhartainn!'

18. An Clachan at An t-Ob

The An Clachan is a small shopping complex that was set up as
one of the Community Cooperative Schemes which were advanced
by the Highlands and Islands Development Board as an answer
to the downturn in the economy of rural areas. An Clachan is
owned by Co-Chomunn na Hearadh – the Harris Community
Cooperative – and is run by a management committee on behalf
of shareholders, the holding of shares being open to any member
of the local community. When the Co-Chomunn was set up first,
it had a wide range of businesses to run – fish-farms, a coalyard, a
building material store – in addition to the shop at An Clachan, but
it was never really successful, and tended to lurch from one financial
crises to the next, until eventually all the businesses were given up,
except An Clachan. Not many of the original Co-Chomuinn in
the Islands are still trading, and my own impression is that it was a
mistake to expect a committee of amateurs, in the best sense of the
word, to be able to run a wide range of different businesses. Almost
by definition, the Co-Chomuinn were set up in areas where there
was a lack of business skills and experience, and it might well have
been better to concentrate on one type of business at a time. An
Clachan has expanded its grocery and vegetable business and now
has twice-weekly deliveries of fresh and frozen food direct from
the mainland, at prices not too different from those charged on the

mainland, as well as running a tea-room, a small exhibition and a much-needed petrol-filling station.

Just to the west of the present day slip for the car-ferry to Uist was the house of Aonghas Ruadh (Angus Morrison). He was the ferryman in his day, and the stone beach below his house was called Mol nam Baraillean – the Barrel Beach – because of the amount of freight that came ashore there; passengers too clambered up among the seaweed to the shore. Aonghas had a brother, Murchadh, who went to Australia with his family in 1857, and took with him Fionnlagh, the son of his deceased brother Tormod, whose wife had married again. In his old age Murchadh returned to Harris, and brought with him Fionnlagh, who was ever after known as 'Straileanach' – the Australian – and was famous for the number of illegitimate children he left in the area.

At one time also, in the 1840s, Ruairidh Hiortach was the 'post-runner' at An t-Obbe: as a Hiortach – a St Kilda man – he should indeed have been fit enough to be a runner. His daughter Oighric got married in 1852 to Iain Martainn (John Martin) from Sgarasta, a cousin of Catriona at An Clachan, and Bard Pabach made a song about it: 'Banais Iain Mhartainn' – John Martin's wedding.

Fiadhachadh farsuinn gu banais Iain Mhartainn
Chualas 's gach ait' an t-iomhradh aic
Gu na shaoil leam an toiseach gu 'm b' ann ann am Manais
Bhiodh i air sgath nigheann Dhughaill aca
Bha mise 'g am bhiodadh nach d' thoirteadh mi ann
Chur crioch air na bh' ann a chursachan
Na gugaichean Hiortach bha corr agus bliadhn'
An crochadh san riasg bha sughanta[46]

Wide were the invitations to John Martin's wedding. / Every place heard the report of it. / If I thought at first it was to be in Manais / that was because of Dougal's daughter. / I was very upset that I wasn't asked / Putting the finish to the courses / with Gugas from Hiort that were over a year / hanging in the peat and succulent!

That is how the song starts, but by the time it finishes the humour is getting rather too broad to repeat here.

Gugas of course are the young of gannets, salted and kept to mature. Today they are still harvested by men from Ness in Lewis

on the rock island of Sulaisgeir, who have a special exemption from
EEC regulations to allow them to continue the age-old practice.

An t-Ob is the terminus for the car-ferry to Bearnaraigh and Uist,
and the journey across on the *Loch Portain* should be a highlight of
any visit to the area. The sea between Harris and Uist is a maze of
islands, reefs and shoals, and the ferry has to make a wide sweep to
the east to find sufficient depth of water for the crossing. I believe
the *Loch Portain* draws only 1.4 metres of depth, and even so, she
cannot make the journey at a very low tide. On a summer's day, with
the sea full of birds and the rocks full of seals, it is a most wonderful
way to spend an hour or so in either direction.

Srannda (Strond)

In the days when Srannda was a farm, with the farmhouse across
on the island of Cilleagraigh, and the farmworkers and sub-tenants
on the mainland at Srannda itself, the tacksmen of Srannda were
Campbells, descended from a John Campbell, who was the foster-
father of Sir Norman MacLeod of Bearnaraigh. Fosterage was a very
formal process then, and all eventualities had to be covered, as can
be seen from the contract of fosterage of 1705 – the oldest known
document in Gaelic referring to Harris.

> This is the condition and agreement on which MacLeod is giving
> his son, namely Norman, to John son of the son of Kenneth, and
> this is the condition on which he is with John, namely, if so be that
> John die first, the child to be with his wife until she get a husband
> for herself, but the guardianship of the child to belong to Angus
> son of the son of Kenneth so long as she remains unmarried, and
> so soon as a man marries her, the child to be with Angus himself
> from that time forward during his life, and if his brother, namely
> Donald son of the son of Kenneth be the longer liver after Angus,
> the child shall be with Donald in like manner . . . [47]

The reference to the Campbell brothers as 'sons of the son
of Kenneth' is odd, and has led some writers to think that they
were MacKenzies – MacCoinnich as a surname, rather than Mac
Choinnich as a patronymic – but their grandfather was Kenneth
Campbell, the warden of the old castle on Pabaigh, and it was as his
grandchildren that they were given the right of fosterage.

Fosterage, as well as being an honour, was a method of cementing relationships within families – 'Cairdeas gu fichead ach comhaltas gu ceud' was an old saying: relationship to the twentieth degree, but fosterage to the hundredth. It was also a commercial transaction, as the same contract shows:

> And this is the stock which John son of John son of Kenneth put in possession of the child Norman, namely four mares, and other four which MacLeod put in his possession, along with three mares which he promised to him when he took him to his bosom; and the charge and keeping of these mares which MacLeod gave to the child shall be with John son of John son of Kenneth, in order to put them to increase for his foster-son; and the care and keeping of the four mares which John son of John son of Kenneth gave to his foster-son shall be with MacLeod to put them to increase for him in like manner . . .

The Campbells of Srannda had farms on Skye also, and many of the families who lived along the shore of Srannda came from that island – Gillieses and Martins among them. When it was thought that the mourners of Anna Caimbeul of Scalpaigh had all been lost – and again that story itself belongs to Scalpaigh – among the families mourned were the Campbells.

> Teaghlach Shrannda riabh bha buadhmhor
> O shuidh Iain air tus na uachdar
> A Mhic ic Chonnich tha sud cruaidh or
> 'N t-oifigeach priseil 'nochd 'sa ghrunnda[48]

> The Srannda family were ever successful / Since Iain himself first had the tack / It is hard on the seed of Kenneth / That the valuable Officer should go to the depths

The farm of Srannda was broken into crofts in the 1830s, and by 1841 there were fifty-seven families there. Other families moved in from the surrounding area, among them a family of MacLeods from Lingreabhagh that included two unmarried sisters, Marion and Kirsty, clann nighean Thormoid (Norman's daughters). They were such good weavers that the Countess of Dunmore, who owned the island then, sent them off to the mainland for training, to Alloa and then to Paisley, and that is why they became known as the Paisley Sisters. When they returned, they in turn taught other Harris women, and that was the start of Harris Tweed as a commercial concern.

Mrs MacDonald of Caolas Stiadair gave more details of the history of weaving in Harris in an article she wrote for *Scottish Home Industries* in the late 1890s, and despite the gushing nature of her prose, the article is so detailed as to be worth quoting at length.

> Fashions of industry change with time, as do other fashions. In Harris, up to the beginning of the present century, hand-weaving formed one of the chief industries of the island. Lint, home-grown, was woven into fine towels and table-cloths of never-ending wear by the labours of the women, assisted, no doubt, by the men in the heavier portions of the work. Certain table-cloths of this date are still to be seen in good preservation, notwithstanding the lapse of years.
>
> Another of the old industries consisted in the making of a fabric called camlet. This was cloth made from very fine wools, combed, carded and spun; cards used in the work may be found to this day in the houses of some of the older families, but the mode of working is of the past. The warp, of six hundred threads, was not thought to be of ideal fineness unless it could be drawn through the wedding-ring of the mistress of the house. It is improbable that these durable textures were ever sold.
>
> It was not till the year 1844 that the people of Harris were shown how they might develop powers of earning money and getting a market for their goods by a new manufacture, for it was then that the late Earl of Dunmore [proprietor of the whole of Harris] sent a pattern of the Murray tartan to be copied in 'tweed', when webs of this material were so successfully made that Lord Dunmore not only used it for his keepers, ghillies, and other retainers, but adopted it for his own wear.
>
> It was then that his noble wife, Catherine, Countess of Dunmore, began to devote her splendid energies to teaching the people how best to help themselves by disposing of the products of their labour – a lesson much needed at that time of difficulty, when the failure of the potato crop was causing great and widespread distress.
>
> The people were encouraged to use the natural dyes extracted from weeds, sea-weeds, flowers and crottle of the rocks, and from the soot on their chimneys. At first there were few varieties in the shades of the webs, but as time went on, and the people gained experience, many pretty colours were produced, and, through the ceaseless exertions of Lady Dunmore, the Harris tweeds became

the fashion, and were soon largely in demand. Webs, good and bad, were sent off at stated intervals to Dunmore, where they were received, measured, and each length ticketed for purposes of sale, the less attractive pieces being reserved for charitable uses at home. Lady Dunmore promptly established an extensive connection with leading tradesmen in Edinburgh and London, and hundreds of pounds were paid quarterly or half-yearly to the workers. It was not until the year 1851 that she visited the island, but she afterwards very frequently went there, stimulating the workers by her presence to yet greater efforts in the new industries. Orders increased, and prices rose as the cloth improved in texture and pattern, and she never wearied nor faltered in her labours till her death, which lamentable event took place in February 1886. She is gone! To the great loss of the people of Harris. The writer can never forget her beautiful countenance, as she smilingly met the workers, who came flocking to Rodil House to receive payment from her own hands, and listened with untiring sympathy as they told her of their various needs and of their love and gratitude.

Her good work is still continued, but not to the same extent. Some ladies, wishing to buy directly from the people, having found that the present writer would forward the Harris products when applied for, now send orders for the stuffs required, and as they also recommend them to their friends, there is in this way a considerable sale. The people are not making less cloth since they lost their benefactress, but they sell it to less profit; for, when needing the necessaries of life, they will accept very low prices from dealers, who, in their turn, have to part with the goods at a low rate to the great city dealers, in order to cover their own expenses. This has reduced the price per yard below its true value. From 3s 6d to 3s 9d per yard is not too much to give the workers, for tweeds so durable and so excellently coloured with healthy dyes that improve with washing. This price, even, barely allows the worker 6d per day for wages. There is very little division of labour, one pair of hands frequently doing all the work, from the fleece of wool to the finished cloth. The looms are only adapted for single-width cloth from 27 to 30 inches wide, but each web measures over fifty yards in length.

There is another Harris industry, the knitting of stockings. In 1857 this work was established by Lady Dunmore, much assisted in this case by Mrs Thomas [the wife of Captain Thomas, Government Surveyor at the time]. This lady still interests herself in seeking out wools to be knitted into socks and knickerbocker stockings, for which she pays the workers. Great thanks are due to the present Earl of Dunmore for his kindness in often giving to the people, without payment, the wool from his own sheep, for the benefit of these various industries.[49]

Srannda developed as a fishing community, and there are still fishermen there, though the village has also become very popular with families from away wanting a holiday house near the shore, with sheltered anchorage for a small boat.

There was a ship came ashore in the Sound a number of years ago, called the *Stassa*, and she had a deck-cargo of timber. It washed in all around the shores here, and of course the people here found good use for the timber. The excise people came around, looking for the timber from the wreck, and they started to check on the timber people had, putting it to their mouths to see whether it tasted of the salt from the sea. So the local people set up the 'Timber-Tasting Society' – and every hen in the area had a new hen-house.

Roghadal (Rodel)

Roghadal is different from the rest of Harris in that it has soil – neither the thin sand of the machair nor the peat moss and rock of the Bays. The soil is rich and red in colour and the Norsemen called it Rodel – 'Red Dale'. On the hill-slope above the village is an Iron Age dun, guarding the Minch and the eastern approaches to the Sound, as the dun at the Teampall at Taobh Tuath watches the west. A good viewpoint is always a good viewpoint, and the Second World War coastguard station is just behind the dun.

The first we know of the history of Roghadal is in 1528, when Alasdair Crotach, eighth chief of the MacLeods of Harris and Dunvegan rebuilt the church of St Clement there; there had been a church there since Columban times. Alasdair Crotach was a warrior; he was *crotach* or hunch-backed, because of a wound he received in a battle with the MacDonalds. This was the time of the collapse of the Lordship of the Isles, and many of the clan chiefs built themselves churches for their own burial, rather than be buried like their predecessors in the Lordship graveyard on Iona.

Alasdair Crotach died in 1547 and is buried in the tomb he had made for himself in St Clement's. The tomb is recessed into the

19. St Clement's at Roghadal

wall, with depictions of a castle, a bishop, the Virgin and Child, St Clement himself and a galley under sail, and below them a hunting scene with dogs and deer, and a tablet in rather odd Latin stating that 'this tomb was prepared by Lord Alexander son of William MacLeod Lord of Dunvegan in the year of our Lord 1528'. The archway around the recess has panels depicting the twelve disciples and at the top a crucifixion, and at the front of the tomb lies an effigy of Alasdair in a coat of mail and holding a sword, with his dog lying at his feet.[50]

Near to Alasdair is the tomb of his son William, who died in 1551, and in a cross aisle another tomb, said to be that of Iain Og of Minginish, but tradition says that many others were buried there too, the last being Aonghas mac Dhomhnaill mhic Aonghais, the man who took his wife off the kidnap ship at Fionnsbhagh in 1739:

Clogaid, luaraich, lann geur
Comhdach Ruairidh nan Lann
Ceithir chinn dheug a' s an aon uaigh
'S truagh a fhuaireadh thu air an ceann

Mail, helmet, sharp sword; / Armour of Roderick of the Swords; / Fourteen heads in the one tomb / A pity to be putting you at their head!

– whoever was Ruairidh nan Lann!

20. Tomb of Alasdair Crotach MacLeod in Roghadal

In the floor of the nave itself was the coffin of the bearers of the Fairy Flag of the MacLeods; they say that there was a metal grid below the lid of the coffin, and as each flag-bearer died and was placed in the coffin, the remains of the previous one were shaken through the grid into the coffin below.

William was one of the less powerful chiefs of the MacLeods and on his death he left only a daughter, Mary; much of the contemporary politics of the clan centred around Mary and her eventual marriage to a Campbell from Argyll. Roghadal was abandoned, and the MacLeod chiefs were thereafter buried at Dunvegan.

In the graveyard itself are several caibeals, or private grave enclosures, for the main cadet families of the MacLeods, and more recent ones for families whose idea of their own importance may not be shared today. There is a caibeal for Sir Norman MacLeod of Bearnaraigh and one for his grandson Donald – 'The Old Trojan' – who was in hiding on Ceapabhal, and one for the MacLeods of Losgaintir.

There is a story that on one occasion two groups of mourners arrived at the graveyard at the same time. A man with second-sight lived in the same village as one of the deceased, and he claimed that he often 'saw' his neighbour lying dead with an arrow in his body – a sure sign that he would die in battle. When his neighbour died in bed, the seer's reputation suffered. When the two sets of mourners reached the gate, they started an argument about precedence, and the argument led to blows and then to the use of weapons. Sir Norman appeared and settled the dispute by giving both parties a row for fighting in a graveyard. The mourners went back for the body, and found that a stray arrow had lodged in it – the seer's reputation revived dramatically.[51]

Although the churchyard was still in use, the church itself had been allowed to fall into disrepair, and it was not until Harris was bought in 1779 by Captain Alexander MacLeod, a son of the Old Trojan, that any attempt was made to repair it. By 1784 it was complete, with a new roof, but unfortunately it caught fire, and had to be rebuilt again. Tradition says that the fire was caused by the masons and carpenters, who celebrated too well after the completion of the renovations; in their drunkenness they managed to set fire to the building.

Captain Alexander took a lot of interest in Harris but his family saw it only as a source of revenue, and St Clement's was allowed to fall into disrepair once again. Then in 1834 Harris was sold to the Earl of Dunmore, and it was the then Dowager Countess of Dunmore who had St Clement's rebuilt to its present state in 1873. Unlike many Victorian 'improvers', the countess' architects kept as closely as possible to the original scheme, with the result that the church is by far the most beautiful building in the whole of the Hebrides.

Roghadal Hotel

As can be seen from the rental of Tarasaigh, seventeenth-century rents were paid partly in cash, but mainly in kind – cattle, sheep, meal, butter and cheese. All this had to be stored, and we find references to MacLeod's 'Keeping-House' in Roghadal. In 1703 Martin Martin mentions a problem the Roghadal people had, no doubt because of the proximity of the 'keeping-house'.

> I have seen a great many Rats in the Village Rowdil, which became very troublesome to the Natives, and destroy'd all their Corn, Milk, Butter, Cheese etc. They could not extirpate these Vermin for some

time by all their endeavours. A considerable number of Cats was employed for this end, but were still worsted, and became perfectly faint, because overpowr'd by the Rats, who were twenty to one; at length one of the Natives of more sagacity than his Neighbours, found an expedient to renew his Cat's Strength and Courage, which was by giving it warm Milk after every Encounter with the Rats, and the like being given to all the other Cats after every Battle, succeeded so well, that they left not one Rat alive, notwithstanding the great number of them in the Place.[52]

When Captain Alexander MacLeod bought Harris in 1779, it was with the intention of living here. He was a different type of landowner: a businessman, much more interested in commerce than in the status of a clan chieftain. He had made his money as the captain of an East Indiaman clipper *The Lord Mansfield*, and now he meant to make Harris a centre of the fishing industry. He set up fishing stations all along the east coast of the Bays and encouraged fishermen to settle there: not just people from the machair but from all over the islands and the west coast of Scotland. He built piers and a net factory in Roghadal and, most important of all, he built himself a new house beside the pier, in one of the most beautiful spots on the whole island. To have a resident landlord, interested in making a success of a local industry, was a new experience for Harris.

John Knox visited Roghadal on his tour of the Hebrides in 1786, and was full of praise for Captain MacLeod and his work.

> About four years ago Captain MacLeod came to settle in Harris, and fixed upon Rowdil Bay as the best adapted to his views; that place being situated on the south-east side of the island, and contiguous to the Sound of Harris. Within the bay of Rowdil, on the north side, there is an opening, through a channel of only 30 yards wide, to one of the best sheltered little bays in the Highlands; from which, on the opposite side, there is an opening of the same dimensions to the sea. This has water for any vessel to enter or depart at any time of the tide; and Captain MacLeod has deepened the south passage to fifteen feet at common spring tides. The circumference of this little harbour or bason is nearly an English mile; and here ships lie always afloat, and as safe as in Greenland Dock. Here the Captain has made an excellent graving bank, and formed two keys, one at the edge of the bason, where ships may load or discharge afloat, at all times of the tide; the other on the graving bank.

21. View of St Clements Church, Rowadill, Harris

He has also built a store-house for salt, casks, meal &c. and a manufacturing house for spinning woollen and linen thread, and twine for herring nets, which he makes for his own use. He has procured some East Country fishers, with Orkney yawls, to teach the inhabitants; and has built a boat-house, sixty feet long by twenty wide, capable of containing nine boats, with all their tackle.

He has raised, or rather repaired, a very handsome church, out of the ruins of an old monastery, called St. Clements. He has also built a schoolhouse and public house; and now he is carrying on good cart roads from the keys to the village, and from thence through the country, to facilitate communication with the west side of the island.[53]

Captain MacLeod made a garden behind his new house, and brought in John MacLeod, a gardener from the Small Isles, to tend it: some say he was from the Isle of Muck itself, but that is probably just being appropriate! There are many of his family still around in the south of Harris, and they are still known as na Gairneileirean – the Gardeners.

The success of Captain Alexander's schemes did not last; the tax laws were against them for a start. It is said that on one occasion a ship laden with salt had to land its cargo hurriedly at Roghadal because of bad weather. Salt at that time had to be checked for tax at Steornabhagh, and the excise insisted that the cargo be loaded again at Roghadal, taken to Steornabhagh, unloaded again there to be measured for tax, loaded again, brought back to Harris and unloaded once more! In any case, Captain Alexander found, like Lord Leverhulme a century and a half later, that you cannot rely on herring; for years you will get a good catch, and then suddenly, for no apparent reason, they disappear for a year or two.

Fortunately at that time there was a boom in the kelp industry. Valuable minerals could be obtained from the ash of seaweed, and at the time of the French Wars, when other sources were closed to Britain, the islands became a centre of the kelp industry. On the Atlantic coast there was the huge cast of tangles after a storm, while on the Minch shore there were acres of rockweed which could be cut. The weed became so valuable that the landlords of North Uist and Harris fought a legal action right up to the Court of Session[54] about the ownership of a set of rocks in the Sound of Harris – the rocks themselves were worthless, but the seaweed around them was of the greatest value.

The argument turned on whether or not you could walk to the rocks at low tide. If you could walk there at a low tide from the shore, then the rocks belonged to Uist, but if not, they belonged to Harris. Men on each side gave different evidence, the Uistmen saying that you could walk there and the Harrismen that you could sail a boat through the channel at the lowest tide. The Uistmen even started to put rocks into the channel to make it fordable, but when it came to the test, they had to give up, and the rocks still belong to Harris.

The trouble was that the weed that should have been used for fertilising the land was used for burning, so the crops suffered. People settled on land that could never support them, and rents were decided by how much of a shoreline there was, not how much land. However much the people earned from the kelp, they found that their rents were put up to match, so although the kelp brought money to the island, not much of it stayed in the people's own pockets! Cutting the weed was heavy work, up to your knees in seawater, and burning it was a filthy job – and the bitter smoke of it cost a few people their eyesight.

After the Battle of Waterloo in 1815 foreign sources for minerals became available again, and the government removed the taxes from imported minerals; the kelp trade collapsed. The tenants lost the income which had paid their rents, and the landlords lost the income which had kept them in luxury. Captain Alexander had been succeeded by his son, who had been in India for many years, and had retired as a society gentleman. He even refused to use the name MacLeod, taking instead his mother's name of Hume, and had no interest in Harris except as a source of income.

His son was no better. He came only once to Roghadal, and that was to empty it. John MacDermid (Iain Ban na Faoilinn) told the story to the Napier Commission in 1883.

> I will tell you how Rodel was cleared. There were 150 hearths in Rodel. Forty of these paid rent. When young MacLeod came home with his newly-married wife to Rodel he went away to show his wife the place, and twenty of the women of Rodel came and met them, and danced a reel before them, so glad were they to see them. By the time the year was out – twelve months from that day – these twenty women were weeping and wailing; their houses being unroofed and their fires quenched by order of the estate. Some of the more capable of these tenants were sent to Bernera, and others were crowded into the Bays on the east side of Harris – small places that kept three families in comfort where there are now eight. Some of the cottars that were amongst these 150 were for a whole twelve-month in the shielings before they were able to provide themselves with permanent residences. Others of them got, through the favour of Mrs Campbell of Strond, the site of a house upon the sea-shore upon places reclaimed by themselves.[55]

Donald MacDonald (Domhnall Choinnich Mhurchaidh) takes up the tale:

> I myself was born in Rodel. I saw my mother with her youngest child taken out of the house in a blanket, and laid down at the side of a dyke, and the place pulled down. My mother was in child-bed at the time. The child was born only the previous night, and my father asked MacLeod, who was the proprietor at the time, whether he would not allow them to remain in the house for a few days, but permission was not given, only he came to the dykeside where she lay, and asked what this was, and when he was told, he asked him to lift her up and remove her to an empty barn, and it was there that

she was put. It was MacLeod himself that took the place and kept it
for two years, and afterwards he gave it to Donald Stewart.[56]

So Roghadal House, Captain Alexander's house, became the factor's
headquarters. John MacDonald (am Baillidh Domhnallach) was
the factor after Stewart, and he was no better. The good lands had
already been cleared, but MacDonald pushed people around from
croft to croft to satisfy his own grudges and to make room for his
own favourites – playing draughts with the crofters, as one old
man said.

Baillidh Domhnallach had a brother James (Seumas Ruadh) who
was the factor in Balranald in North Uist and this Seumas Ruadh
had a daughter Jessie, who was engaged to be married to the assistant
factor, Donald MacDonald from Monkstadt in Skye. Donald was
dismissed for being too lenient to the crofters, and a new assistant,
Patrick Cooper, was employed: Jessie was now expected to marry
him instead! This was too much for Jessie and she sent for Donald
to be ready on a certain night, with a ship to take her away. All went
according to plan except the weather, for a storm blew up, and they
had to make for shelter in Harris, where Jessie's uncle locked her
up in his house in Roghadal, and sent Donald away. Donald did
not give up as easily as that, and he found another boat and crew
in Harris. They raided the house in Roghadal, and Donald took
advantage of the uproar to smuggle Jessie out of a back window.
On this second elopement they got clear away, and eventually went
to Australia.

Baillidh Domhnallach was not the man to take such an affront
to his family dignity quietly, and everyone that he could discover of
the raiding party was put out from his croft. Donald MacDonald
(Domhnall Choinnich Dhuinn) from Lingreabhagh was the
steersman of the boat, and he was sent as a cottar to Aird Asaig. The
family of MacLeods known as the Fidhleirean – the Fiddlers – were
even more harshly dealt with according to Iain Fidhlear, who gave
the story to the Napier Commission in 1883.

My brother had a vessel, and he came in the vessel with Donald
MacDonald from Monkstadt. The factor MacDonald had his
revenge upon me and my brothers for this act, though we were
quite innocent of it. One of my brothers was at the time in Borve

and another in Scalpay, and I had a sister in West Tarbert. The four of us had lands at the time, and he deprived us of them all. One of my brothers went to Australia, where he is still. That is how I lost my land – the sole cause – and I did not get lands since . . . The end of it was that my family, when they grew up, scattered in to all parts of the earth; and some of them are dead in a foreign land, and others I know not where they are – and I am alone.[57]

One cannot but have sympathy for Iain Fidhlear, but was his evidence accurate? Kenneth MacDonald, the factor for North Harris, tells a different story in his evidence to the Commission.

Another remark I may make with regard to the evidence of John MacLeod. He said his brother was forced to leave Harris. Nothing of the kind. Allan MacLeod was one of the best tenants we had – never falling into arrears. He left of his own free will, and he went to Australia, and now goes to church in his carriage. He was a most industrious man, and a man who was never in arrears.[58]

Who are we to believe? It is always tempting to believe the oppressed rather than the oppressor, but when we look at Scalpaigh we find that the brother there was not evicted, and his family still have the same croft today. I do not doubt that Iain Fidhlear was evicted, and for the cause he claimed, but other parts of his evidence are suspect.

22. Rodel Hotel

This is always the problem with the evidence that was given to the Napier Commission. Because our sympathies today are with the crofter and against the estates, we tend to assume that the evidence of the crofters must be correct, but this need not be so. In most cases, witnesses are giving evidence of what had happened many years before, perhaps not even in their own lifetime, and we have to allow that their recollections may have beeen inaccurate, exaggerated or even downright untrue.

Latterly Rodel House became a hotel, and the window out of which Jessie eloped was one of the sights shown to the visitors, but gradually the building fell into disrepair until only the bar was left open. Now a reconstruction programme has been completed, and the hotel is once again open, run by Donnie MacDonald, a grandson of the former owner, and his wife Dena – and if you want to taste seafood as it should be cooked – unfussy, and with all the goodness of the freshest of ingredients showing through – then you should visit the dining room at Rodel Hotel!

Bearnaraigh (Berneray)

Bearnaraigh was always one of the most fertile parts of the islands, and many of the families there are of great antiquity. The MacPhaics, for example, who today for some inexplicable reason go under the name of MacKillops, claim descent from Paul Balkason, one of the half-Viking rulers of the islands in the twelfth century, while the Fergusons claim that their one-time favourite name of Robert derives from a henchman of Bruce who was in hiding in the island in the months before Bannockburn. This type of oral tradition is often looked on with suspicion, but there is in fact a gap in the known history of Bruce at this period, and since the MacDonalds of the Isles were among his main supporters, it could well be the case that he and a henchman were in the Hebrides in that period.

Formal history on the island dates from the time of Norman MacLeod, later Sir Norman, a son of Sir Ruairidh Mor, fifteenth chief of the MacLeods of Harris and Dunvegan. He was born in Bearnaraigh and there is the remnant of a building there with the inscription *Hic natus est illustris ille Normannus MacLeod de Berneray, eques auratus* – Here was born the illustrious Norman MacLeod of

23. The Gunnery of MacLeod of Berneraigh

Bearnaraigh, a distinguished knight – though it is thought to have been MacLeod's gunnery rather than his house.

Sir Norman was given a liferent of Bearnaraigh by his father, a liferent which included not only the island itself but also Nisabost, Geocrab, Aird Asaig and Bunabhainneadar on mainland Harris. In the wars of Cromwell, Norman was a confirmed Royalist and fought at the battle of Worcester in 1651, a fact commemorated in a tablet to his memory in the family caibeal at Roghadal.

> Sir Norman MacLeod
> Of Berneray
> 1614–1709
> Seirbhiseach dileas Cruin
> Third son of Sir Roderick Mor
> MacLeod XV Chief and Isabel
> MacDonald of Glengarry;
> Fought Cromwell's armies at Worcester, Stornoway and Loch
> Garry; knighted for Loyalty and Valour by King Charles II
> A generous patron of Gaelic culture
> Closely associated with
> the bardess Mary MacLeod

Sir Norman was the great patron of Mary MacLeod (Mairi ni'n Alasdair Ruaidh) who wrote many of her songs in his praise:

> Gur muladach tha mi
> 'S mi gun mhire gun mhanran

Anns an talla am bu ghnath le MacLeoid
Shir Tormoid nam bratach
Fear do dhealbh-sa bu tearc e
Gun sgeilm a chur asad no bosd[59]

I am sorrowful / Without laughter or song / In the hall where
MacLeod used to be / Sir Norman of the banners / There are few
of your kind / From whom never came vaunt nor boast

So much so that MacLeod of Dunvegan became jealous and exiled
her to Scarba, off the coast of Argyll. She was forgiven on condition
that she stopped writing songs, but she got round this by describing
all her later poetry as croons, lullabies or the like.

Sir Norman married twice, his second wife being a daughter of
MacDonald of Sleat and North Uist. She was supposed to bring a
dowry of 20 000 marks, but her father was unable to pay it, and
Sir Norman got possession of the Clachan and Baile Mhic Phail
areas of North Uist instead, which is why you find many families
of Harris origin in that area today, among them the Morrisons of
Ruchdaidh, who claim the chiefship of the Morrisons of Lewis and
Harris, on genealogical evidence which is shaky, to say the least.
When the dowry was finally paid, Sir Norman used the money to
buy a wadset (a long-term transfer of property in security of a loan)
of a large part of mainland Harris: Huisinis with Scarp, Losgaintir,
Tarasaigh, Horgabost and Seilibost.

It was in Sir Norman's time that they had the great sandstorm
of 1697 in Bearnaraigh and in Pabaigh. A gale came from the
north-east, after a spell of dry weather, and lifted the entire surface
of the ground from the machair at Loch Bhrusda, and blew it to
the south until it covered the whole village of Siabaigh, along the
south shore of Bearnaraigh. The evidence given in the boundary
dispute between Harris and North Uist in 1770 includes reference
to Siabaigh and its tenants.

Rory MacLeod, grieve at Bernera, aged 54 years, depones that
his grandmother by his mother's side was Mary MacLeod, alias
Ninhormoid vic Ean vi Gillichalum, who died fifteen or sixteen
years ago, above 100 years old; that upwards of thirty years ago she
told the deponent that she could herd cattle when Sir Normand
MacLeod went to the Battle of Worcester; and that she lived in
Siabay at that time with her mother, then a widow, to whom Sir

Normand allowed a little land; that thirty years ago, and frequently thereafter she told the deponent that she remembered Shiabay in Bernera when it was all corn and pasture ground, and no part of it over-run with sand; and that it was then possessed by tenants; and was so until the sand over-ran it.[60]

On Sir Norman's death — which was in 1705, not 1709 as on the grave-slab — Bearnaraigh passed to his son William, who also inherited the wadset. In a judicial rental of 1724,[61] William answers for 'the four pennies of Eye, the three penny lands of Raa and the four pennies of Pabaill, all in Taransay, the two penny lands of Scarp, the two and a half penny land of Horgisbost, the two penny land of Shelibost and the three penny land of Housinish' as well as the liferent lands of Bearnaraigh, giving him 65¾ pennies out of 93½ penny lands of the whole of Harris.

In 1730 MacLeod of Dunvegan decided to increase all the rents in Harris, and William gave up the lease of Bearnaraigh and moved to Losgaintir. Bearnaraigh passed to his nephew Donald, known as the Old Trojan.

Many of the stories of the Old Trojan belong to the period just after the 1745 Jacobite rebellion, and his subsequent hiding at Uamh Ulladal in the Forest of Harris and at Gob an Tobha at Taobh Tuath, but intrigue was nothing new to him, as he had already been involved in the kidnapping of Lady Grange and her captivity in remote St Kilda. Rachel Chiesley was a lady of very uncertain temper, verging at times on insanity. Her husband had been involved in Jacobite plotting and she had learned the secret and threatened to give it away. She was spirited away from Edinburgh to the remote island of Heisgeir off North Uist, but after two years the people there decided they could take no more of her temper, and insisted that she be removed. She was taken from there to St Kilda for eight years, but her reason finally failed and she was eventually taken back to Skye, where she died in 1745.

It was the Old Trojan too who was most involved in the dispute mentioned already about the boundary between Harris and Uist, and the consequent rights to the kelp on the rock of Grianam and other rocks in the Sound of Harris. The case reached the Court of Session in 1770, and began with the proprietors of Harris and North Uist establishing their claims.

The said Sir Normand MacLeod of MacLeod his predecessors have, in virtue of their charters and infeftments, been in the immemorial possession of certain islands, and of a considerable number of rocks, lying interjected betwixt their said lands of Harris and the island of North Uist, which belongs to Sir James MacDonald; and particularly, they have been in the immemorial possession of the islands of Bernera, Torgay, Haay, Suersay and Votersay, and also of the two rocks called Grianam and North Rangus, and of several other rocks lying interjected, as said is, as all parts and pertinents of their said lands of Harris, otherwise called Ardmenoch. The said rock of Grianam yields some little pasture, but the principal value of it, and of North Rangus, which yields no pasture, consists in the seaweed growing on them.[62]

Among the points of evidence given by the Old Trojan is the story of a stranded whale.

Depones; That he heard that the tenants of Borve in Bernera had found, and secured with ropes, a whale, on one of the rocks now in dispute; and that some of the North Uist tenants had carried it away under silence of night, by order of Ranald MacDonald late of Baleshare, factor on North Uist, who manufactured the blubber of the whale; and it was generally talked, that the late William MacLeod of Luskinder complained of that to Sir Donald MacDonald; and that Baleshare was obliged to pay to Luskinder, as then possessor of Bernera, the value of the whale; and this the deponent heard from severals, and, as he thinks, from the present Luskinder, but in that he cannot be positive.[63]

The end result of the case was that all the islands north of the channel of Rangass were judged to belong to Harris, so that boundary today runs close along the shore of North Uist.

Even though the kelp industry failed long ago, the islands are still valuable to Bearnaraigh for grazing sheep and for cutting peat, for Bearnaraigh has no peat of its own, but relies on peat cut on the off-shore islands, which is then brought home by boat.

From the Old Trojan, Bearnaraigh passed to his son Norman, the villain of a kidnapping scandal from Fionnsbhagh in Harris, and from him to his daughter Isabella, the last tackholder of the island.

In 1830 MacLeod of Harris took a court case to evict his cousin Isabella, and it was then that Bearnaraigh was broken into crofts

24. Landing peats at Bearnaraigh

for the first time. The northern township, Ruisigearraigh, stretched from Beinn na Ghainmheachadh (Sand-hill) in the north to the head of Loch a' Bhaigh, while the southern township, Borgh, included Siabaigh, now restored to fertility after the sand-blow.

Siabaigh was the home for a few years of Angus MacAskill, the Cape Breton Giant. His father Norman (Tormod Aonghais 'ic Neill Mhoir) came from Pabaigh, and settled for a few years near where the cemetery is now, but the place was still bad for sand-blow, and after a few years most of the neighbours went off to Cape Breton. Norman went to Cuidhtinis in the Bays of Harris for a few years, but eventually he too went to Cape Breton with his family, to Englishtown.

One of my favourite stories of Bearnaraigh concerns two young boys, Domhnall Alasdair 'ic Neill (Donald Morrison) and a friend, who were out fishing on the west side of Bearnaraigh, when a storm blew up and took them out to sea in their little boat. The Bearnaraigh people had given them up for lost – and the other boy did indeed die of exposure – but Domhnall's granny insisted that he was still alive: 'Tha Domhnall a' tighinn dhachaidh, agus aghaidh air an tigh' – Donald's coming home, and he's facing the house.

The rest of the family could not believe her: apart from anything else, the harbour on Bearnaraigh was on the east coast and, as their house sat, anyone coming into the harbour would have their back to the house.

As it turned out, Domhnall had managed to stay alive, and eventually was picked up by a sailing ship going to the West Indies, and taken there. He cast around for a chance to work his way back to Scotland, and at last the chance came, and he found a ship that was bound for the west coast. Pabaigh at that time was famous for its whisky, so Domhnall persuaded the skipper that he should call in there for some whisky, and took the chance to jump ship.

At that time too, the people of Pabaigh and Bearnaraigh shared a newly built church on Bearnaraigh, and the Pabaich used to sail round to the east side of Bearnaraigh on a Sunday to go to church. As it happened, the first Sunday after Domhnall arrived on Pabaigh, the sea was so calm that the Pabaich did not bother to sail round the island, but just beached their boats on the west beach of Bearnaraigh, opposite Pabaigh, and walked across the machair from there; so Domhnall did come home, and he was facing towards the house.[64]

At this time there was a ferry from Port at the south end of the island across to North Uist, at a place called the Leac Bhan (the White Flagstone) quite close to where the causeway now reaches the shore. They say that there were actually three stones, and if you stood on Leac an Tasdain, the ferryman knew that you were willing to pay a shilling, and would come for you immediately; standing on Leac na Sia Sgilinn meant that you were willing to pay sixpence, and the ferryman would come for you whenever he was ready; on the other stone – I forget its name – you were not willing to pay anything, and he would come when he had some other reason to do so!

The crofters in the southern township of Borgh did not enjoy it long. Borgh is the more fertile part of Bearnaraigh, and the factor soon had his eye on it for a sheep-farm. Malcolm MacLeod (Calum Ruairidh Ailein Bhain – Malcolm son of Roderick son of Fair Allan) told the story to the Commissions of 1883 and 1894:

> We are in Bernera 45 families who have not so much as a turf of land to maintain ourselves and our families. Many of us formerly

had land, and this makes us feel the want of it more now . . . There were 40 crofters in Borve previous to 1848 and then the number was reduced to 20. They were only left in possession for five years. The rent paid by the original 40 was laid on the 20. It was on account of its being too heavily rented that they left it. They were evicted and deprived of their stock by the proprietor and the ground officer.[65]

Our land was taken from us, and every head of sheep and cattle which we possessed, and no crofter on the other end of the island was allowed to give us a foot of land to till. We began to fish lobsters to maintain our families, and at once the factor MacDonald sent the ground officer to stop us, he being angry with us because we were not going to Australia. Some of us then came to this end of the island, where we are now, along with the crofters and others, still in Borve. I am ashamed to tell you the manner in which some of the people lived at that time. They lived on shellfish – limpets. Those who had boats went out to the rocks once or twice a day when the ebb occurred at forenoon and evening. All this occurred because of the Clearing of Borve to give it to William MacNeil. We fish lobsters summer and winter, and still we are unable to provide ourselves with food and clothing. From want of nets, we cannot go to fish herrings, though the lochs on either side of us were full of them. Every year we think we can fish out of the Atlantic what will buy nets for us, but because we have our wages pledged for food before the fishing begins, we must deny ourselves many things in order to keep up our credit.

In order to deliver us out of this womb of poverty in which we are enclosed, we beg of your honours to assist us in getting the land, of which there is plenty in the island, restored to us; for it is unseemly that the big sheep should die eating the fatness of the land at one side, and we banished from our fathers' land which ought to be ours, and forced to brave the dangers of the sea in order to obtain food.

We asked land of the proprietor, and he promised it to us in his own house at Rodel – he gave us a promise, but nothing else, and we never got the land.[66]

William MacNeil of Caolas Bhearnaraigh in North Uist, but of the family of the MacNeils of Pabaigh, took the lease of Borgh first; it then passed to his brother-in-law John MacDonald (Seonaidh Scolpaig). After his death, Borgh was let to Roderick Campbell from Harris, and he was the farmer at the time of the agitation to have the farm broken up into crofts once more.

25. At Bays Loch, Isle of Bearnaraigh

The cottars on Bearnaraigh began to put pressure on Campbell to give up the farm; his stackyard caught fire and was destroyed – though his own grieve's son-in-law got the blame for that – and before that a boatload of cattle coming to the farm was turned back at the Riof; one of the Bearnaraigh boys threw a rock at the boat, and it went right through it. There was real trouble then and some of them ended up in court for piracy on the high seas. When Campbell's lease ran out in 1900, Borgh was broken up into twenty-four crofts.

A great number of families emigrated from Bearnaraigh to Cape Breton in the 1820s, settling especially in the area around Grand River, L'Ardoise and Loch Lomond, in the south of Cape Breton: There was no pressure on the crofters to leave the estate at that time only the pressures of increasing numbers, the turn-down in the kelp industry, and probably the return of sand-blow to Siabaigh; migrants also knew they faced the challenge of pioneering in a new land. One of them, Murdo Morrison (mac Choinnich Bhain Iain Fhionnlaigh) wrote some verses on his own difficulty in getting hay in 'Oran air Gainne an Fheoir' – A Song on the Shortage of Hay.

Nuair a dh' eirich mi 's a mhaduinn
Bha e trom a' sileadh sneachda;

Chaochail 'n inntinn bh'aig Lachluinn
Cha toireach e sgath dhomhsa

Dh' fhalbh mi 's bha mi bochd 'nam inntinn
'S ann a thadhail mi aig Sile;
'S ann a thoisich i air griocan
'Tha sinn fhein gun roineag'

Smaoinich mi gu'n tillidh dachaidh
Cha robh reusan dhol na b' fhaide
Dh'fhalbh mi gu math trath 'sa mhaduinn
Sios gu cladach L'Ardoise[67]

When I rose in the morning / It was heavy with falling snow /
Lachlan changed his mind / And wouldn't give me any. / I left
with a heavy heart / And then I met Sheila / And she started
complaining / 'We haven't got a shred.' / I thought I might as well
go home / There was no reason to go further / I left early in the
morning / To go down to the shore at L'Ardoise

Murdo was living in Cape Breton, at a place named Ferguson's Lake,
because so many of the Fergusons and other Bearnaraich had built
their houses around it.

Pabaigh (Pabbay)

Pabaigh was a rich island, with deep ploughing ground, and it was
so good for crops that it was known as the granary of Harris. Part
of the island was destroyed in a sandstorm in 1697 which even
blew away a whole village, and dumped sand on what had been
acres of arable land. The estate records of 1698[68] refer to 'Pabbay,
having been formerly a fourteen penny land, is now reduced to ten
pennies, on account of sand-blow'. The village of Baile-Meadhanach
(Midtown) disappears from the rentals and only three villages are
left: Baile-mu-Thuath (Northtown), Liongaigh (Lingay) and Baile-
na-Cille (Kirktown).

The MacLeods had their castle there in the days when they were
a sea-power, before they moved to Dunvegan on Skye. Ian Borb
MacLeod, the sixth chief of the clan, was a famous warrior – no
doubt that was how he got the nickname of Borb, or truculent. He
headed the right wing of the island army at the Battle of Harlaw

26. Teampall Mhoire, on Pabaigh

in 1411, and it was there that he got a deep wound in his forehead, which never completely healed. He seems to have lived in peace after that, probably a peace inspired by fear of him, but he always enjoyed swordsmanship, and it was in a fencing bout on Pabaigh that the old wound burst, and he died there in about 1467.

There was a battle there too, and 'MacIain' – who is believed to have been Donald Munro Morison, a son of John Morison (Gobha na Hearadh) gathered a tradition about it for an article in the *Celtic Magazine* in 1880.[69] The date of the battle must have been about 1405, at a time of feuding between the MacDonalds and the MacLeods, while Iain Borb was still a youngster.

> One day the inhabitants of the island discovered to their terror that a large party of MacDonalds were approaching in their war galleys, evidently with the intention of attacking the island. Hastily collecting their families, they placed all the women and children in places of safety at some distance from the hamlet; then separating, they hid themselves in the numerous creeks and coves of the island. Landing without opposition, and leaving one man in charge of the boats, the MacDonalds advanced exultingly to the village which, to their pleased astonishment, they found deserted. Confident in their numbers and strength, they gave themselves up to collecting all the booty they could lay their hands on.

So soon as the MacLeods saw their foes thus engaged, they all rushed to the boats, seized the sentinel before he could give the alarm, and set the whole fleet adrift, the tide soon carrying them far away. Then hurrying to their own boats, the MacLeods pulled with a will to the neighbouring island of Berneray and sought the assistance of their kinsmen there. The MacLeods of Berneray willingly offered their aid to destroy their mutual enemy, and accompanied the Pabbay men back to their homes.

Finding themselves unable to resist the deadly onslaught of the MacLeods, the MacDonalds beat a retreat to where they had left their boats, but, to their despair, they found them gone and encountered instead the determined attack of the men left in charge of the MacLeods' boats. Many of them threw themselves into the raging sea, preferring a watery grave to the dishonour and death before them. Not a single man of the invaders was left to tell the mournful tale.

There is a whole area in the south-east of the island, between the Seana-Chaisteil (old castle) and Abhainn Liongaigh – Lingay River – looking towards Bearnaraigh, where the great sandstorm of 1697 first blew away the soil, and then dumped loose sand on top, so that today it is all a clayey marsh with moving sand hills on top. That must have been the site of the battle, for that is where the shepherds used to find bones and bits of swords and armour as the sand-hills moved before the wind.

Neil Morrison, Bard Pabach, mentions Lag a' Bhatail – the Plain of the Battle – in his *Oran an Eagail* or Song of Fear:

Tha e soilleir ri dhearbhadh
Gu'n do mharbhadh na ciadan ann
Le gaoth thioram a Mhairt
Bheireadh an aird bho an t-siabuinn iad.[70]

It is a sure fact / that hundreds were killed there. / The dry winds of March / bringing them up in the sand.

Baile na Cille village is built around an old church, Teampall Mhoire – Mary's Chapel, of which the west gable and parts of the side walls are still standing. Its stonework is quite different from that in the Teampall at Taobh Tuath and St Clement's at Roghadal, and it may date from an even earlier time than their 1528. The ground around the Teampall is raised to a considerable height, well above the base of the walls, presumably from its use as a burial ground. In those days coffins were a rarity, as timber was far too precious to be left to rot in the ground, and so bodies were buried in a shroud. This took far less space than a coffin, which explains why the old graveyards in the islands are so small. It also meant that once the depth of ground available for burials had all been used, bodies could be laid on the surface and the earth heaped over them, thus gradually raising the level of the surface of the whole graveyard.

William MacLeod, the ninth chief of the MacLeods of Harris and Dunvegan, had no sons, and the chiefship passed to his only daughter, Mary. There was great dispute in the West Highlands about whom she should marry, and eventually Campbell of Argyll married her to a relation of his own, Duncan Campbell of Auchinbreck, in 1567. Mary gave up her rights in favour of her uncle Donald, and in return Campbell obtained tacks of some of the best land in Harris for his followers. One of them, Kenneth Campbell, became the warden of the old Castle on Pabaigh, and it is from him that almost all the Campbells on Harris today are descended.

Alexander MacLeod, tacksman of Baile mu Thuath, the North Town of Pabaigh, gave evidence in a dispute about the boundary of North Uist and Harris in 1770.

> Depones that in the sound betwixt the island of Eansay and the north part of the island of Berneray, in the deponent's neighbourhood, there runs a bank of land called Druimnabeast; That this bank runs opposite to the north part of Berneray, and the deponent has frequent occasion to cross it in boats on his way to Berneray, and on his way to the island of Eansay, and to the islands of Groay and Lingay, where the deponent casts his peats; and that the channels in the said bank shift frequently, and the channel the deponent takes at one time, will not perhaps be passable in a fortnight thereafter. Depones that the said bank called Druimnabeast is a large bank of sand about three miles long; but that the deponent cannot say whether there are any quick-sands in it or not, for he never walked or put his foot on any part of it. And depones that there are great tracts of blowing sand on the islands of Pabay and Berneray, and that the sand has over-run great tracts of these two islands.[71]

It is interesting that MacLeod mentions cutting his peats on Groaigh and Liongaigh, for these are islands away at the eastern end of the Sound of Harris, opposite Roghadal. There was very little peat on Pabaigh – probably it had all been cut out over the generations – and they had to go to this group of islands, still called the Pabach Islands. The tides in the Sound are odd, with one tide coming from the Atlantic and another from the Minch, and they say that if you know the tides and are careful, you could sail from Pabaigh to the islands on a tide, and return at night on another.

Baile mu Thuath had always been a farm and the resident MacLeods were clann Alasdair Ruaidh, the family of Red Alexander. The Alexander of 1770 was the last of the family to live on Pabaigh, for he was another of the tacksmen who left Harris to go to Carolina after the failure of the 1745 Rebellion. Not that MacLeod was Jacobite – or at least not openly – but after Culloden the whole relationship between the chiefs and their tacksmen changed. No longer was it the ties of relationship that mattered: the preferred tacksman now was the one who could offer the highest rent. Many of the tacksmen did not approve of this change of status – nor could they afford the new levels of rent – and they decided to emigrate with their sub-tenants and farm-workers, to set up a new clan system in Virginia or the Carolinas, with themselves as the new clan chiefs. Of course it did not work; with so much land available, the sub-tenants did not see why they should be subordinate to anybody, and many of them headed off on their own, as far as Georgia and Tennessee. Then when the War of American Independence started, the tacksmen came out on the British side, and lost everything; Alexander's two brothers were killed in 1776, and he himself, after a period in prison, died in 1782.

When Alexander MacLeod gave up Baile mu Thuath to go to America, the farm was let, along with Baile Liongaigh, to William MacNeil, son of a merchant in Dunvegan in Skye, and many of the travellers going to remote St Kilda in the early eighteenth century enjoyed his hospitality on the way there. William died in 1828, and his gravestone is still visible, outside the south-east corner of the Teampall. He was succeeded by his son Major John MacNeil.

The Revd John MacDonald of Ferintosh visited Pabaigh a few times on his way to St Kilda, and describes one such visit in his journal for 1827.

Next day (Friday) we got only as far as Pabbay, the wind being still rather unfavourable. There we took our quarters with Mr McNeil, once tacksman of St Kilda, and a gentleman remarkable for Highland hospitality. In the afternoon the inhabitants, having heard of our arrival, assembled for sermon. After sermon I examined the school in the place, supported by the Inverness Society, and was gratified with the progress and proficiency which the scholars had made, about forty of whom were present.[72]

In Cape Breton, I have seen a Gaelic New Testament with this inscription on the fly-leaf: 'Gifted by the Inverness Education Society to John Morrison, Pabbay in Harris, 21st June 1827.' The Testament must have been one of those brought to Pabaigh by the Revd MacDonald, and then taken by its recipient on his long journey to a new home across the Atlantic.

A few years ago, we carried out research at *Co Leis Thu?* for a descendant of Major MacNeil, who had done a great deal of research himself into the later history of the family. He found that the major – he was only a captain at the time – married when he was on duty at Curaçao in the West Indies, then came back to Pabaigh with his wife and family; but when his father died, instead of taking over the whole tack, he only got a double croft in Liongaigh, around the old farmhouse, and the rest was broken up into smaller crofts. Major MacNeil died on 23 July 1834 – his wife had to notify the War Office about his pension, so we know the exact date – and the family shortly after left to go to Glasgow, where Mrs MacNeil died in 1841.

When the MacNeils left, the old farmhouse was given to Ruairidh Cubair – Roderick MacLeod, the cooper, or barrel-maker – from Aird Asaig, as an inducement to come to Pabaigh, where they were needing as many barrels as they could get.

Pabaigh was famous for the making of whisky, and although that was illegal, the estate made no objection, for the sale of the whisky paid the rent. There are lots of stories about gaugers – the excisemen – coming to Pabaigh to try to catch the Pabaich with the whisky, but they did not succeed, partly because the ferrymen from Bearnaraigh were in the deal with them, and used to make a special signal with the sail as they came round the Carradh Liath (the north-west point of Bearnaraigh), and that gave plenty of time to hide the evidence.

There is a story of one time when the gaugers went to the house of an old woman – and a very upright, sharp-tongued woman she was too – and questioned her about whisky, and what a tongue-lashing they got for suggesting that a respectable old woman like her would have anything to do with illicit whisky. After the men had left, with their tails between their legs, the old woman stood up from her 'chair', and as she lifted her long skirts, revealed that it was a barrel of whisky she was sitting on!

But things were changing. The factor in Roghadal wanted Pabaigh as a sheep-farm, but since the Pabaich were paying their rents out of the profits of the whisky, he could not use the excuse of rent arrears to get them out. So the gaugers were encouraged to make more strenuous efforts to catch them with their illegal produce, and on one of their raids, either the Bearnarach skipper did not know about the signal, or forgot to make it, and the Pabaich were caught red-handed. That was enough for the factor, and the whole population of the island was evicted, whether they had anything to do with the whisky or not.

In 1841, at the time of the census, there were 323 people on Pabaigh, in 65 households; in 1843 Liongaigh was cleared, and in 1846 Baile na Cille. The whole population of the island were evicted, apart from one man and his family, and he had been brought in as a shepherd to Liongaigh. One or two other shepherds were brought in, and a ferryman. All the rest were cleared off the island: some to Cape Breton, some to Bearnaraigh (and most of these left for Australia a year or two later) and the remainder scattered around Harris and the island of Scalpaigh.

There is a sad little story about one of these families. Alexander MacKinnon was one of those who were cleared, probably from Liongaigh, and he ended up at Cape North in Cape Breton. His son Roderick was married to a daughter of Iain Choinnich Iomhair, who had emigrated from the machair, but he died young – they say that he was shot during a row in a gambling saloon in the Yukon or Alaska at the time of the gold-rush there. His eldest son, Alexander, went off south to earn money in New Hampshire in the United States,

27. Ruins of house on Pabaigh

and though he kept in contact – and no doubt sent money home – it was thirty years later before he got the first chance to return home to Cape North to see his mother. Only when he met her again did he realise that he had lost his Gaelic, and she had no English![73]

After the clearance, Pabaigh was let to William MacNeil of Caolas Bhearnaraigh in North Uist, a grandson of the old tacksman. When he died in 1863, the island passed to John Stewart of Easaigh, a son of Stewart of Losgaintir. He brought in a new shepherd, Neil Morrison from Cleit na Duthcha, who remained on Pabaigh from about 1863 to 1873. Much of his poetry was written there, so he is called the Bard Pabach, even though he spent only a relatively short time on the island.

His two best-known songs of this period are *Oran a Chianalas* – Song of Homesickness – and *Oran an Eagail* – Song of Fear – and the latter suggests that he found life on the island, alone with his family and Domhnall Bessa, less than agreeable.

> Gur h-e mis' tha fodh mhulad
> Tha leann-dubh air mo sharachadh
> Ann an Eilean Dubh Phabbai
> 'S beag a th'agam-s' a dh'abhachd dheth

Nuair a bhios mi gun mhoine
A' tional otraich nam baghannan
Gur h-i feamainn na ceilpe
'Bhitheas a' goil a bhuntata dhomh.

Geamhradh fad' air bheag cuideachd
'S e thug buileach droch snuadh orm
M' aite comhnuidh 's mo thuineach
Dluth air tulach nan uaghannan

'Nuair a chiaras am feasgar
Bidh an t-eagal ga m' chuairteachadh
Chan' fhalbh mis' gun mo bhata
'S car na m'omhaich mu'm builear mi.[74]

How sorrowful I am / And tired by depression / in the black isle of Pabaigh / Little joy I have from it. / When I am without peat / gathering rubbish from the bays / it is the kelp of the seaweed / That boils my potatoes / A long winter with little company / Has put me in a bad frame / My dwelling and my home / beside the hill of the caves. / When the dusk comes / It surrounds me with fear / I will not go out without a stick / My head turned / lest something should strike me.

Today, Pabaigh is occupied only by a few shepherds at lambing and shearing times.

It has only a very poor landing place, and all attempts at making a better pier have so far been swept away in the winter Atlantic storms. Without good sea access, it is probable that Pabaigh would have had difficulty in maintaining a population, and would have emptied like so many other off-shore islands.

But Pabaigh never got the chance.

PART FOUR: AN TAIRBEART AND NA BAIGH

An Tairbeart (Tarbert)

The name An Tairbeart is from the Norse words for a place where boats could be pulled across from the head of one loch to another; in this case from the East Loch to the West Loch. Anyone going from North to South Harris has to pass An Tairbeart, and one of our first stories about An Tairbeart is about such a journey in the 1500s, when the Morrisons of Ness raided Harris as part of the troubles following the collapse of the Lordship of the Isles. The raiding party headed down for Harris, but at the narrows of the Cadha, the steep hill leading south from An Tairbeart, they were intercepted by a party of MacLeods, led by Donald of the three Donalds – Donald son of Donald son of Donald – wielding a timber snatched from a roof.

> Domhnall na tri Domhnall
> Chlann MhicLeoid 's e air a' chearraig
> Le cabar dubh a tigh a nabuidh
> Tillidh e 'namhaid 's a' Chadha[75]

> Donald of the three Donalds / left-handed and of clan MacLeod, / with his neighbour's sooty rafter / will turn the enemy in the Cadha.

This is often quoted as one of the prophecies of Coinneach Odhar, the Brahan Seer, but like many of these 'prophecies' it describes events which had already happened.

It was in the early 1850s that An Tairbeart began to be an important village, when the first church was built there, at the head of the East Loch. The story of that church begins on the island of Tarasaigh, where John MacDonald, the farmer, built himself a fine new two-storey house at the Uidh. The roof was of Ballachulish slate – one of the first in the Islands – but it was too heavy for the walls and the weight started to force the walls apart. So the roof had to be taken off, but rather than waste it, it was brought across to An Tairbeart, and the new church was built underneath it. A manse was built nearby, and there was a graveyard just across the road, behind where the bakery was later.

28. An Tairbeart

In the time of the Revd MacIntosh MacKay in the 1860s, a new church was built at the eastern end of the village, near the present pier, and the old church became a school, and then a store, and latterly the masonic lodge. The manse became the doctor's house, which is why the old people still call it Manse an Dotair. The graveyard is long disused, and they say that the last to be buried there was a sailor who came off a foreign ship.

Joseph Pennell, who visited the islands in 1887, gives a description of a Sunday in An Tairbeart.

It was on Sunday mornings that there was the greatest stir in Tarbert. Then the people came from far and near to meet in the little kirk overlooking the loch. We were told that comparatively few were at home. This was the season when they go to the east coast, the men to the fishing, the women to the curing-houses; but we thought they came in goodly numbers as we watched them winding with the road down the opposite hill-side, and scrambling over the rocks behind the town. Boats one by one sailed into the loch and to the pier, bringing with them old women in clean white caps and tartan shawls, younger women in feathered hats and overskirts, men in bonnets and blue sailor-cloth. They were a fine-looking set of people, here and there among them a face beautiful with the rich, dark beauty of the South – all that is left of the Armada. As they came up upon the pier they stopped in groups under the shelter of a boat-house, for the wind was high, the men to comb their beards and hair, the women to tie one another's bonnet-strings and scarfs, to smooth one another's shawls. And all the time scarce a word was spoken; they were as solemn at their toilet as if they already stood in church.

The Islanders are as melancholy as the wilderness in which they live. The stranger among them never gets used to their perpetual silence. Their troubles have made them turn from the amusements they once loved. The pipes now seldom are heard in the Hebrides. Their one consolation, their one resource, is religion, and to them religion is a tragedy. Nowhere was the great conflict in the Church of Scotland fought with such intensity, such passion, as in Skye. The same Sunday in Harris, we met people coming home over the hills, and still they walked each alone, and all in unbroken silence. And this Sabbath stillness lasts throughout the week.[76]

Pennell's comment about the remnant of the Armada is a common one, but the dark, Iberian colouring seen in some parts of the Bays is far older than the Armada, and in any case, it is unlikely that survivors from its wreck would have stayed alive long if they had come ashore. The dark features and polished blue-black hair are almost certainly a reversion to the old Bronze Age type, before the days when the fair, Iron Age Celts came to the Islands.

Pennell's other point about the people walking each alone must be true, for do they not still say that you can tell the Hearaich by the way they walk in single file, even when they are alone?

It was after the new church and the pier were made that An Tairbeart began to grow into its present shape. Much of that was due to Bean Mharaig, the farmer's wife from Maraig. Her husband, Kenneth Morrison, from Skye, had the farm at Maraig, but he died, and she moved in to run the inn in An Tairbeart at the head of the bay, just between the church and the graveyard. She wasn't the first to have an inn there – the MacAulays from Aird Asaig were there before – but she must have made a success of it, for she is remembered as being very wealthy as well as very stout. 'Uiread ri Bean Mharaig' – just like Bean Mharaig, they used to say of anyone really hefty. Her daughter married Donald MacLeod (Domhnall Ban Griasaiche or Fair-haired Donald the shoemaker) and they had a large family, including seven marriageable daughters, most of whom were set up with a shop, a house, and a husband – and some say that that was the order of priority too – and that was the start of the Main Street.

There was a smithy on the Main Street, with Eoghann Gobha as the blacksmith. He was a son of Gobha na Hearadh, the hymn-writer and blacksmith of Leacli, and in his old age he became blind, and he used to go along the street led by his grandson, a son of his son Seonaidh Og and Jessie Gibson from Ireland. 'Eireannach Beag' – Little Irishman – Ewen used to call him: 'Eireannach Beag, I can hear your father in the smithy. He's making horseshoes, from the sound of it – but if that's how he is making them, he's not the smith his father was!'

I remember a package of letters being donated to the Comunn Eachdraidh (History Society) in An Tairbeart; Eoghann Gobha had written to his half-brothers and sisters in Canada, asking for assistance in his old age and blindness, and these were the replies. One or two enclosed a little money – even his sister in Bruce County, whose children were bad with the 'hupencove' – but all suggested that he write to his brother Roderick, who was rich; Roderick wrote back too – with eleven pages of good advice.

One of the others who built a house on the Main Street was Norman MacLeod (Tormod mac Neil) and he was a first cousin of Donald Ban Griasaiche. From being a merchant and farmer with his own big house in An Tairbeart, he went down in the world until he was lodging in a garret of the house that used to be his own. In 1889 he wrote a letter telling his life story, which was published in the *Scottish Highlander*. The letter is rather long, but worth quoting in full for the picture it gives of the merchant class of Harris at the time.

Landlord oppression in Harris – told by a nonagenarian

Tarbert, Harris, 24th May, 1889

Sir; I am under the necessity of applying to you to put my statement of oppression and cruel treatment by the landlords and factors since the year 1828 in print, so that the original cause of the Highlanders being poorer than other people in Scotland may be seen – landlords and factors preventing me and other poor people in former times giving education to our children, as you will see by my statements herewith. You will see my sons, by their education, wealthy merchants in the East Indies since 30 years, carrying on a lucrative business. They have that benefit for my fightings against the proprietors and their factors for several years. No person in Harris dares venture to state their treatment from factors or land-owners, else they are put out of their crofts. Please excuse my troubling you with the said statement. I am, etc.

Norman Macleod, senr., Tarbert
the oldest man in Harris, 90 years of age

Statement of oppressions at Tarbert, Harris, in 1846 by the landlord and his factor, Captain John Macdonald, Late Factor of Harris.

I, Norman Macleod, senr., merchant, was born at Tarbert, Harris in February 1800. I am a son of Neil Macleod, tenant at Tarbert. My father was a tenant at Tarbert paying rent for the 6th share of East and West Tarbert for the period of 92 years, at a rent of £6 sterling per annum. In the year 1828 my father gave me one hundred pounds sterling to purchase goods in Glasgow to commence as a general merchant at Tarbert, Harris. When I arrived at Greenock, I called upon a second cousin of mine, Messrs Maclellan, owners of 18 three masted ships. This friend went with me to Glasgow and opened accounts for me in 18 of the largest warehouses in the city. Dealing with these ware-houses for upwards of 50 years upon a large scale I made some money. Times were much better then than now, because the estate of Harris was wholly inhabited with tenants in good circumstances, being in possession of Sheep, Cattle, horses and money in abundance. I would be certain sure to have square accounts with my customers at the end of every twelve-months to the amount of £600 sterling, going to Glasgow every August. The landlords and factors had not then commenced clearing the crofters' land for themselves illegally, which was the original cause of the destitution in Harris in 1846–47. The late factor of Harris, Captain

Macdonald, took a spite at me for taking my children from the estate school when the teacher was not able to give my children sufficient education. With that spite the Factor would not allow me to build huts to give education to my children, outside of my own dwelling-house. The factor then pulled down to the ground five huts I built for educating my children. I told the factor that it was most cruel of him to prevent me or any other person from educating their children at their own expense. Then I told the factor at once that I would put my children under the roof of my own dwelling-house, where neither proprietor nor factor could take the roof off it for 57 years to come, that being the length of my lease.

I then wrote Dr Maclachlan at Edinburgh, to supply me with students for eight years – to send me one every year, and that I would pay board, lodgings and wages at my own expense to the students. When I got my children well educated at home I sent some of them to the East Indies – namely Singapore and Manilla, where two of my sons have been doing a lucrative business for 30 years, that by their good education, independent of the cruel landlord and factor that prevented their education, namely Captain Macdonald, factor of Harris, under Lord Dunmore. In the year of 1848 I took a farm called Banvenedra, with stock of cattle and sheep at a valuation, which cost me £1200 sterling, and paid ready cash for them. The rent for the farm was £52 sterling per annum, on a lease of 14 years. The factor, Captain Macdonald, broke the lease 10 years before the expiration and sold 80 sheep for £50 of rent, due in May, and would not give me delay for three months, till Falkirk market in August, when I was to sell my wedders, £150 sterling worth. The factor left on that day in the fanks 400 sheep and 30 head of cattle without grass or farm to keep them alive. I have built a slated house and kitchen and fanks, by plan and specification of the factor, which cost me £470 sterling, and he never paid me a penny for the whole affair.

The same factor, Macdonald, pulled down shop, fishing stores of mine, with salt cellar and fishing materials at Tarbert, and left it upon the streets under the rain &c. The whole affair cost me £420 sterling. This is only a small history of the factor's cruelty and oppression and tyranny. I have seen this with my own eyes, done by the factors in Harris, of whom Captain Macdonald was the worst in my time. Captain Macdonald, late factor of Harris, oppressed and ruined me, reducing me from having 700 sheep and 40 head of cattle of the best stock of the late Mr Stewart of Luskentyre, until he left me penniless. There is no law to be seen in Harris, and no wonder when factors, sheriffs and petty officers co-operate with other planning mischief against the poor class. They are like the Unjust Judge in Scripture who had not the fear of God nor regard for man.

We never received our share of the law of Scotland in the district of Harris – poor yet, and no wonder, when landlords, sheriffs, hotel keepers, police constables, and petty officers prevented poor people from setting their herring nets even in the salt seas. I have seen the above statements myself with my own eyes, and shall prove it.

In February, 1883, Hornsby, hotel at Tarbert, took my bull, worth £25 sterling, for trespass. He said that Kenneth Macdonald, factor of Harris, gave him authority to make use of my bull for himself without paying me a penny.

The present factor, R. Matheson of North Harris, is the worst that ever came – taking gardens that I possessed for 70 years, after being planted and manured with 10 sorts of seeds, and refused to pay me a penny for the labouring of it, nor compensation. He locked my fishing sheds upon me that I cannot cure fish should thousands of barrels be caught daily here. Under these illegal oppressions the only small bit of garden I had since 70 years was taken from me on the 16th inst. by Matheson, factor for North Harris. Under these circumstances I shall be under the greatest obligation to Mr Alexander Mackenzie, Scottish Highlander, to give room to the above statements.

Norman Macleod, senr[77]

29. An Tairbeart

You feel sorry for MacLeod, but he was far from being the average Harrisman in his circumstances, and the whole affair sounds much more like two wealthy men falling out. It seems strange too that he should have been in such poor circumstances, when his sons were doing so well in the Philippines.

There is a copy of a letter which one of the boys in the Philippines sent to his aunt in Cape Breton:

Manila, 14 June 1899
Mrs Mary MacLeod
North River Bridge
Vic. Co.
Nova Scotia

My Dear Aunt

Failte oirbh, agus gu ma fada a bhios beo agus ceo as bhur tigh (Greetings to you and may your life be long and smoke from your house) . . . Altho' Spanish has been almost my daily speech since I arrived in this part – 33 years ago – I can still handle Gaelic fairly well, reading it with ease, thanks to my small collection of good Gaelic books; agus 's aithne dhomh mo sgriobhadh, ged nach urrainn dhomh sin a dheanamh ro mhath (and I know how to write it, though I do not do that so well). But this is not to be wondered at, when I remember that I quitted my Highland home for ever at the early age of fifteen. I hope your knowledge of Gaelic is sufficiently strong to enable you to understand the few phrases incorporated in this letter. Your having emigrated so long ago, about 1845, must make your recollection of Harris very dim. I cannot, however, say the same for myself, for my recollection of Tir nam Beann, nan Gleann 's nan Gaisgeach (the land of mountains, glens and heroes) is as fresh as ever. I remember well the places where I used to roam as a boy – an Tota Ghlas, Beinn an Tanga, Uamha mhor a Laganain Bhuidhe, etc. etc. and few things would give me more pleasure than to visit them once more before I die; I trust that wish may be gratified some day.

Tha mi a nis a co-dhunadh ann an dochas gu ruig an litir seo sibh ann an tir nam beo slan agus falainn. 'S mise, le mor run agad urram, mac bhur brathair (I finish now in the hope that this letter will reach you hale and hearty in the land of the living; with great love from me to you, your brother's son) Alexander S. MacLeod

Alasdair mac Thormoid mhic Neill mhic Thormoid mhic

Thormoid mhic Iain mhic Neill (son of Norman son of Neil son of Norman son of Norman son of John son of Neil.) Am bheil an t-sloinntireachd ceart? (Is that pedigree correct?)

In my genealogical work over the years, we have been in contact with some of the family in Cape Breton, some now in New Zealand, and a descendant of one of the boys who went to the Philippines.

As well as the Main Street, there were some houses too at Cnoc a' Charrain, near the present Scott Road. They were poor landless cottars living there, many of them from the old village of Stiocleit, on the southern shore of the West Loch. At one time there were three old cailleachs there – Morag, Flora and Maggie. None of them had very much, but Maggie had a fancy piece of china that the others coveted, and she had promised it to Morag. In time Maggie died, and Flora took the chance to sneak into her house and take the plate. Morag was pretty sure what had happened, but was afraid to tackle Flora directly. So she started going around Flora's house at night, moaning to herself, 'Thoir air ais an rud a chaidh a ghoid, thoir air ais an rud a chaidh a ghoid' – 'Put back what was stolen, put back what was stolen.' Flora heard the voice, and got so frightened that she put the plate back in Maggie's house; Morag went in and took it, so she did get the plate after all!

An Tairbeart nearly became the centre of Lord Leverhulme's schemes for Harris, instead of An t-Ob, as reported in Nigel Nicolson's book *Lord of the Isles.*

> Obbe was not the best possible site. Tarbert would have been preferable, for it had deep sheltered water, and it would not have been beyond Lord Leverhulme's scope to dig a canal through the narrow isthmus linking the East and West Lochs Tarbert, and so provide his boats with access to the sea on both sides of the Hebrides. Why Leverhulme discarded the obvious claims of a Tarbert canal is not clear. Perhaps he feared its proximity to Stornoway, or did not wish to harm the interests of the thriving community of fishermen on the Isle of Scalpay at the entrance to the East Loch. Or perhaps it was for the more personal reason that once the decision had been taken to rechristen Obbe 'Leverburgh', it became unthinkable to abandon it.[78]

The idea of a canal was not new: it had been suggested by John Knox in his *Tour Through the Highlands of Scotland and the Hebride*

Isles in 1786.

> When the herrings are in West Loch Tarbert, the fishers on the
> east side drag their boats across the isthmus; and so vice versa
> when the herrings are on the opposite side. Apparently, a navigable
> canal might be made through it, at no great expence; but at least
> a good smooth road might be made. By means of which and a
> number of horses, large empty boats, wherries, and even small
> decked vessels, might be dragged upon wheels or sliders from one
> side to the other.[79]

The Harris Hotel has long been a feature of An Tairbeart, and
Sarah Morrison, who runs it now, is the fourth generation of the
family to do so. Here is the description of the hotel, as shown in the
Leverhulme sale documents in 1928.

> **The Harris Hotel** with lands and fishings are let to Mrs Cameron
> on yearly tenancy on terms of an expired lease at an annual rent
> of £100.
>
> **The Hotel**, stone and slated, is a few minutes' walk from Tarbert
> Pier and Post Office. It looks south and west, has a large garden in
> front, and contains –
>
> **On the Ground Floor** – Large Dining Room, Smoking Room,
> Sitting Room, Gunroom, Bedroom, Hotel Parlour, Kitchen, Scullery,
> Pantry, Office, 2 Stock-rooms, and Bar with Cellar.

West Loch, Tarbert

30. West Loch, An Tairbeart

31. Harris Hotel

On the First Floor – Drawing Room, 11 Bedrooms, large Servants' Bedroom. Bathroom with Lavatory Basin and w.c., Bathroom with w.c., Bathroom with Lavatory Basin and separate w.c.

On the Second Floor – 3 Visitors' Rooms.

Outside are Milk House, Wash House, Larder, Coal House, 2 Stores, Urinal, and Lavatory.

A short distance from the house are 3 Garages for 5 Cars, large Workshop with Loft over, Barn, Byre for 3 and 2 Calf Pens. A small Garage and Stockroom are claimed by the Tenant.

There are 25 to 30 acres of grazing which go with the Hotel.

Excellent Salmon and Sea Trout Fishing goes with the Hotel. Loch Laxadale and the chain of lakes are well known for providing excellent sport, and there are Brown Trout in Loch Braigh-nah-Imrich.[80]

Louis MacNiece visited An Tairbeart and describes the hotel in *I Crossed the Minch*:

The hotel in Tarbert is the highest grade thing I saw in this island. It has a smoke-room with leather club chairs and copies of the *Scottish Field*. On the other hand it has a very original bar – dark as bars should be (no decent bar admits the light of the sun) and traversed by horizontal bridges the width of pew-ledges on which a man when standing can comfortably rest his glass. Pew ledges is an apt comparison, for the drinkers stand silently about as if in church, their eyes reverently lowered. Once in a while, they drink and then relapse into devotion.[81]

The main hotel still stands much as described, though with major extensions since that date, and it must be one of the few family-run hotels still in the West of Scotland – with all the personal welcome and friendship that was a hallmark of the family hotels – and is so often lacking in the corporate-owned ones.

There were plenty of characters in An Tairbeart. Kenny a' Bheiceir had the bakery, and was a great source of stories about An Tairbeart and its people.

Padruig Ruadh had the shop next door, though the red hair that gave him the name had long gone by the time that I knew him. Anyone coming into An Tairbeart had to pass his shop – and little chance you had of doing so, for Padruig would be at the door, calling you in, and asking who you were and what you were doing.

Padruig's wife had had the shop at first, but I do not think that he bought much new stock in; after he died, some of the stock was taken to Harris House for a sale of work, and it had the post-war Utility Mark on it.

Next door again was Duncan (Donnchadh na Banndraich), who had survived the Gallipoli campaign in the First World War. Mr Cameron from the hotel invited a group of men all over the age of

32. Duncan MacAskill's shop in An Tairbeart

33. Pier Road, An Tairbeart

ninety to a dinner party at the hotel, but Duncan couldn't go – he was too busy in the shop!

So you could go on, up along the whole Main Street. There was Bean Angaidh's – Mrs MacDonald's – with all sorts of things piled everywhere in utmost confusion: Harris socks beside the cheese, and paraffin beside the milk.

I remember Cathie Ruairidh's shop too; it had narrow double doors, and there was no way I could get through them with a rucksack on without getting stuck.

Dolaidh Phadruig's shop stocked everything under the sun. On one occasion a visitor wanted insect repellent against the midges, and was praising her own usual potion as against the one that Dolaidh stocked: 'Well, lady,' he said, 'That might work for the midges you have in England, but the midges here would just look on it as salad dressing!'

The greatest character of them all was Sandy Mor – a fool to himself for drink, but clever with it and very witty, and you couldn't help but like him. At one time, he was living in three sheets of corrugated iron against the wall of the garden of the bank, and gave his address as Bank Buildings, An Tairbeart. Another time, the minister found him lying by the roadside – 'Drunk again today, Sandy?' says the minister. 'So am I!' says Sandy.

In due course, Sandy went into Harris House, the local Old Folks' Home, and he was the life and soul of the home, just the kind of person that was needed to keep it alive. He could cause his problems too, but he was so quick and so full of fun that he always got away with it. One Christmas, Sandy obviously had a supply of drink in his room, and the matron went looking for it. She found a bottle of whisky wrapped up in a stocking, so Sandy was on the carpet: 'You know that there's a rule here that you are not allowed to keep any drink in your room,' says Matron. 'Yes,' says Sandy. 'Why, were you thinking of changing it?'

Matron knew she had lost already, but she had to carry on. 'No, I wasn't, but if you know the rule, why have you got a bottle in your room?'

'Me!', says Sandy 'Where did you find a bottle in my room?'

'In a stocking,' replies Matron.

'Oh,' says Sandy 'Thainig Santa' – 'Santa came!'

Direcleit and Ceanndibig (Diraclett and Kendibig)

These villages were a part of the farm of Losgaintir at the time of the lease of 1803,[82] which mentions the 'sub-tenants or cottagers in Sticlat and Keandibig and the herd in Dereclet' . John Lane Buchanan, in his *Travels in the Western Hebrides*, tells of a dispute between the tacksman of Losgaintir and one of his sub-tenants there:

> I was told a laughable squabble that happened between this tacksman and one of his poor subtenant's wives that lived at a paltry place near Diraclet, called Ceandibeg. This woman had a strong sheep that she could not catch, for want of a dog bred to that purpose, as is the custom in the island, so that the lamb was not marked when the tacksman collected his sheep. The tacksman seeing a large and fat lamb following the poor man's ewe, ordered one of his scallags to carry it home for his dinner. But the poor man's wife to whom the lamb belonged, happening to be present, remonstrated stoutly against such an act of injustice, urging that the dam that the lamb followed and by which it was suckled, sufficiently proved it to be her property. But the tacksman, deaf to all her arguments, renewed his orders to his scallags to carry off the lamb. But the fellows knowing the virago they had to deal with, were rather backward to carry their master's orders into execution. Xantippe held better than the tacksman could draw, crying out in the Gaelic language

''S fearr cumal cailliach no tarruing bodaich,' that is 'An old woman holds better than an old man can pull.' She held the lamb as firmly as a cat holds a mouse; and, after a long struggle, the tacksman of Luskintire was obliged to give up his expected prey, and yield to substantive justice.[83]

In the 1830s Direcleit and Ceanndibig were made into crofting townships, but in 1851 all the crofts were cut in half to make room for families evicted from Borgh in Bearnaraigh. It is interesting looking around the tobhtaichean – ruins of houses – in Direcleit today, for you can tell which ones belonged to the old village and which to the Bearnaraich. The old houses made use of the natural rock, for parts of the house walls and for shelter, while the Bearnaraich, used to the flat machair, built their houses in the open. Both villages were cleared in the 1860s, on the excuse that they were too handy for poaching in the deer forest of Losgaintir – which was probably true!

Most of the crofters went to the area around Owen Sound in Ontario, but one or two were left in little houses around the shore. The Kerrs' house was so near the shore that a high tide came right in to it. Kenneth MacDonald (Coinneach Ceit) was related to the MacKenzies in the Glen at Carraigrich, on the other side of the East Loch, so they gave him a little piece of land there, and he used to row back and forth across the loch to plant and tend his potatoes. That is the type of story which can actually give a lot of help in tracing families. Ceit, Coinneach Ceit's mother, was from Shieldaig in Wester Ross, and had come to Harris as a servant in the manse in Sgarasta, before she married Murdo MacDonald (Murchadh Dhomhnaill Bhain) from Stiocleit. The MacKenzies in Gleann Carraigrich had been in Seilebost, to which they said were to have come as road-builders, but no one knew where they had originated. But if Coinneach Ceit was related to them, it must have been through his mother, and so the MacKenzies in Seilibost must have had connections with Shieldaig area.

A lot of families evicted from other places found temporary homes in these villages. Peter MacDonald (Padruig mac Dhomhnaill 'ic Uilleim) was born on Tarasaigh in 1825, then his people were moved to Seilibost, then to Borgh on Bearnaraigh. From there he was cleared to Miabhag and then to Ceanndibig, then to Drinisiadar, then finally he died in Aird Sleimhe. They used to say that when

Padruig arrived in a village, all the other families started packing – it was sure to be their village's turn to be cleared soon!

Ceanndibig and Direcleit were broken into crofts again in 1884, as a part of the move to break up the deer forests, and because they are so handy for An Tairbeart, there are quite a lot of new houses there too.

When the road was being made south from An Tairbeart to the Bays, two of the crofters in Ceanndibig wouldn't allow the road to go through their crofts, along the old track along the shore-side, and that is why the road climbs up the steep hill of Sail Cheanndibig and along towards Horsacleit, before branching down to Miabhag.

It was at Direcleit, too, that the two ladies saw the ghost bus. They had been out visiting, and on their way home they got the fright of their lives to see the bus from Steornabhagh coming towards them, then heading off the road into the rocks of the moor! They ran to the nearest phone to report the accident, and while they were there, the real bus passed them. What is really strange is that when they made the new road there, the line they took was where the ladies saw the bus heading into the moor.

When the people were cleared from Direcleit, some of them moved up the hill to Cadha, on the hill side of the modern road. Until recently there was still a little cottar settlement there – houses with no rights to any land, though they all had their unofficial plots of potatoes.

The track through Cadha has now been laid out as a part of the Harris Walkway. Unlike the rest of the walkway, this section has been tarred, so it makes a nice evening stroll from An Tairbeart – up the hill from the road junction at the end of the Main Street, through the gate on the right, and up through the old village. There are magnificent views over the harbour and East Loch Tairbeart, then down again to the main road at the side of Loch Direcleit, and back along the road to An Tairbeart.

Horsacleit and Stiocleit

Horsacleit was a shooting lodge, built about 1900, though it is originally a Norse hill name – Horse Rock. It sits under the shelter of Uabhal, the south-eastmost shoulder of Beinn Losgaintir, not far

34. Peat-cutting at Stiocleit

from where a bomber with an Australian crew crashed at the end of the war. The road today runs away south from Horsacleit to round the shoulder of Uabhal, before turning west towards the machair, but at one time the old route from the machair was across the saddle between Uabhal and Beinn nan Leac – the Hill of Flagstones – and so down to Stiocleit, on the shore of West Loch Tairbeart. The village there is mentioned in the lease of Losgaintir in 1803, but it was cleared soon after. The loch beside the village was dammed, and a fishing loch made, which drowned most of the arable land of the village. One or two of the crofters were given lands in Diracleit, and the cottars given sites on Cnoc a' Charrain in An Tairbeart.

Since then, Stiocleit has been used mainly as a peat-cutting area for the people in An Tairbeart. One of the last to live in Stiocleit –

not in the village itself, but on the Aird, the headland on West Loch Tairbeart – was Coinneach Stiocleit (mac ni' Dhomhnaill 'ic Alasdair: Kenneth son of the daughter of Donald son of Alexander). He was a bit simple, but a hard worker, and his fee for a day's work was a penny, but it had to be paid as two halfpennies, because he used them as washers on his boat! He was a very good otter hunter too, and took much of his living from the skins. He died in 1882, and was one of those to be buried in the old graveyard behind the bakery in An Tairbeart.

There was another village out beyond Stiocleit – perhaps hardly a village, there was probably only one house there – at the shore in the mouth of the deep valley of Biosdal. I never heard anything about who lived there except Eoghann Ban a bha ann am Biosdal – Fair Ewen that was in Biosdal – but who was he? The only thing that is remembered about him is that his wife died in Biosdal, and the mourners had to climb down the steep slope from the saddle at the top of Beinn Losgaintir; when they got the coffin into Ewen Ban's boat to sail round the point to the graveyard at Losgaintir, with Ewen Ban himself at the oars, there was no room for anyone else, and they all had to climb back up the mountain again.

Uamh Ard

If you continue along the main road from Horsacleit, around the shoulder of Uabhal, you come to a road junction at the Uamh Ard which used to be one of the visitor attractions of Harris, because of the signpost there. One arm pointed down the Bays road and said 'Rodil' and the other pointed down the machair road, and said 'Rodil'! Both were quite correct, as the two roads met at Roghadal, but many a tourist stopped to take a photograph of it.

Miabhag nam Bagh (Meavag)

Miabhag is typical of the little fishing townships that were set up in the days of Captain Alexander MacLeod of Bearnaraigh after he had bought Harris in 1779. At the head of the bay you can still see the carradh – the fish trap; a wall built out across the bay just a little below high water level, so that the fish would swim into it with the high tide, and be trapped behind it with the falling tide.

There was a family of MacLeans who lived on the Aird – the headland – away off the road. They had a black house, and it was the ceilidh house where all the youngsters of the village would gather in the evenings. There were five of a family and all lived into their seventies and eighties and none of them were married. When the last of them died, there were forty-odd cousins to share what little he left, and some of them were cousins on both sides and so had double shares – and most of the first cousins were dead, and their families shared their shares. One of the relations was in Maraig, and he got a letter from the lawyers with a cheque. 'The old bodach on Aird Mhiabhaig left us £210,' he shouted to his wife. 'Are you sure?' she asked.

'Well, no,' he answered, 'it's £2.10!'

There are still the ruins of the old watermill in Miabhag, and of the mill-lade which drove the wheel. It was the MacAulays who were millers at An t-Ob who had the mill in Miabhag also, and one of them had the unusual name of Mata – Matthew. His son Aonghas Mhata, who moved back to An t-Ob, was a great teller of tall tales, but as one of the neighbours said: 'You couldn't call Aonghas Mhata a liar, for you were never expected to believe him!'

Drinisiadar (Drinishader)

Drinisiadar was another old fishing village but it also included a little farm at Caolas Sgeire Buidhe – the Narrows of the Yellow Rock. At one time this belonged to a Widow Campbell and her deaf and dumb son, and Tobhta Bhalabhain – meaning the ruins of the deaf and dumb man's house – is still pointed out there. He died and another son emigrated to Goderich in Ontario, so the widow went to live with another son in Scalpaigh, and the croft passed to a Kenneth MacLennan from Miabhag – Coinneach an Thailleir: Kenneth son of the tailor. He was over in the Scalpaigh islands one day in 1866, cutting seaweed along with Norman MacDonald from Direcleit (Tormod Dhomhnaill Alasdair) to take back to Caolas Sgeire Buidhe for fertiliser, but they over-filled the boat and she was swamped; both men were drowned. Great-grandchildren of Kenneth still live on the croft, among them one of the last Harris Tweed weavers still to use natural dyes in her weaving.

When they were clearing Ceanndibig, they found new crofts for some of the people by taking bits off the crofts in Drinisiadar for them. The Drinisiadar people were less than pleased about this, and quite a few of them went off to Canada, to Manitoba.

Drinisiadar is also the scene of one of the old stories told by Donald Morrison (an Sgoilear Ban), who made his collection of stories in Steornabhagh in the 1840s.

> At Drinishader, by East Loch Tarbert, there dwelt by himself Malcolm MacUrchy Mhoir – a MacDonald – a turbulent, wild man, whose character was viewed with suspicion by the neighbours. There was a tenant called Angus MacInnis Mhic Illespic – a Morrison – who held lands in an adjacent village and this man Morrison missed a young cow. He travelled over many parts of Harris without finding her, till at last he came to MacDonald's house and asked him if he had seen any trace of the cow, MacDonald replied that he had seen the cow; indeed, he would serve him with a part of the meat before he should leave the house. Morrison, feeling himself to be in danger, complied in every way. But for all that, MacDonald killed him in cold blood. MacDonald then severed the head and feet from the murdered man and putting the body into his own cow's hide, he buried it in the sea.
>
> It was not long before the mangled body and the cow-hide were found and suspicion rested on MacDonald of Drinishader. The rumour spread through the Isles and MacDonald, finding that he was not safe in Harris, took boat and fled to Skye, the seat of the Laird of MacDonald. The Laird of MacLeod was married to a daughter of MacDonald of Skye, but he wrote a threatening letter to the effect that it was disgraceful in MacDonald to screen a hateful murderer and so MacDonald of Drinishader was sent back to Dunvegan and thence to Rodel. There he was hanged in the Glen and left upon the gallows for a long time thereafter, until a storm brought the corpse to the ground. It is said that the night after he was hanged, the two shoes were stolen off his feet.[84]

The old folk had a slightly different version where the body in the hide came ashore in Scalpaigh, and Murdo was hanged right enough: not at Roghadal, but over a rock still called Cnoc a' Chrochadair – the Hangman's Rock – near Scadabhagh.

Plocrapol

Plocrapol is officially part of Drinisiadar, but is worth a separate mention, as it was the home of Marion Campbell, famous world-wide for her home-spun, vegetable-dyed Harris Tweed. Different plants give different dyes at different seasons, and Marion was an expert at selecting plants to give the colours she wanted for her tweeds.

Her grandfather Angus Campbell (Aonghais mac Alasdair 'ic Choinnich) was one of the Harris witnesses to the Napier Commission in 1883.

> The people of the Bays of Harris have no wool of their own, but they purchase wool elsewhere, and their wives through the night manufacture it into cloth. I myself get it for them – as much as 500 stones in one year from tacksmen through Uist and elsewhere, at prices ranging from 14s to 26s per stone. This enterprise was carried on through the kindness of the Dowager Countess of Dunmore and Mrs Thomas, and except for the proceeds of this manufacture, I do not know how these people could live at all. The people are quite accustomed to work bad land. There is no good land for them. The little good there is, they were driven out of it.
>
> I have of such land as is going a sufficient amount to maintain myself, and my family are springing up, and there is nothing left to distribute among them. A month ago my fourth son left the island without being too communicative with me about the matter; but he took some of the neighbours into his confidence, and I got a letter from Glasgow, and he is now upon his way to Queensland. His letter was, that when the oldest – Alexander – was to settle down he could get a portion of the croft, and when the second was to settle down – Murdoch – he was to get a share, but what was to remain to him in the land of his birth? – and, therefore, he would require to go away.
>
> I have paid road assessments since I was seventeen years old. The only thing I asked them finally for, in return for these assessments, was put out a bridge upon the river Luskin upon the road leading to the churchyard. For I have seen the coffins carried upon our shoulders dragged through the flood – six men strung together, and following the course of the stream in order to keep themselves from being swept away with the bier upon their shoulders.[85]

Scadabhagh (Scadabay)

Scadabhagh was another of the fisheries villages, around the beautiful natural harbour of Loch Scadabhagh, where one of the last of the herring drifters in Harris was based – The Constant Friend. One interpretation of the Norse name is the 'tax' or 'Skat' bay, where the Norsemen collected their taxes from the island. Nearby is Aird Bhi, and it is said that there was a great battle there between the Norsemen and the islanders.

There was another battle there too, between a cailleach from Harris and one from Skye. We have met the Harris cailleach already, hammering limpets on Aird Nisabost, but when she tired of limpets, she would go fishing on the east coast of Harris. She had a chair on the top of a cliff near Scadabhagh, and from there she would cast her line out into her favourite fishing ground in the Minch. There was another cailleach in Trotternish in Skye, and they were great rivals at fishing. Anyway, this day they were both out fishing, and their lines became tangled in the centre of the Minch. Now the Minch at this point is about twenty miles wide, so they must have been using pretty long lines – but what was that to a cailleach who had wielded a twenty-foot long limpet-hammer?

She gave a tug to the line, but it was well caught, and all that happened was that the Trotternish cailleach gave a tug back. She gave such a tug that the Harris cailleach and her chair were pulled off the cliff and landed on the shore below; but she gave such a tug in return that the Trotternish cailleach was pulled into the sea and drowned. If you don't believe me, go round the shore between Reibinis and Plocrapol, and you will see Seidhir na Caillich – the cailleach's chair – still there, turned to rock by the shock of its fall from the cliff.

There was a family of Campbells in Scadabhagh – a branch of the Campbells in Srannda – and they were both good fishermen and good businessmen, and they prospered well. They were fish-curers too, and had their own boats trading with the Baltic. It was there that Eoghann Ruadh was drowned, crossing the bar into the harbour at Danzig. Ewen's brother Lachlan was one of the men who gave evidence to the Napier Commission in 1883 about the conditions in the island, and he was described as: 'Looking like a

Viking with a look of power in a face rarely seen, with his strong features, great beard and iron-grey hair rising four inches above his forehead'.[86]

Greosabhagh (Grosebay)

The old track south from An Tairbeart came along past Horsacleit, then cut south under the shoulder of Greosacleit down to the sea at the head of Loch Greosabhagh. There were no roads along the shores then, linking the villages of the Bays, but only a series of paths, connecting the track into Greosabhagh, for example, with the villages on either side. These paths were used to give access to schools from the villages which did not have schools of their own, and were maintained, partly by the parish council and partly with grants from the Congested Districts Board. There is a note in their minutes for 1902:

> Bridge across the Grosebay River and two junction paths: This is an extension through the village from where the path stopped last year, and a path of 70 yards to connect the village with the main road. A bridge of ten feet span will be required.[87]

If you want a really spectacular walk, you should take the path from Greosabhagh that cuts into the hills behind Loch Mhic Neacail and climbs steeply up to the ridge above Stocinis. When you get there, you can see one of the volcanic dykes than run across the island – brown, gritty rock instead of the usual grey gneiss – and you can follow it all along above the villages until it crosses the road at the Uamh Ard. This is a part of Frith-Rathad na Hearadh – the Harris Walkway – a chain of tracks and quieter roads which can take you from the shoulder of the Cliseam in the north, around the Bays and through Bealach Creig an Eoin to Seilebost on the machair. The paths have been upgraded and signposted by Harris Development Ltd, a local group aimed at boosting the development of the Island, to give the visitor a series of walks along less-frequented roads and paths.

When Greosabhagh was settled in the 1780s along with the other villages in the Bays, there were two families from Uig in Lewis who came to the village, MacAulays and MacLeans; there were two MacAulay brothers, Roderick and Sorley, sons of Neil. Sorley is a

most unusual name in Harris, and almost every man of that name
in the island can be traced back to this Sorley MacAulay.

Collam and Cliubhair (Collam and Cluer)

This joint village straggles along the shores of Rubha Cliubhair,
and seems a very odd shape for a village. In the old days of the kelp
industry, it was the shoreline that mattered, not the land, and the
boundaries were set where streams divided the shores. So Collam
looks across a stream to houses which count as part of Greosabhagh,
and the far end of Chliubhair has only a little rivulet to separate it
from Stockinish. When the road was made to link up all the villages
in the Bays, the section at Cliubhair was one of the most difficult,
and it is hard to imagine now how some of the cuttings through the
cliffs were made without the use of modern machinery. No wonder
that the road was called the Golden Road by one of the mainland
papers, who reckoned its cost a ridiculous sum to be spent on a few
crofters – and the Golden Road it is called still.

When the machair side of the island was broken into crofts again
in the 1920s, it was from Cliubhair and Stocinis that many of the
new settlers came. Alexander Ferguson, the Cliubhair Bard, was
keen to go, yet saw the problems of moving:

35. Mol Ban at Cliubhair

Bu toigh leam fhin, bu toigh leam fhin
Bu toigh leam fhin dhol do'n ait'
Far an robh mo sheanair og
Air an iodhlainn mhoir a tamh.

Ged tha' m machair breagh gu leor
'S e cho comhnard ri lar
'S iomadh rud tha gann san stor
A tha pailt gu leor sna Baigh.[88]

I would like, I would like, / I would like to go the place / Where my
grandfather was young / To live on the great meadow / Though the
machair is beautiful / It is as flat as the floor / There is many a thing
scarce there / That is in plenty in the Bays.

In the end, he stayed behind in Cliubhair, though many others from
the area went across to the new crofts on the machair.

Roderick MacDonald (Ruairidh Dhomhnaill Fhionnlaigh) who
lived in Cliubhair, had a large family – twelve altogether – two girls
to start with and then seven boys in a row, so of course the seventh
son was known as an Dotair (the Doctor) because of the old story
that a seventh son in a row had healing powers. At one time they
used to say it was the seventh son of a seventh son, but as families
got smaller, they had to be satisfied with one generation. The boy
was actually called Neil, but I doubt if he ever heard much except
'Dotair', and his family are still known as clann an Dotair.

Caolas Stocinis (Stockinish)

Stocinis means the 'cleft headland' in Norse, and when you look at
Stocinis island you can see why – it is split almost in half by a deep
steep-sided rift. Much of the gully is filled by a tidal loch, and at
one time it was dammed and used as a natural lobster pond. Loch
Stocinis itself is a long narrow loch, running deep into the rocky
lands of the Bays, and at one time there was a ferry here, across the
narrows of the loch to Sruparsaig, an outlying croft of Geocrab.

Some of the Stocinis people used to cut their peats on the island,
but most of them were up on the hill, little patches among the rocks
and lochs. There was no chance of getting a cart to where these peats
were – even if they had had a horse – so all the carrying had to be in
a creel on the back. A tarasgeir (peat-iron) was used to cut the peat

36. The rocky landscapes of the Bays – Loch Stocinis

and the wet slabs were laid out on the surface of the ground to dry. When they were dry enough to be handled, they would be turned and stood up on end in little stacks of three or four peats, and as they dried they would go into bigger stacks. If they were to be stacked at the peat-bank, the final stack would have a greabhadh – the outer wall built into a pattern, often a herring-bone, and the top turfed, so that the finished stack would throw off the water. Then every day someone would have to go out to the moor with a creel, to bring home enough fuel for the next day.

Maybe the peat-banks would be on the other side of a loch, or across a gully, and that is where they used the blondin. That was a wire slung between two poles, one on the one side of the loch and the other on the other side, and a creel hung on it, so that the creel could be loaded on one side of the loch, then slid along the wire to the other end and unloaded there, and there was a rope attached to the creel so that you could pull it back again to the start. Not many cut peats in such difficult places now, but you will still see bits of blondins in the moor.

Leacli (Leaclee)

Leacli, at the head of Loch Stocinis is probably best known today as the source of the song which has become a kind of national anthem for the island.

37. Taking home the peats

Chi mi'n tir san robh mi nam bhalach
Tir nan suinn, Leacli 'nam shealladh
Chi mi'n tir san robh mi nam bhalach

'S ged 's creagach cruaidh e,
cha toir mi fuath dha
Far bharr a' chuain
aite 's boidhche sheallas

Chi mi'n tir san robh mi nam bhalach[89]

I see the land where I was a boy / Land of heroes, Leacli in my view /
Though it's hard and rocky / I will not turn my back on it / From
the ocean wave / The most beautiful sight / I see the land where I
was a boy

A hundred years ago, it would have been better known as having
been the home of John Morrison (Gobha na Hearadh) the Harris
blacksmith and hymn-writer. Iain Gobha belonged to the blacksmith
Morrisons from Stangigearraidh at Sgarasta, but his grandfather had
moved to Roghadal when Captain Alexander set up his base there,
and Iain himself set up a smithy in An t-Ob.

In the 1820s the Church of Scotland was divided by the evangelical movement, which had turned against some of the old-style ministers, who had been showing more interest in their farms than in their congregations, and whose religious teaching had been very poor. Iain Gobha was very firmly of the evangelical camp, and so fell foul of the religious establishment. He had to leave An t-Ob and go to Leacli, where he opened a smithy on the croft of his son-in-law Donald MacLeod, who had a shop where the Taigh Geal now stands – the Taigh Geal was a white house as opposed to a black house. Iain Gobha spent most of his days gathering funds for the Free Church of Scotland, and in particular for their church at Manais. He died in 1852, leaving his third wife as a widow with six young children, and the best that the Church could do for the one who had spent his life working for them was to pay the fares of the widow and children over to Canada. It was to Tiverton in Ontario that they went, although some of her sons later moved on to the copper-mining area of Calumet in Michigan.

There was another preacher in Leacli at that time too – Aonghas mac Dhomhnaill 'ic Thormoid (Angus Morrison). He was such a good preacher that he was nicknamed Pol Beag na Hearadh – Little Paul from Harris – and his descendants are still known as clann Thormoid Phoil – family of Norman son of 'Paul' – rather than by their proper name, clann Thormoid Aonghais.

There was another famous man in Leacli: Calum mac Fhionnlaigh mhic Iomhair, Malcolm MacKinnon. This was the time of Mac an t-Sronaich, an outlaw who wandered the hills of Lewis and Harris in the 1830s and '40s. He was connected to the Lewis gentry, so he was safe enough from official pursuit, even though he had committed a few murders, so people were very much afraid of him. Anyway, Calum was coming up from the shore below his house at Leacli, with a creel full of cuddies, when Mac an t-Sronaich sprang at him from out among the rocks. With the rope of the creel round his shoulders and chest, Calum could not get the free use of his hands to fight, but he managed to get his teeth into Mac an t-Sronaich's hand, and bite him in the joint between the finger and thumb until the blood ran. Mac an t-Sronaich had to let go, and that gave Calum a chance to get rid of the creel, but by that time Mac an t-Sronaich had taken fright and run away. They say that Calum was the only person to beat Mac an t-Sronaich in a fight, but he had the sense to know that that would not be the end of the affair. He had a large family of sons, and the house was only small, so they used to sleep in the sabhal, or barn. That night, Calum took them all into the house for safety, and sure enough, in the morning, all that was left of the sabhal was its smouldering roof – Mac an t-Sronaich had come in the night to take his revenge.

Mac an t-Sronaich's father had the Inn at Garve in Ross-shire, but his grandfather had been the Revd Alexander Stronach, minister of Lochbroom near Ullapool. His first murder was actually unintentional: a girl from Skye called Marion MacLean (Mor ni'n Mhanuis) had been down south working on the harvest on a farm in Lothian, and was on her way home with her wages and a necklace of beads which she had bought for herself. Mac an t-Sronaich's sister admired the beads, and he decided that he would get them for her. The inn was full and Mor and his sister had to share a bed. During the night, Mac an t-Sronaich came into their room: he saw the glimmer of the beads in the moonlight, and throttled the girl wearing them. What he did not know was that Mor had given his sister a loan of the beads to wear for the night and so it was his own sister that he had killed.

He had never been very sound mentally, and after the murder he went off and became a wanderer in the hills, especially in the islands, living by threats and theft, though it is claimed that it was a man from Caolas Scalpaigh who was responsible for him being caught at last.

Mor eventually made her way home, and latterly she was married to a man from the island of Scarp, and lived at the Aird Bheag, on the west coast of Lewis.

Leacli was one of the places most affected by an outbreak of typhoid in the late 1800s, and so great was the fear of infection that most families in the village left their old houses, and built new ones further from the shore, across the present-day road. The old ruins still stand near the shore, and few of the old folk would even touch the stones in them, in case the germs of the fiabhruis – the typhoid – might still be alive among them.

At one time there were four MacKinnon brothers and their families living at the out-end of Leacli: Lachlan, Ruairidh, Aonghas and Domhnall. Ruairidh was one of the emigrants to Australia in the 1850s, Domhnall went to Steornabhagh and Ruairidh to Scalpaigh. Lachlan stayed on at Leacli, and his daughter Anna lived there for a time, then moved in to An Tairbeart to keep house for a bodach there. This bodach had a bad chest, and the doctor asked Anna one time if he was coughing much. 'Oh no,' she replied 'Nothing but tea' – so ever afterwards poor Anna Lachlainn was known as 'Coffee'.

Aird Mhighe (Ardvey)

Aird Mhighe is a tiny village of only two crofts, but it is at the end of the most important cross-island route: the coffin road to the machair through Bealach Creig an Eoin, the Pass of the Rock of the Eagle. The land of the Bays is so rocky that there can be no burial grounds on that side of the island, and in any case, all the old burial grounds were on the machair, and people continued to use them after they moved to the Bays. Coffins had to be carried on the mourners' shoulders along the path through the peat-bogs to the pass – heavy work, and they would usually stop for a breather once the sands of the Atlantic coast were in view. It was the habit to build a cairn of stones wherever the coffin rested, and if you follow the coffin-path today, you will find little cairns of stones all the way down from the summit of the path to the shore.

There is the story too of an old lady who was taken in her coffin over the bealach, and when the mourners stopped for a rest at the top, they heard a noise from inside. The old lady wasn't dead at all, but had had some kind of seizure, and so they had to carry her all the way back down again, this time without the lid on the coffin!

The path is the natural route to and from the machair, and it appears in a story from the mid 1500s.[90] There had been a dispute about the chiefship of the MacLeods in Dunvegan, which had been taken by force by Iain Dubh – Black John. When the rightful heir took power again, he determined to wipe out all Iain Dubh's brothers and sisters together with their families. Alexander was the warden of the castle on Pabaigh and Allan had the tack of Seilibost, while Alexander's son Norman was fostered on Tarasaigh with Finlay Morrison and his wife Beathag Choinnich mhic Aonghais.

Word was sent from Dunvegan to Finlay on Tarasaigh, to kill the young boy, but the ties of fostership were too strong and he warned Beathag that Norman was in danger. She got their own two sons to launch the boat and take her across to Horgabost, then headed for Seilibost, only to hear the uproar as Allan's family were being attacked by the soldiers from Dunvegan. She headed through the darkness through Bealach Chreig an Eoin, hoping to find a boat in Loch Stocinis, but the only boat there was the one which had brought the soldiers to Seilibost. She took the risk, hailed the boat and asked for a passage back to Skye for a widow and her child, wanting to get back to her own people there. She had no money, but she had a large silver brooch, and she offered that to them as a fare. The crew felt sorry for her and let her on board, but they would not take the brooch: they would be well enough paid when they took the returning soldiers back to Dunvegan. So Beathag and the young boy travelled back to Skye along with the murderers of the rest of his family. Once safely there, he got the protection of MacDonald of Duntulm, and Bannatyne MacLeod of Losgaintir, writing in the *Bannatyne Manuscripts* in the 1830s, tells us that the brooch was then still in the possession of a descendant of Beathag in Edinburgh.

After the road crosses the bridge across the head of Loch Stocinis, it starts to climb into the moor, and a little track runs back down to the tiny township of Liceasto. Most of the crofters who settled there were Morrisons, and it said that they were descendants of Iain mac Iain Duibh from Bearnaraigh. We have no idea who Iain Dubh was, but his reputation must have been bad, for it was his name which was always cast up to the Morrisons if they were in any dispute.

Geocrab

Geocrab was the home of Domhnall Og (Donald Morrison), who gave evidence to the Napier Commission in 1883.[91]

> Before my father's time, there were no tenants in Geocrab at all. No person can conceive what kind of place it is without seeing it. At first the land was held on the run-rig system – they had it among them in common. They had no lots among them, but the hill was divided in to four parts, each of which was divided between two. The lots were better, but people in these times preferred to have

38. Geocrab

them in common. I have seen a woman weeping at being separated from her neighbours by the division of the crofts.

Domhnall Og had a big family of six boys and two girls. The croft in Geocrab was small enough for one family, so as the boys got older they looked for land for themselves. Roderick was the first to go, in 1873, and he went to the Eastern Townships in Quebec. This was an area up in the hills near the border with the United States, and a great number of families from Lewis had gone there over the years, so it was a Gaelic-speaking area, with its focus around the town of Stornoway. By this time most of the land in the main area had been taken up, and the new settlers were heading further east, to the shores of Lac Megantic. Roderick prospered and sent for his brothers Ewen, who was living at the time in Fionnsbhagh, and Sorley, who had got a new croft in Cuidinis. Their sister Marion and her husband decided to go too, and when their widowed father heard this, he joined the party as well, at the age of seventy-nine. A few years later another brother and sister, Peter and Kirsty, decided to go to Manitoba, so out of that large family, only Donald and John were left in Harris. Domhnall Og himself died in Quebec in 1894 and is buried in a cemetery at Marsboro' Mills, in the forest beside Lac Megantic.

Ruairidh from Geocrab was a great friend of the factor, and though there is no doubt that Ruairidh was very clever, he was not the best of neighbours to have. An old man living in Fleoideabhagh had a housekeeper, and Ruairidh suspected that all was not as it should have been between them. When he visited them one night, they asked him if he had seen the tongs for the fire – they hadn't seen them since his last visit. Ruairidh told them that he had put them in the housekeeper's bed last time, so it was a wonder that she hadn't found them: the old man had to marry the housekeeper!

Another Geocrab man married when he was away at the East Coast fishings and settled for a time in Wick. He was always boasting to his wife about the farm he had, and eventually he persuaded her to come to Harris: she took one look at the rocks of Geocrab, and took to her bed, and I am told that she stayed there for the rest of her time on the island.

When Lord Leverhulme was trying to develop Harris in the 1920s he built a carding mill in Geocrab, and the power supply was from turbines driven by water piped down the hill from Loch Udromul. The pipes are still there, but the mill is now a salmon hatchery.

There is a story about a murder which took place at Geocrab – at least, on the road on the hill above the village. Two men – a young lad from the village and an older man from Lewis who was married there – had set off home from An Tairbeart; the older man arrived home alone, and the lad's body was discovered by the road the following morning. Nothing could be proved, but the Lewisman's byre kept burning down until he took the hint and left the village, going to live in Steornabhagh. Of course the rumours followed him there, and the story goes that a Harris man was going past his house in Steornabhagh when he saw chalked on the door: The Harris murderer. 'Nach eil sin uamhasach!' 'Isn't that terrible!' he said, and scrubbed out the word Harris, changing it to 'the Lewis murderer'.

Aird Sleimhe and Becrabhig (Ardslave and Becravig)

These little villages, of three crofts each, are officially treated as one. Among the families here were MacMillans, a most unusual name for Harris. The story is that they originally came from Lochs in Lewis, where the name is common enough among the descendants of a

Murchadh Bard (Murdo the Bard) who went there from Argyll as a shepherd in 1740. In the time of the press-gangs – who kidnapped young men for naval service – Murdo's son John had lost two sons in this way, so he sent the other two to Harris for safety, where you can tell their descendants from their use of the Christian name Maoldomhnaich. This is usually translated into English as Ludovic or Louis.

Alec Mor in Direcleit used to tell a story about a relative of his, Alexander MacLeod – also Alasdair Mor – who lived in Aird Sleimhe. Alec said that you should always carry a pocket-knife, and gave Alasdair Mor as the reason. 'Alasdair was coming home with a bundle of heather on his back, and he slipped and fell on the edge of a peat-bank. As he fell, the rope holding the heather caught on a projecting snag at the edge of the bank, and slipped up under his throat. He couldn't break the rope and the knots holding it were out of reach, and he hung there until he was throttled. Now if he had had a knife in his pocket, he would still have been alive now' – though I doubt it, for he was born before 1800!

It was in Becrabhig that Iain mac Ruairidh (John MacDonald) lived. He had his own ship, and on one occasion he sailed her down to Ballachulish to collect slate, but met with a storm and was shipwrecked near Connel. As he had no money, he could not buy materials to mend the ship, and as he could not write, he could not send word home. He was a year in Connel, earning enough money to repair the boat, but at last she was finished, and he set sail back to Harris. The people in Becrabhig had long given him up for lost, and in fact had gone into mourning for him, when one of the men saw the boat coming into the loch. 'Well,' he said 'if he was alive, I would say that that was Iain mac Ruairidh, from the way he steers the boat.'

The problem of illiteracy affected the islands until a proper education system was set up. Wealthy merchants like Alexander MacLeod in the Philippines could write home, but the average emigrants had no way of contacting those they had left behind. As a Lewis bard put it, to those without reading and writing, the parting was like a death; often it was only by chance that families made contact again, as in another letter we have. A lady in Baile Ailein in Lewis is writing to her sister in Cape Breton, after a seaman from

Lewis had met one of the Cape Breton family on a ship – and it was not the old lady herself who did the writing, but her grandson, who was just out of school. And of course there was the old lady who had had a letter from her son, but, since she could not read, she asked the minister to read it to her: 'But, just in case there's anything private in it, would you put your hands over your ears while you read it?'

Manais (Manish)

Manais was the site of the Free Church built largely by the efforts of Gobha na Hearadh (John Morrison of Leacli). The first minister here was the Revd Alexander Davidson, and he was married to one of the Garneileir MacLeods from Roghadal. She had the reputation of being a bit mean – and with fourteen children to raise, no doubt she had to be!

At that time you could buy molasses for the cattle, and many a pail of molasses came from the shops in An Tairbeart, and was used as treacle on bread or on porridge. Mrs Davidson went one better: she thinned it down with hot water and gave it to the servants instead of tea. Of course, tea was quite a novelty then in the Bays, and there is the story of the two cailleachan who had visited the manse and watched Mrs Davidson making tea for them. 'Oh well,' said one of them after they left. 'The mean-ness of nighean a' Ghairneileir [Mrs Davidson] that only gave us the souse [or bree] and kept the meat for themselves!'

Tea wasn't the only thing that came from An Tairbeart. Mairi Liath was the midwife, but she had a shebeen as well, and she used to get the boys to bring her a pige of whisky from Steornabhagh; on one occasion the boy had carried it carefully all the way to Manais, but he slipped going down the rocks at the Carnan Mor, and the pige was broken – and there was all her profit running down the rock into the sea!

There is a family of MacLeods here, and they are descended from Ruairidh Ban Drobhar, a cattle-drover from Lewis. They say that he first saw his wife when she was washing clothes in the Abhainn Garbh (Rough River) at Geocrab; perhaps he was attracted by more than her skills at laundry, for the means of washing heavy clothes then was to trample them in the stream, with skirts tucked up high to keep them dry.

Fleoideabhagh (Flodabay)

Fleoideabhagh is a typical fishing settlement from the 1780s, and one of the original settlers there was a Neil MacLennan or Niall Saighdear: Neil the Soldier, and not just any soldier but a Chelsea pensioner. While in the army he had married Mary Rae from Limerick in Ireland – in fact he married her in the Woolwich Barracks – and eventually they went home to live in Fleoideabhagh. They were fairly well-off for their day, for Neil had his pension – it was not much, but it was cash, and who else had cash in that day?

Mary had no Gaelic, and no one else in the village but Neil had any English, and they say that one day Neil decided to get up early and head off to An t-Ob on an errand. When Mary woke up Neil had gone, and no one else in the village had enough English to be able to tell her where he was; she thought that he had gone off and deserted her.

Cuidhtinis (Cuidinish)

Cuidhtinis has had a very chequered history. It is a typical rocky Bays township, yet it was cleared for a farm in the 1850s, and its people sent to Australia. There are two wings to the main village – Cnoc Esgan to the north-east and Sruthmor to the west, and when the village was cleared, a few families were left in Sruthmor as cottars. Cnoc Esgan was the first home of the Cunninghams of Harris; when Captain Alexander set up his fishing stations, he brought tradesmen and teachers across to the island, and the Cunninghams were brought from the Small Isles to teach fishing. When Cuidhtinis was cleared they spread to Geocrab and to Scalpaigh, and Scalpaigh is where you find the name today.

Cnoc Esgan is famous for something else too: when Cuidhtinis was re-settled in 1885, one of the crofts in Cnoc Esgan was taken by Sorley Morrison (discussed in the section in Geocrab), but he didn't like it and went off to Canada; the croft was taken over by James MacLeod – Seumas Aonghais Ruairidh Bhain – from Manais, and then by his nephew Malcolm, called Calum Sheumais because he was brought up by his uncle James. Then people began to see a light at Calum's house – not in the house itself, but sometimes in front of and sometimes above it; this light was sometimes red and sometimes yellow. Sometimes it would start at the road end, about the size of a torchlight, and would move towards the house, getting bigger all the time; sometimes it would go past the house and down to the shore, and you could even see its reflection in the sea. The strange thing was that as you went to the house it was in front of you almost until you reached the house, and then it would disappear from your sight, but people at the road end could still see it! It was so common that you just expected it: you would never think of telling that you had seen Solas Taigh Chaluim Sheumais – the light at Calum Sheumais's house – though you might mention that you *hadn't* seen it. Well, the old man died, and the house went empty – and the light stopped. People decided that the light must have been some effect of the Tilley lamp in the window through mist rising from a boggy patch in front of the house, or some other practical explanation, but then new people moved into the house and the lamp went back in the window – but the light was never seen again.

At the far end of the Cuidhtinis road was the house shared by Domhnall-Iain Raoghaill – Donald John MacLennan – and his wife Cairistiona Bheag, with his brother Donnchadh and sister Ciorstaidh. Domhnall-Iain has to shoulder a large part of the blame for getting me hooked on genealogy, for he and I spent many evenings talking about the families of the area, trying to fit together the pieces of the jig-saw, while Cairistiona Bheag supplied us with oatcakes, crowdie and cream. Many of my stories of the Fionnsbhagh area came from Domhnall-Iain, and Ciorstaidh and Donnchadh had their own contributions to add. Ciorstaidh Raoghaill was an expert on orain luadhaidh – waulking songs.

From the other end of Cuidhtinis, from Sruthmor, comes the story of Donnchadh Ban Taillear – Fair Duncan the tailor. He was a travelling tailor, as they were in those days, going from place to place and staying in the house where he was working. His work was not just in Harris, but in Lewis as well, and it was in Marbhig in Lochs on Lewis that he had a girlfriend, Ciorstaidh Alasdair. Being a tailor he was good with his hands, and he made her a little locket carved out of wood in the shape of a heart, and gave it to her as a keepsake. Matters were progressing well until Donnchadh caught smallpox – and very badly he took it too – and for a long time he couldn't travel. He couldn't write either, and Marbhig was a long way away for news to travel, and Ciorstaidh wasn't hearing from him at all. At last he recovered, but he was badly scarred with the pockmarks, so he grew a great big beard to hide them. When he was able, he set off for Marbhig, but the first house he came to, there was nobody in it at all. And the same with the second. In the third there was an old cailleach lying in bed and he asked her where everyone was. 'At Ciorstaidh Alasdair's reiteach', was the answer. Now in these days they always had a reiteach – a sort of betrothal party – before a wedding, and everyone in the village would go to it. So Donnchadh went to the reiteach, and sure enough it was his Ciorstaidh who was getting betrothed: after not hearing from him for so long, she thought he had forgotten her and she had agreed to marry a boy in her own village. Donnchadh stayed quietly at the back of the room, and of course nobody recognised him with the big beard, but in due time he was asked to give a song or a story to help the evening along. So he did, and his song was 'That he didn't know where Ciorstaidh's heart was, but he knew where his heart was, for she was wearing it round her neck'. With that she recognised him; she left the other boy in the reiteach and married Donnchadh instead, and went back with him to Sruthmor.

Early in the 1900s the Lewis and Harris Fishing Association built a fishing lodge at the mouth of the river from Loch Holmasaig, and they called it Finsbay Lodge, even though it was in Cuidhtinis. It was a timber building, very fancy, and utterly out of keeping with its surroundings. I only know of one picture of the Lodge, and I feel fairly sure that it is a fake; to me it looks as though a drawing of the Lodge has been superimposed on a photograph of the area, perhaps to show what the Lodge was intended to look like. It didn't last very long and eventually there was a fire and it burned down. The foundation can still be seen – and a fair amount of the timber is in houses in Cuidhtinis today!

The lodge was beside a rocky hill called the Cnopa Dubh, and there were the ruins of a few houses there, and the stones were used in building the Lodge – all except one ruin 'where the fuamhar was'. Fuamhar means giant, and this giant was the Cape Breton giant, Angus MacAskill. Angus had been born on the island of Bearnaraigh, but his family had come to Cuidhtinis when he was

Finsbay Hotel, South Harris.

39. 'Finsbay Lodge'

still a baby; the Cuidhtinis people used to say that there was nothing special about him as a baby except the size of his thumbs – which, in its own way, is pretty convincing, for if you are going to make up a story, you would surely make up a better one than that.

One night Angus's father was out fishing at the mouth of the loch, and his boat was upset by a cairbean – a basking shark. He had to swim for the nearest island and spent the night there, which is why it is called Sgeir MhicAsgaill or MacAskill's Rock today. Whether that was the reason or not, the family soon left Cuidhtinis and went to Englishtown in Cape Breton, and there are MacAskills there still.

Angus grew to a height of seven feet nine inches, and he was broad in proportion. The MacAskills in Englishtown have opened a Giant MacAskill Exhibition, where they have some of his clothes and other mementoes.

Fionnsbhagh and Aird Mhighe (Finsbay and Ardvey)

At one time the villages of the machair had grazings extending right across the island, for the fishermen in the fishing stations of the Bays had no interest in the land at first. Fionnsbhagh was the first exception, for it was taken away from the grazings of Sgarasta to

40. Collecting the mail at Fionnsbhagh

make a kelp-farm – a farm where the important crop was sea-weed. MacNeills from Skye had the farm at one time, along with the inn at Roghadal, and it was not broken into crofts until the late 1820s, when three crofts were made in Fionnsbhagh and two in Aird Mhighe. As other villages were cleared, more and more people were squeezed into Fionnsbhagh and Aird Mhighe until by 1870 there were eight crofts in Aird Mhighe and six in Fionnsbhagh, and many landless cottars on the shore as well.

One of these cottars was called Fannag Iain Oig: Fanny daughter of Young John (for his father was John as well), and she lived with her mother in a very poor little house on the edge of the shore. One of the neighbours had built a new house for himself, and he told Fannag to take the old one – and old as it was, it was still better than hers. In due course the mother died, and they noticed that Fannag was having a few visits from a man in An t-Ob, but they didn't think anything of it. Then one morning, when they got up, Fannag had gone – and so had the most valuable thing she had, the roof of the house! Her boyfriend had come before daybreak in his boat, and had taken Fannag and her 'dowry' back to An t-Ob; those roof timbers were on a house in the Clachan there until it was knocked down a few years ago.

One of the more colourful characters in Aird Mhighe was Aonghas MacCuthais (Angus MacCuish), a son of MacCuthais Mor who had been frightened by the uilebheist at Gob an Tobha. He was born in 1789, and as a young man he married Catriona Ruairidh Rois from Srannda, but she died giving birth to her first child, and the child died too. Aonghas then went away to the mainland to work on the construction of the Caledonian Canal, but he was diddled out of his wages by the foreman there, so he left and joined the army, and was sent to Ceylon. He remained there for over twenty years, and when he returned to Harris, he took one of the new crofts in na Buirgh. It was while he was there that he married again, in 1850 to Mairead Dhonnchaidh – Margaret, daughter of Duncan MacLennan, another of the new crofters there. When na Buirgh were cleared again in 1853 Aonghas, better known as an Saighdear – the soldier – obtained the croft at No. 1 Aird Mhighe, where he and Mairead had a family of seven, the youngest being born when he was eighty-three years of age.

It was from Fionnsbhagh that the ship *Celt* left in 1852, taking passengers to join the emigrant ship *Hercules*. The last few years had been very difficult in the Hebrides, especially in the poorer areas like the Bays, for the potato crop had been ruined by blight three years running, and no other crop could be grown in such poor land. What little money people had had been spent in buying food, and once that had gone nothing was left but scrounging the rocky shores for limpets and other shellfish. Earlier emigrants had gone to Cape Breton, but the blight was just as bad there. On the other hand, Australia was desperate to attract settlers, but the sea voyage was long, and the fare accordingly high.

The Highlands and Islands Emigration Society was set up in 1852 to advance the money for assisted passages to Australia. The bulk of the first group of sponsored emigrants were from Skye, but in December 1852 the *Hercules* set sail with 742 emigrants from Harris,

North Uist and Skye. Such a large ship could not come to the Islands, so the steamer *Celt* was hired to take intending passengers to Campbeltown. The emigration officer at Fionnsbhagh described the scenes there as the most harrowing he had ever witnessed in the whole of his career.

> Sturdy Highlanders grasped each other by the hand, whilst the muscles of their faces and bodies quivered with emotion. Women hung on the necks of friends, and were in some cases removed by force; to say they sobbed aloud would faintly express their sorrow. It would be difficult, perhaps impossible, to describe it. As the vessel steamed out of the bay they stood on the poop, threw their arms into the air, giving full vent of their grief, as they gazed for the last time on the black peaty glens and bleak rocky hills, over which they had long been accustomed to roam, and to which they were so devotedly attached.[92]

The *Hercules* took on extra passengers from Skye to make up the numbers, and one of them was a youth who turned out to have smallpox. The disease spread like wildfire with the crowded conditions on board, and the ship, already buffeted by ferocious gales, had to take shelter off Cork in the south of Ireland. By then 237 of the passengers were suffering either from smallpox or from typhus, and fifty-six of them died. In April 1853 the *Hercules* set sail again, with only 380 passengers on board, the rest either being too ill to sail, or occupied in nursing their relations, and eventually following on other ships. Strangely enough, the death rate among the Harris emigrants seems to have been less than in those from other areas – were they in a better condition at the start of their journey, or did they have more immunity to the diseases?

There was an earlier intended emigrant sailing from Fionnsbhagh too; in 1739 Norman MacLeod, son of the Old Trojan of Bearnaraigh, had been involved, along with the sons of MacLeod of Dunvegan and MacDonald of Sleat and North Uist, in a scheme to solve the employment problems in their plantations in Virginia and the Carolinas. It was difficult to find willing emigrants at the time, especially for the conditions that they offered, so they decided to try kidnapping. Their ship, the *William* came into the loch at Fionnsbhagh, where the women from Sgarasta had come for the summer shielings, bringing the cattle and sheep across to fresh

41. The emigrant ship HMS *Hercules*

grazing and taking the pressure off the arable lands until the crops had been safely taken in. The women were decoyed on to the ship, and imprisoned there. Word got back to the men back at home in Sgarasta, and they crossed the moor to Fionnsbhagh at night and raided the ship which was still at anchor in the loch. The leader of the raiders – Aonghas mac Dhomhnaill 'ic Aonghais – took his own wife off the ship first, but when asked to go back for the others, said 'Bitheadh a h-uile fear a' toirt sgarbh a creig dha fhein' – 'Let each man take his own cormorant off the rock': a phrase still in use in Harris.

People in other islands were not so lucky, or so daring, and the *William* eventually sailed for America, but was detained off Donaghadee in Northern Ireland. Most of the unwilling passengers escaped, and a few managed to make their way home and tell their story. Duncan Forbes of Culloden was a great supporter of the

Hanoverian government, and he got to hear of the story of Long nan Daoine – the shipload of people – and it is said that he used this knowledge to blackmail MacLeod and MacDonald into supporting the government in the rebellion of 1745.

In 1888 the government arranged an assisted emigration scheme to enable crofters and cottars from Lewis and Harris to settle in the Canadian prairies. Twelve families from Harris sailed from Glasgow on the *Buenos Ayrean* on 2 June 1888 to settle at Killarney in southern Manitoba, among them Dougal MacKenzie from Fionnsbhagh (Dughall mac Dhughaill 'ic Dhomhnaill 'ic Ruairidh) his brother Donald, his wife's brother Roderick MacKay (Ruairidh Chaluim Iain) and their cousin Hugh Morrison (Uisdean Mhurchaidh Uisdein). A government report of 1890 described their progress:

> House – 14 x 16, double boarded, with clay between. Has built small log addition 14 x 12.
>
> Stable – log and turf.
>
> Ploughing etc. – 40 acres ready for crop. Well 42 ft, but no water in.
>
> Stock – one yoke of oxen, one cow, one yearling heifer, one calf, three pigs and 20 chickens
>
> Crop 1889 – 26 bushels wheat from 7 acres. No oats. No barley. 18 bushels potatoes. 13 or 14 loads of hay
>
> Remarks – 6 acres ready on land of Donald MacKenzie, brother, Morrison, cousin, and MacKay (brother-in-law). John MacKay, Donald MacKenzie, and Hugh Morrison all earned £50 during the year after paying board. Mary Ann MacKinnon, cousin, out at service, earning $10 per month all the time. Has paid MacKenzie half of the passage money back. Says it is not easy to get the fish out of Pelican Lake, but is going to try again this winter. Donald MacKenzie has 6 acres broken, value $15. John MacKay has 5 acres broken, value $12.50. Hugh Morrison has 10 acres broken, value $25.[93]

The following year's report shows their progress.

> Dougal and Donald MacKenzie from Harris have each 160 acres, and between them they had eight acres of wheat, which yielded 11 bushels to the acre in 1889, while this year they had 40 acres, from which they expected to thresh 30 to 33 bushels per acre, and it looked like doing so. Roderick MacKay, who has his father with him, had about the same in crop. MacKay had 11 head of cattle, 2 pigs and 20 hens. Both the MacKenzies and the MacKays said that

they were pleased they had come out, and that they would have no hesitation in inviting their friends to do so if they got the chance. They and several others complained that 160 acres was too little, and that the Home Government, should intercede with the Canadian Government in order that they might get another 160 acres.

Dougal MacKenzie's cattle have done well, and he keeps his house with the produce of his dairy and poultry. He does not consider the winter so severe as in the old country. He would not leave Canada, even although he could get the same amount of land to farm in the old country as he has in this. He has a good school and church near his homestead.

A final note to the report adds 'Many other instances may be given of what men with a moderate amount of brains and energy can do when settled in Canada.'[94]

Of course, not all the settlers did so well as the MacKenzies, and some of the settlers got so badly into debt with the local traders that they had to give up the land. But the MacKenzies certainly were successful, and their descendants still live at Ninette in that area.

These MacKenzies were always an enterprising family, and scattered all over the country. Our first notice of them is in Seilibost on the machair, and when that was cleared, one brother, Tormod, went to the Glen at Carraigrich, and the other, Domhnall, to Ceann Dibig. From Ceann Dibig Domhnall and most of his family (including a son Panny – a sure sign of their Seilibost origin) went to Gearraidh na Monadh in South Uist, with another son, Calum, in Fintry near Glasgow, and a daughter, Rachel, married a shepherd on the isle of Rum. Only one son, Dougal, remained in Harris, as he had already married in Fionnsbhagh before his parents left Harris, and as we saw most of Dougal's family went to Manitoba. Again only one son, Murdo, remained in Harris, and I was lucky enough to have the friendship of three of his grandchildren: Seonaidh Dhughaill (John MacKenzie) in Bearnaraigh; Seonaidh Ailig (also John MacKenzie) in Sruth Mor; and Mairi Sheochdain (Mrs Mary MacCuish) in Horgabost.

Borsam

Borsam is a little village near Fionnsbhagh. It was one of the last villages in South Harris to get a road – but it was too late. Only one house is inhabited in the village now, and that by only one man.

Among the families who were there once were MacLeods, and one of them, Tormod Ruairidh Iain (Norman, son of Roderick son of John) who was seventy-five years old at the time, told his family's story to the Royal Commission in 1894:[95]

> My father lived in Horgabost before he was married, but the people were removed from there before I was born. My father had a holding in Horgabost, and my grandfather, but I cannot say how many were there along with him. I was born in Borve, but when I was a youngster a company of soldiers came to remove them; they were put out by force, against their will. I remember that I was a young lad at the time, and ran out of the township before them. That was from Little Borve. My father and many others went away to the moss with all their stock at that time, and Mr Donald Stewart got the land my father was in. They did not care where they went if they got that land cleared for Mr Stewart.

There is a story too about how Norman came to have that name. His mother had lost several children, and an old woman advised her not to name the next child after any of the dead ones, but to give it a name which was not in the family at all. The next child was another boy, and the first person she saw after the birth was Norman MacKenzie (Tormod mac Ruairidh) from Seilibost, and so the boy was called Norman.

Lingreabhagh (Lingerbay)

Lingreabhagh is officially part of the township of Roghadal, but in the 1840s it was cleared to add to the grazing of the farm there. Ceann a' Bhaigh was on the other side of the stream from Lingreabhagh proper and in the 1840s it was tenanted by Alexander MacSween, from Roag on Skye. He had a barque named *Isabella* after his wife, with which he traded with Skye, mainly in timber; there is an entry for him in the 1841 census, at Ceann Loch Reusort, on the boundary of Lewis and Harris, delivering timber for the construction of a gamekeeper's house there.

One of the MacSweens decided to go to Canada, to Manitoba, with his wife, Catriona. Life in Manitoba was hard, especially in the winter, and there was snow the like of which they had never seen before. In the winter Torlach made some money from logging, and one winter's night there was a heavier than usual snowfall, even for

Manitoba; he couldn't get home and Catriona was left alone. Two strangers came to the house asking for shelter, and Catriona wasn't very keen to give it, but you couldn't refuse on a night like that, so she let them sleep in the kitchen. Torlach had built the house himself and there were cracks in the partitions between the rooms, and through a crack she heard the men plotting to kill her and steal the little money she had saved. So she climbed out of a window and ran away, but when Torlach finally made his way home, he found her lying dead in the snow.

In Ceann a' Bhaigh also was Iain Alasdair Ruairidh (John Morrison), who gathered so much land for himself in the area that he was known as 'An Diuc' – the Duke of Lingreabhagh. It was to Ceann a' Bhaigh, too, that the MacLean shepherds from Pabaigh retired.

A hundred years before that Lingreabhagh had had a brief moment in history. Prince Charlie was returning from Scalpaigh and the abortive attempt to secure a ship in Steornabhagh, and was heading for the relative safety of Uist. Ned Burke's journal, published in *The Lyon in Mourning,* gives an account of the journey from 'Glass' – Eilean Glas, or Scalpaigh:

> From Glass, having no wind, we rowed off with vigour. About break of day, the wind rising, we hoisted sail . . . Then we passed by Finsbay, in the Isle of Harris, where we spied a man-of-war, commanded by one Captain Ferguson, under full sail, and our little sail was full too. He pursued us for three leagues, but we escaped by plying our oars heartily, they being better to us than arms could have been at that time. The water failing the man-of-war, he was not in a condition to pursue farther. We steered upon a point called Roudill, where the Prince expressed himself as formerly that he should never be taken in life. After this the said Captain Ferguson, being anxious to know what we were, endeavoured to make up with us a second time, but to no purpose, the water being at the ebb, and we continuing still to row in amongst the creeks. Seeing this he turned to the main sea, when we sailed to Lochmaddy.[96]

He does not mention the actual place where they skulked in the shallows among the rocks, but the local people will show you Stac a' Phrionnsa – the Prince's Rock – at Lingreabhagh, behind which they hid from the man-of-war.

Lingreabhagh is best known today for the proposal to make a super-quarry there, or rather, for the farce of the local public enquiry into the proposal. This was held sixty miles away in Steornabhagh and took six years to reach a decision; the government then decided to ignore the recommendation of the Reporter anyway. There are arguments both for and against the super-quarry, but somewhere in the process the local people were forgotten, and were left for six years not knowing what was going to happen, while all the time the lifeblood of the community – its young people – drained away. The amount of money spent on the enquiry could have been spent on rejuvenating the economy of the south of Harris, but instead we have a worthless report, and nothing else to show for the whole sorry saga.

Those who were in favour of the project based their case on the need for jobs in the area, for without jobs the young people cannot stay. Redlands Aggregates, the would-be developers, could hardly have made a worse job of their public relations, and allowed themselves to appear as oppressors, wanting to tear out the heart of a community. Public opinion, at first in favour of the quarry, turned against it, encouraged by a very strong campaign on behalf of the opponents, who counter-argued on the number of potential jobs that could be lost if the quarry plan went forward. At this point, the local authority, who until then had been in favour, turned against the project. The result of the local inquiry was that the Reporter recommended that, on balance, the project should be permitted, as the environmental damage would be more than offset by the economic gains to the island, but the government decided not to accept her recommendation – and how many million pounds of public money were wasted?

In the meantime, the population of Harris continues to fall, as more and more young families leave to look for work, and of course none of the jobs that were promised if the quarry was turned down have materialised. One would have thought that if the conservation bodies were so keen on preserving Harris they would have tried to create jobs here, and so they have – six part-time mink-trappers.

PART FIVE – THE FOREST AND SCALPAIGH

Aird Asaig (Ardhasaig)

Aird Asaig sits on the shore of West Loch Tairbeart, under the shadow of the hill of Gillabhal. Coming down from the north you can see why the Norsemen gave it that name, for the face of the mountain is ridged with ravines – *gil* in Norse.

Aird Asaig was the headquarters of a family of MacLeods, known latterly as the fidhleirean – the fiddlers. For generations they were the assistant keepers of the deer forest of North Harris, under the Campbells of Scalpaigh, and of course 'forest' in a deer forest doesn't mean trees, just wild country. There is something strange about this family's origins. They are the same group as Tormod mac Neill and Domhnall Ban Griasaiche in An Tairbeart, and we gave Tormod mac Neill's pedigree as mac Neill mhic Thormoid mhic Thormoid mhic Iain mhic Neill – son of Neil son of Norman son of Norman son of John son of Neil. Tormod himself was born in 1800, and if we allow the average of three generations to a century, that takes us back to about 1600.

There is a descendant of Tormod mac Neill who retired to Skye, and he knew the same patronymic, and he referred to the Neil at the head of the tree as *Niall a chaidh a' chrochadh ann a Lit'* – Neil

42. The hills of North Harris

43. The bridge at Ceann an Ora, Aird Asaig

that was hanged in Leith. Many a MacLeod in Lewis and Harris was hanged, but why bother taking one to Leith? There was one famous Neil MacLeod hanged in Leith, and he was one of the many illegitimate sons of Roderick, the last chief of the MacLeods of Lewis. When the MacKenzies were taking over that island he had stood out against them from his rock fortress of Berisaigh in Uig, until he was finally captured, taken to Edinburgh and hanged there in 1613. But what have these MacLeods in Lewis to do with Harris? A paper in the Privy Council Minutes of that time has a complaint against MacLeod of Harris: that he was harbouring a son of Neil of Berisaigh. Could it be that MacLeod of Harris gave him the post of sub-forester, and that he was the ancestor of the Fidhleirean? If so, it would solve another problem, too – the caibeals around St Clement's in Roghadal were built as grave-enclosures for families

44. Spinning wool at Aird Asaig

of some social standing, and on Tarasaigh we have Caibeal nam Fidhleirean in Cladh Che. Could it be that they still felt that their descent was that little bit above the rest of the local people?

John MacLeod (Iain Fidhlear) who had been evicted from his croft in Aird Asaig, warned the Napier Commission of the effects of the Clearances.

> There is not a family in the whole of Harris where there are two sons, but one of them at least is in the service of the Queen, perhaps two, and neither they nor their fathers can obtain a foot of the soil upon which they could live. It would appear that, when Britain becomes involved in a struggle with another nation in the future, they must send for the deer and sheep of Harris as well as its young men – and then they can see which is the best bargain![97]

45. Dyeing wool at Aird Asaig

Bunabhainneadar (Bunavoneadar)

This is one of the few wholly Gaelic village names in Harris, and means the mouth (bun) of the river (abhainn) which comes down between two groups of hills (Eadarra) – and the mere fact of it being in Gaelic suggests that the name, if not the village, is relatively recent. Before An Tairbeart was made and the villages settled in the Bays, travellers to the south of Harris would have taken a boat from here to Losgaintir, and W.C. MacKenzie's *History of the Outer Hebrides* contains a record of such a journey in 1753, when Captain Barlow of the Buffs was coming through the island, looking for rebels and firearms:

> Began my march on the 11th June taking Lieut. Nicolson and Twenty of his men with me. We came to Kiose where I left 1 Corpl. and 4 men, as People who Travel that Country must necessarily pass through that place. We came afterwards at Ballallan where I left a Sergt. and 10 men. The next day being the 12th I march'd to Bonnevenitre or the Ferry House which stands upon the side of Loch Tarbet. I found there a French Firelock which had been newly oil'd and clean'd without a Lock, in a hut where there were only two old women. I asked for the Lock, but they told me it had been took away by one Mr McLeod, Factor to the Laird of that Name. Not being satisfied with this Answer, I caus'd the whole house to

46. Bunabhainneadar

be search'd, and look'd into every Chest and Cupboard, but could find nothing, so I brought the Firelock away. This place is about 12 miles from Ballallan and 26 from Stornway. The whole country that we march'd through is one continued Bogg, impassable at all times for Horses or Cows, and the same in the Winter for any Human Creature.[98]

If Captain Barlow did not think much of this part of his journey, he liked the rest even less.

From Bonnevenitre I came part by Land and part by Water to Loskiner. From Loskiner I march'd to Rowdill where I waited several days and could hear nothing of the Brigg. At last the Master sent me a letter over land by his Pilot, acquainting me that he had done all in his power to make the harbour of Rowdill but could not do it, and that he lay in Fins Bay unable to move until the wind changed. By this time my Party began to suffer very much for the want of Provisions, Meal particularly, as none could be got at that Place, and as to my own part I thought I should have been eat up with Rats and Lice. In this miserable situation I was obliged to hire an old leakey Boat to Transport myself and Party to the Ship in Fins Bay, and thanks to Providence we all got there. We continued Wind bound Four Days longer before the wind shifted and we were able

47. Whaling station at Bunabhainneadar

to sail, and in that Time had terrible Storms of Wind, Rain, Hail and Snow. It was very astonishing to me to have such weather in the Month of June, who had never seen the like!'

When Lord Leverhulme owned Harris in the 1920s, one of his projects was to re-open Steisean nam Muc – the old whaling station which the Norwegians had built there. Like most of his projects, it failed after a year or two, and all that is left of it now are the rotting wharfs and the brick chimney. At its peak, it provided work for many of the men of north Harris, but it also provided a smell which pervaded the whole area, and sank into the men's clothes and skin. The water-power for the plant was taken from the river above the village, and as the old pipes burst they used to send up beautiful fountains of water.

At the mouth of the river there is an island – though they say that it only became an island when they started work on the river for the power for the factory – and on the island there are the ruins of a house. They say that there was a boy of the name of MacDonald, and that he was a very good poacher. On one occasion MacLeod had been on the hill after deer, and never a deer could they see, so in the end they sent for the poacher, to see if he could find any, when the keepers couldn't. He did, and so MacLeod had good sport after all. As a reward he gave MacDonald this site for a house, but only if he changed his name to MacLeod. He did that, and some of the MacLeods around An Tairbeart are descended from him, and should rightly be MacDonalds.

As you head out west beyond Bunabhainneadar you pass on the shore the old village of Teilisnis. Like most of north Harris, it was cleared in the early 1800s, but being less easily accessible the buildings there have not been demolished to any great extent, and you can still see the houses and the byres and the corn-drying kilns. Big houses they were, and that shows you how well off they were before they were all put out of the place. Some of the MacLeods were there, but there were Campbells too, who were related to them by marriage, and Morrisons as well.

Tolmachan and Miabhag nam Beann (Tolmachan and Meavag)

At one time there were villages all along this shore. Norman Cunningham from Scalpaigh, giving evidence to the 1894 Commission, describes them:

> My grandfather came from Tolmachan; there is nobody there now – it is deer forest. There were three or four crofts there. There were crofts along the whole south coast of North Harris at one time – Teilisnish, Tolmachan, Meavaig, Branndarsaig, Cliasamol and Husinish, all on West Loch Tarbert. They were cleared of crofters about 79 years ago.[99]

Robert Matheson, the factor for north Harris, gave a rather different history to the Commission:

> Until about 70 years ago the ground now afforested was used by the tenants of the west side of South Harris, and the islands of Bernera, Taransay and Pabbay, for summer grazings for horses, and about this time was formed into two sheep farms on which deer were also kept along with the sheep. Over forty years ago the present deer forest was formed. The hills now under deer had at no time been in possession of crofters, but, while as sheep grazings, there were about eight cottars, two or three of which were situated at or near the site of the present castle, three or four at Loch Meavaig, and two at Bunaveneadar.[100]

It depends of course on the definition of a crofter, and whether they were talking about the periods before or during the sheep farms.

Tormod Fidhlear – Norman Cunningham's maternal grandfather – had given evidence in a boundary dispute between the owners of Lewis and Harris in 1805:

> Depones that he has been born in the Forest of Harris, and that his father and his grandfather lived in the Forest of Harris the most of their days; that his father died about fourteen years ago at the age of eighty; that he herds the cattle of Captain Kenneth Campbell, Uiy in Taransay, in Tolmachan; that the grazings of Tolmachan extend through the Forest of Harris to the march of Lewis; that his father was the herd of Uiy's cattle at Tolmachan since ever he remembers; and that his grandfather has told him that he had charge of the cattle sent from Uiy to summer pasture in the forest.[101]

The forest was actually cleared twice: first the crofters were put out to make room for sheep, and many of them sent to places like Reinigeadal and the Pairc area of Lochs in Lewis. Then the sheep and the shepherds were cleared out to make a deer forest, and anyone who was left over from the first clearance was sure to be caught in the second. When the people were put out of Tolmachan itself to make room for the sheep, some of them were put for a year or two into a new village further into the hill – and you can tell when that was done, for they called the place Waterloo, after the battle in 1815. But that didn't last long and they were all sent over to the other side of Tarbert. There were crofts too on the other side of the loch at Miabhag: Miabhag nam Beann – Miabhag of the Mountains – to distinguish it from Miabhag nam Bagh – Miabhag in the Bays – and it was resettled in 1919 after being raided by some of the cottars in Aird Asaig.

Branndarsaig and Cliasamol

Travelling through north Harris now, you would not even know that Branndarsaig was ever there, for you have to go down along the river from where Cliasamol school is today, down to the river-mouth, and there you would find the old houses of the village.

There was a family of MacInneses there – five brothers of them – and when Branndarsaig was being cleared they decided that they would go off to Cape Breton, and the place they were offered there was at Wreck Cove near St Anns – just a little pocket of land before you hit the mountains. Four of the brothers decided to settle there, but the fifth one didn't like it at all – they say that he didn't even get off the boat, but just stayed on board till she left again to come back to Harris. However that was, he certainly did come back to Harris, and got land for a while at Ceanndibig, and then got a croft in Caolas Scalpaigh, where his people are still.

Cliasamol had been a village too – you can see that from the lines of deep feannagan or lazy-beds – though the man that called them that in English had never worked one. In the days of the deer forest it became a deer-park, and even when the rest of north Harris was settled, it wasn't re-crofted until 1919.

Cliasamol School stands on the hill above Branndarsaig, and was built to serve the children of Cliasamol and Miabhag. With the typical logic of Inverness County – the local authority of the time – the school was built half-way between the two villages. If they had built it in Cliasamol, then the Miabhag children would have got wet on a bad day, and if they had built it in Miabhag, the Cliasamol children would have got wet; to be fair they built it half-way, so both lots of children got wet!

Cliasamol appears in a rental of the 1770s as 'Clashmul and Isle Soay' so the tack must have included the islands of Soaigh Mor and Soaigh Beg in West Loch Tairbeart. At the time when crofts were being made along the north Harris coasts, there were two attempts to establish crofters on the islands, but without any lasting success. First Donald MacDonald – Domhnall Iain Fhionnlaigh – went there from Scarp, but he moved on to Bunabhainneadar, and the isle was later let as two crofts to cottars from Molinginish, Murdo MacDonald – Murchaidh Iain Dhomhnaill – and Finlay Campbell – Fionnlagh Ruairidh Fhionnlaigh – better remembered as Murchadh Shoaigh and Fionnlagh Shoaigh, though they too left after a few years and settled in An Tairbeart.

Abhainnsuidhe and Leosabhagh

These were little villages on the shores of Loch Leosabhagh, but both were cleared at the 'time of the sheep'. John MacLeod (am Fidhlear Mor) – the Big Fiddler – a brother of Norman whom we met at Tolmachan, was among those cleared for sheep, and he went across to Tarasaigh to herd there for his brother's employer, Captain Kenneth Campbell of the Uidh; it was no doubt he who built the caibeal in the graveyard there.

At the head of the bay was Ob' an Doill – the Blindman's Bay. The blind man was Alexander Martin, and he was a weaver and tailor; it is said that despite being blind, he could weave a web of cloth so fine that it could be passed through a wedding ring. When they came to build the castle at Abhainnsuidhe, they wanted rid of the Taillear Dall, but he always earned enough from his trade to be able to pay his rent on time, so they couldn't use arrears as the excuse. The factor sent one of his henchmen up to Ob' an Doill, to see if he could find an excuse. He was given a meal by the Taillear, and the meal was salmon from the river; so he ate the salmon but put the skin and the bones into his pocket to take back to the factor to prove that the Taillear's boys had been poaching, and so he was evicted

Abhainnsuidhe Castle was built in 1867 by the Earl of Dunmore, who had bought Harris from a grandson of Captain Alexander as a shooting lodge. It is said that one of the reasons for building it was to impress his son's fiancée, who had been very disparaging about the old house in Roghadal. By the time it was finished they had spent so much that they had to sell the castle to the Scotts – and I don't think that she married him anyway!

48. Abhainnsuidhe Castle

Gobhaig (Govig)

Gobhaig is off the main road, down to the shore, and it was the Gobhaig crofters themselves who built the road down into the village, when the local authority would not do so. The present village is at the head of the bay, but there are old ruins further out on the loch, at a place called Tamna. At one time the Tarasaigh people used to cut peats there, as the best peat on the island had been cut out over the centuries, and when Tarasaigh was cleared one family came across to live at Tamna, in the little shieling they had made there. They were Morrisons and they had the unusual Christian name Ceithinn in the family – the more unusual since they made it Cain in English. They were blacksmiths, and a few of them had gone, over the years, to work in Uig in Lewis. Uig was MacAulay country, and the Morrisons and MacAulays had been at feud for generations, so Morrison wasn't the best of names to take there. So the first group that went there took the patronymic of MacCheithinn, which was translated as MacKinnon in English, though it has nothing to do with that name. The next ones to go kept their trading name – Smith – and when the family at Tamna finally made their way across to Uig, they kept the name Morrison – so that there were MacKinnons, Smiths and Morrisons there, all of the same family.

Donald Morrison – An Sgoilear Ban – has a story about a Cain Morrison, who will be the same man. Apparently he was the steelbow tenant of Losgaintir for a short time – presumably after the lease to James Hogg fell through. (Steelbow meant that the tenant got a lease of the farm and its stock, and had to return the same amount of stock at the end of the lease, having enjoyed the profits in the meantime.) Anyway Cain had been steelbow tenant, but at the end of the lease he fell out with the MacLeods, the farmers, who claimed some of his own goods in payment of a claimed debt. Some of Morrison's goods consisted of meal he had bought from Kenneth Campbell of Scalpaigh, but had not yet paid for, so he told Campbell he had better try to get the meal back himself, as he was sure he would never see the money for it.

Kenneth Campbell had the measure of the MacLeods, and knew that they would never allow him the meal by normal means, so he went to Losgaintir and told Mrs MacLeod that he wanted the meal and would break down the door of the storehouse if necessary to get it. She ran to the door of the store, as he knew she would, and sat down in front of it, where she and Campbell spent a considerable time in threatening and abusing each other. In the meantime, Campbell's men had made a hole in the thatch of the roof at the back of the store, and taken out the forty bags of meal, and loaded them on to his boat. Then Campbell told Mrs MacLeod that if she had not been such a loud scold, she might have heard them, and might not have lost her meal!

Beudarsaig (Bedersaig)

The village of Beudarsaig consists of two houses beside the road to Huisinis, but that is the third site that the village has had. First it was at Buaile nam Bathach – the cattle fold – on the hill above the present village; then, when the place was re-crofted in 1885, the houses were at the glen below the road, but as new houses were built they were built at the roadside. The family who were at Buaile nam Bathach were MacDonalds, and their descendants became keepers and shepherds on the Lewis side of Loch Reusort at Teallasbhagh and Crolla. The last of the Crolla family was Ceit, and when she left Crolla she came for a time to Luachair, on the Harris side of the boundary. Ceit had a brother, Murdo, who was of near-genius ability, though all his learning had been acquired in the little school at Luachair. He would have gone to university, only he died before he could begin there. The *Stornoway Gazette* did an article on him once, including a very nice obituary of Ceit herself – which she enjoyed very much when she read it! Ceit always claimed that her MacDonalds were one of the families who had come to the Islands from Glencoe after the massacre, and if Ceit told you history, you could be sure that it would be right.

Beudarsaig was the home of Tormod Alasdair and his wife Magaidh Iain Reinigeadal. Tormod was a great story-teller, but, as he said himself, a good story was never worse for getting better, and it was not always a good idea to believe his tales too implicitly. He was a great character, and many an evening and early morning we spent yarning about Scarp and its people, while Magaidh, whose people came from Bunabhainneadar and Reinigeadal before that, and was not really interested in history, pottered about in the kitchen and made us endless cups of tea. That was my base for many a wander in the hills of north Harris, over at the Lag Mhor and the back of the Taran. Tormod had been a very strong man in his day and a great hillwalker – and poacher – but he was less able by the time I knew him. But I still remember going out with the Scarp boys to gather sheep at the Lag Mhor. Tormod was no longer able to climb the hills, but he went in the little boat along Loch Reusort, moving the sheep along the cliff ledges by whistling at them – he knew every inch of the area so well that he lost not one sheep.

Huisinis (Husinish)

Huisinis is at the end of the north Harris road, and was a very old important dwelling-place, to judge by its Norse name – House Headland. In historical times, Huisinis was a part of the tack of Bearnaraigh, and the Bearnaraigh people used to winter their horses in the hills above Huisinis, to save the grazing at home.

At the back of Aird Mhanais, the western end of Tarasaigh, there is an area at Aird Tro walled off from the rest of the island, and it has been said that this is where the Bearnaraigh horses were taken ashore for a night or two's grazing on their way to Huisinis – which could also explain why it was from Bearnaraigh that the Tarasaigh people got help in the battle in 1544.

Robert Matheson, the factor, gives a description of Huisinis Farm to the Royal Commission in 1894:

> This small farm, which is in Lady Scott's possession, extends to 1067 acres, of which about 10 acres are arable, and part of which her Ladyship gives to the cottars of Scarp rent free for the purpose of planting potatoes, the other portion being kept under cultivation by a shepherd. There is at present a stock of about 240 sheep kept on the farm, and which are used for the purpose of supplying table mutton while Lady Scott and friends are in the islands; a less number would not be sufficient for this purpose.[102]

Matheson did not recommend the crofting of Huisinis, when the other villages along the shore were being re-crofted, but it was nonetheless broken into three crofts in 1900 for crofters from Direascal, along the shore of Loch Reusort.

There are old graveyards in Huisinis, and John Murdo from the hotel in An Tairbeart has a story about a stone from one of them.

> It is a long time since we first heard about Clach Huisinis – the Huisinis stone. It was apparently in the graveyard above the houses in Huisinis for years and years, and there was something about it, for no one would go near it. Anyway, this day, one of the An Tairbeart 'gentry' was in Huisinis and heard about the stone, and he thought to himself that the stone would be better in An Tairbeart, that it would be safer there, not knowing what might happen to it.
>
> Without asking for permission, he got the stone lifted, and placed in the back of the post bus to be taken to An Tairbeart. Now the old man who lifted the stone on to the back of the other – neither of them were well shortly after that. One of them had a wound in his back, and the other man's fingers twisted and he couldn't do fine work ever again. The man who took the stone to An Tairbeart – he wasn't well – and the post who took the stone up to An Tairbeart in the back of the bus, he broke his leg, and badly. And Alasdair, who had been working on the stone, he broke his arm playing football shortly afterwards.
>
> When we found the stone, it was in a garden in Taobh Siar Tairbeirt, and I went with another chap to take it down to the Comunn Eachdraidh – History Society. It was underground and dirty and we dug it up, and we lifted it into the lorry, and we took it down the village and put it in the door of the shop the Commun Eachdraidh were using. That was three years ago, and I have not had anything worse than dandruff![103]

Scarp

The island of Scarp lies off the far end of the Huisinis road. At one time it was a little farm on its own, but in about 1810 the farmer at Huisinis moved his farm workers across to the island where he made eight crofts, later extended to sixteen. When north Harris was cleared, Scarp was left very isolated, with easier contacts to Breanais in Uig than to the rest of Harris.

The story was told by Norman MacDonald (Tormod Dhomhnaill Sheumais) Norman of Donald of James to the Napier Commission in 1883.

49. The village of Scarp

The isle of Scarp was formerly in the possession of eight farmers who could sustain themselves with comfort. They were allowed a wide range of hill pasture on the mainland opposite. Thither they sent their cattle in summer, and getting the island thus clear managed to bring most of the arable land under cultivation. About sixty year previous to this, thirteen villages, extending from the head of Loch Resort, and scattered along the west coast to Bunamhuin Eadara, were cleared of their inhabitants, and taken possession of by a certain tacksman, named Alexander MacRae. He deprived us of the hill pasture then. When Lord Dunmore owned North Harris, he divided Scarp, seventeen years since, into sixteen crofts, which were further subdivided by the people among their family and friends. The number of people has greatly increased. About 200 souls live on the island today. This increase, along with the consequent overcrowding on one another, the scantiness of the land, and its inadequacy to maintain the people, have mostly led to the present poor circumstances.

It may be said, for all the land yields, that the people wholly depend on the sea, and that in a manner specially precarious, owing to the rough coasts. The place is not suitable for heavy boats. The coast is very wild, and we can only use light boats. When we work at lobsters in the winter, we have to launch the boats every morning, even supposing it were in frost or snow, and in launching them we

50. Taking the peats home to Scarp

have to wade through the surf up to the waist, and remain in that condition until night again.[104]

Scarp was the site of the third church built by Alasdair Crotach of the MacLeods in 1528, along with those at Roghadal and Taobh Tuath, and although there is no trace of it now, the graveyard down at the shore is known as the Teampall, and the same story of the treasure hidden where the three uidhean can be seen is told on Scarp also.

The story of Herr Zucker's unsuccessful attempt in 1934 to set up a rocket mail from Scarp is well known – the rocket exploded and the singed letters were spread over the shore – and so is the story of Kirsty, who had twins, one at home in Scarp and the other in hospital in Steornabhagh, and so managing to have one in Invernessshire and the other in Ross and Cromarty, different counties and different registration areas.

Tormod Alasdair in Beudarsaig used to tell the sad story of the boy who was born without any arms or legs. His brother used to carry him about in a creel, and they say that he even took him across to the mainland, to see if they could get help there. On one occasion the brother was working at potatoes in Scarp, and he set the creel with his brother in it at the side of the lazy-bed. The boy in the creel had a cold, and started to sneeze, and the force of the sneezes made the creel roll over, and he rolled out, and down the slope on to the shore, and into the sea, and was drowned – but as usual with Tormod's stories, you could never be quite sure if they were wholly true!

Crabhadal (Cravadale)

The only access to Crabhadal from Huisinis is over a cliff path, the Stiamair. It is a beautiful walk in the summer, but tricky in poor weather, and there are one or two nasty patches where the track crosses the head of a gil, or gully. At one time there had been a village on the shore, but that was cleared, and the shepherd and keeper's house was on the inland side of the loch. It is a beautiful spot on a summer's day, but the mountain cliffs are close behind the village, and their shadow reaches almost to the house, even in the summer.

I remember hearing that Donnchadh Rabh from Sruthmor bought a cow from the shepherd at Crabhadal once, but refused to pay for it till he saw it safely across the Stiamair. But for all that, it is a beautiful walk on a summer's day, across to the beach at Meilein beside Crabhadal.

Direascal and Luachair

Another couple of villages were resettled in 1885, Direascal, about half-way up Loch Reusort, and Luachair at the head. The people in Direascal had great trouble with the deer coming into their crofts, and I suspect that the estate had as much trouble with the Direascal people coming into the deer forest. In 1900 they were shifted to the former farm of Huisinis.

Before they left Direascal, there was one young boy of school-age, and the nearest school was in Luachair, where there was a Sgoil nan Leddies, that is a school run by the Ladies' Society in Edinburgh. So they started to make a road for him to go to school, and as usual they started in the middle and worked towards both ends. Before the road was finished, the Direascal people had moved to Huisinis, so the road was left unfinished, which is why you can still find the track of the road, from not-quite Direascal to fairly close to Luachair!

There had been a small farm in Luachair at one time, tenanted by MacAulays from Uig – Domhnall nan Luachrach and his family – but it was cleared for the big sheep-farms, and mainland shepherds brought in.

There was a family of MacRaes, from Kintail, shepherding there at one time: at least William was from Kintail, but his wife Jessie Johnston had been born in Beattock in Dumfriesshire, a far cry from Luachair. One day when the men were away from the house, gathering sheep, she saw a man coming towards the house, and realised that it was Mac an t-Sronaich the outlaw. She got her husband's gun, and her little daughter Mor – Marion – gave her the ammunition, and she began firing the gun out of the window, to scare Mac an t-Sronaich and to attract the attention of her own men. The MacRaes later went to Australia, all except Mor, who married in Scalpaigh, and it was she who used to tell the tale of the day she had loaded the gun for her mother.

The whole area between Loch Reusort and the north Harris road is one of wild beauty, though there is danger there too, and there are many parts where it is unwise to walk alone, without someone else to go for help in case of an accident, for the backs of the hills there are not visible from any inhabited area.

My own favourite walk – or it was when I was fitter – is from Abhainnsuidhe through the hills to Direascal and back to Huisinis. It starts in the valley just on the east side of Abhainnsuidhe, then up past the Hydro dam at Loch Chliostair and along the side of Loch Aisebhat.

The head of Loch Aiseabhat is almost at the bealach – the watershed. Suddenly the ground drops in front of you, down towards Loch Ulladal, and to the side rises the great rock-face of Sron Ulladal. It was in a cave there that Donald MacLeod, the Old Trojan, of Bearnaraigh was hiding in 1746, before he moved to Taobh Tuath.

Martin Martin describes it in 1703:

There are several caves in the Mountains, and on each side the Coast; the largest and best fortify'd by Nature, is that in the Hill Ulweal, in the middle of a high Rock, the Passage leading to it is so narrow that one only can enter at a time; This advantage renders it secure from any attempt, for one single Man is able to keep off a

Thousand, if he have but a Staff in his Hand, since with the least touch of it he may throw the strongest Man down the Rock. The Cave is capacious enough for 50 men to lodge in; it hath two Wells in it, one of which is excluded from Dogs; for they say that if a Dog do but taste of the Water, the Well presently dryeth up; and for this reason, all such as have occasion to Lodge there, take care to tye their Dogs that they may not have access to the Water; the other Well is called the Dogs Well, and is only drunk by them.[105]

Seonaidh Ob' an Doill (John MacKay) mentions the cave too, in his '*Oran nam Beannaibh*' ('Song of the Mountains')

An teid thu leam, a ribhinn mhaiseach,
An falbh thu leam, a ribhinn og;
An teid thu leam dhan eilean aghmhor
Far an d'fhuair mi m'arach og?

Chi thu 'n Cliseam, chi thu Langa,
Uisneabhal gu bonn le ceo;
'S iad as boidhche 'nam an t-samhraidh
Annta gheibh damh seang a lon.

Chi thu Cleiseahal 's am Beidig,
Oireabhal 's na feidh 'nan drobh
Chi thu Ullabhal 's an Uamha
'N am a' chruaidh-chais aig MacLeoid[106]

Will you come with me, my bonny girl / Will you come with me, my young girl / Will you come with me to the lovely island / Where I was in my youth? / You will see the Cliseam and Langa / Uisgebhal with its base in clod / So bonny in the summer-time / Where the slender deer find pasture / You will see Cleiseabhal and the Beidig / Oireabhal with its herds of deer / You will see Ullabhal and the Cave / Where MacLeod was in his time of peril

Not only men have hidden in Uamh Ulladal. I remember hearing about two keepers who were coming back to the castle from Luachair; they went up to have a look at the cave. They could hear a noise inside, and the braver of them shouted, 'Come out of there, if it's the devil himself!' A big black billy-goat looked out at him, and he got such a fright he collapsed and had to be carried back to the castle!

The path goes down to the head of Loch Ulladal, but the bottom of the valley is very boggy, and it is better to keep to the drier ground on the side of the hill to above Lochan an Fheoir, and then to cut through the little valley to Direascal, and round to Loch Brunabhal. From there I would head back into the hills, along Gleann Bhearraraigh, to Creag Bhearraraigh, the rock-wall which closes the head of the glen. A long climb takes you on to Braigh Bheagarais, between Ceartabhal and An Tiorga, high above the deep gully of Gleann Chrabhadail with its loch narrow loch. I remember when I got here once, coming down from Braigh Bheagarais on a windy day, and seeing clouds of smoke issuing from the glen below me. I could hardly imagine that anyone would be burning heather on such a day, but when I got lower and could see properly into the glen, I realised that it was not smoke at all – the wind blowing across the top of the deep gully was causing waterspouts, travelling along the surface of the loch and out to the sea. Needless to say I did not go down the glen and round to Huisinis that day, but went back to Abhainnsuidhe along Gleann Leosaid.

When I arrived back to Beudarsaig, and told Tormod about the waterspouts, he said that he remembered being one day at the mouth of Loch Crabhadal and seeing great rifts cut in the peat where the spouts had crossed on their way to the sea. He told me too that on one occasion some of the Scarp people were working at their peats there when they saw spouts coming from the glen and had to get away quickly. He added that one was not quick enough, and got caught by a spout and drowned; but he had a sparkle in his eye as he told me, and I think that was another of his stories.

There is another good walk through the hills, starting at Miabhag nam Beann, and up the glen to Loch Scourst, under the rock-face of Sron Scourst. The Sron is in view ahead of you all the way up the glen, and does not suddenly appear, like Sron Ulladal, but it is still very impressive. A low watershed is reached, and then the track runs gently down to Loch Bhoisimid, which is said to have inspired J. M. Barrie, who was staying at Abhainnsuidhe at the time, as the original of 'The Island that likes to be visited' in his play, *Mary Rose*.

Above Loch Bhoisimid is another Sron – Sron Ard – and an old track leads under it to Loch Chleistir and to the pass between Stulabhal and the Rapaire. The track is quite indistinct in places, and if you lose it, you have to avoid the temptation to go up Gleann

51. Loch Siophort, from the Lewis border

Stuladal itself, and instead keep to the north of the small cliff-face of Creag Chleistir. This is debatable land, over which the estates of Lewis and Harris fought a court case in the 1800s. From the pass below the Rapaire, the track zigzags down to the head of Loch Langabhat, the great inland loch which wanders its way through peat bogs through the centre of Lewis. From the loch, there is a steep climb up Tom Ruisg, and then a gentle slope down Gleann Bhiogadail to Bogha Glas on the shore of Loch Siophort.

Bogha Glas, Aird a' Mhulaidh and Scaladal (Bowglas, Ardvourlie and Scaladale)

These villages are on Loch Siophort-side, near the boundary with Lewis; the dispute about the boundary here began in 1804 and was still running in 1850. The evidence given then gives some of the earliest stories from that area. The first story dates from 1805 and comes from the Lewis side of the boundary, from a Malcolm Matheson, tenant in Peighinn Dhomhnaill in Uig:

> Depones that his father, who died about twenty years ago, told him that, when he was a boy herding John MacAulay of Brenish's cattle, Donald Campbell, the present Scalpay's father, and the said John MacAulay met at Braidhanfhiachlachan on purpose to fix and

renew the march, and they whipped his father soundly in order that he might remember the circumstance and recite it to posterity; that his father told him, that when he was whipped, the gentlemen gave him five shillings a-piece for allowing himself to be flogged.[107]

Duncan MacKay of Aird a' Mhulaidh adds a more detailed marker:

> Depones that he has heard, since ever he remembers any thing, that coal had been deposited at the foot of Claichantoppan, as a march mark; that by coal, he means charcoal of peats or wood, which from his earliest information, he had been taught to consider as an article generally used as a march mark; that he heard Donald MacLeod, his great-grand-uncle, MacLeod's forester, residing at Hillisnish, Murdo MacLeod, the deponent's great-grandfather, for some time conjunct forester with his brother at Hillisnish, and Malcolm Campbell, residing at Scarista, and two men from the Island of Barra, whose names he knows not, were present at laying the said coal.[108]

Norman MacDonald, also at Aird a' Mhulaidh, brings the story up to date:

> Depones that he saw the coal dug up in his own presence, at the foot of Claichantoppan, in September 1802; that this was done in the presence of Rev Dr John MacLeod, minister of Harris, the deponent's brother John MacDonald, Angus MacLeod tenant at Smuaisiveg in Lewis, and Finlay MacLeod, sub-forester of Harris; that he himself dug for the said coal, of which only a small part was taken up, and much left in the ground; the sod being immediately closed in, and the remainder of the coal covered up.[109]

Donald MacDonald of Bunabhainneadar remembered another marker:

> Depones that he heard from several people a particular stone once stood at Eeuntom-na-laig Aird, in the line of the march, but which was long ago removed; depones that in the same line of march, nearer to Loch Resort, he saw a particular stone stuck in the earth, of which a foot and a half or two feet was above ground; that the first time he saw this stone was about two or three years ago, and John MacKay, who once lived at Kenloch Resort and now near Loch Rogue, was along with him at the time, and that this was the

same person who took away the stone from Eeuntom-na-laig Aird to Stornoway.[110]

Further details come from the re-opening of the case in 1850. Norman MacLean from Einaclet, Lewis:

> Depones that he knows a place called Eeuntom-na-lag-ard; that he saw a stone there about 2½ feet long, four-sided, with sharp corners as if it had been made with a plane; that he does not know who put the stone there; that there was writing on the stone; that he does not read and cannot say what the writing was.[111]

Donald MacKay of Srannda ends the story:

> Depones that he is in his seventieth year; that when he was 15 years of age he was on board of a smack at Scalpay; that at that time a man came to Scalpay and informed Mr Campbell that the stone at Eeuntom was taken away; that the man who told about the stone was a Harris man, and he said that the stone had been taken away by MacKay of Kenresort; that the late Angus Campbell of Ensay was also present; that Scalpay said to Ensay that they knew what was on the stone that was taken away; that there were the letters TOH on one side, and TAL on the other side; that the words used by Scalpay were – 'I don't care though they have taken the stone, they have not taken the hill.'[112]

As it turned out, they had taken away the hill – for the boundary line when finally fixed left Eeuntom well on the Lewis side of the boundary.

I wonder what the disputing estates would say if they knew that most of the North Harris Estate has been the subject of a community buy-out, and is now run by the North Harris Trust, who are hoping gradually to make good some of the neglect suffered by the estate over the years, and once more develop its economy and its population.

The grazing on the hills above the villages is claimed to be the best in the whole of north Harris, but it doesn't do to be saying so. There is a story that two brothers had the grazing at one time, and at the sheep sales the factor was praising the quality of the wedders they were selling. 'Ah!' says one of the brothers, 'There's no better grazing in Harris than Mo Bhiogeadal.' By the time of the next sheep sales, the brothers had been evicted and the factor had the grazings of

Mo Bhiogeadal for himself: 'Cha dean e chuis a' bhi moladh Mo
Bhiogeadal' – 'It doesn't do to be praising Mo Bhiogeadal!'

It was on the old track along the shore below Aird a' Mhulaidh
that Mac an t-Sronaich carried out one of his murders. Fionnlagh
Chaluim Iain 'ic Choinnich (Finlay MacAskill) in Eilean Anabuich
was getting married, and his brother Eachann (Hector) had gone to
Steornabhagh to buy whisky for the wedding; whisky then did not
come in a bottle but in a pige, an earthenware flask. As he was coming
home along the shore between Bo Glas and Scaladal, Eachann was
attacked by Mac an t-Sronaich, who killed him to get the pige,
which was dropped in the struggle, and all the whisky was lost. It
was Murchadh Aonghais Iain Bhain – Murdo MacDermid – who
told me that story first, and showed me the pieces of the pige, which
could still be seen lying in the drain beside the track, even if I did
suspect that he renewed them every year before the tourist season!

The villages were taken out of the deer-forest in 1884 to make
crofts for cottars from the Island of Scalpaigh – two at Bo Ghlas and
two at Scaladal. Donald Morrison at Mol na Hearadh, the nearest
croft to the Lewis boundary, told the Royal Commission of 1892:

> Nothing could be more useful to us than the land, if we could get
> it. I can prove that it would be to the benefit of the crofter to get
> more lands. I was for twenty-one years a cottar in Scalpay. I went
> to Bowglass with only five sheep and a cow; I have today got twenty
> one sheep with lambs, and four cows.[113]

Maraig (Maaruig)

There is a little seam of fertile soil in Maraig, so there was a farm
there in the old days. There was an old Celtic church there too,
dedicated to St Luke, which will be an anglicisation of Moluag of
Lismore. There is no trace of the church now, but the graveyard
around it is still in occasional use.

In the earliest available rental of Harris, in 1680, Maraig is
tenanted by John Campbell, the Forester of Harris: 'Set to John
Oige the lands of Marwgae for wch he payes fourtie merks'.[114]

Martin Martin, a few years later tells us that

> There are abundance of Deer in the Hills and Mountains here,
> commonly called the Forrest; which is 18 miles in length from East
> to West; the number of Deer computed to be in this place, is at least

2000; and there is none permitted to Hunt there without a Licence from the Steward to the Forrester. There is a particular mountain, and above a Mile of Ground surrounding it, to which no Man hath access to Hunt, this place being reserved to Mack-leod himself, who when he is dispos'd to Hunt, is sure to find Game enough there.[115]

By 1684 John Campbell had also become tacksman of most of the Island of Scalpaigh.

Set to Ean oige ye three parts of Scalpa & Marrig for wch he payes yearly four score & sax merks eight shills. & eight pennice.

By 1698 he had taken over the whole of Scalpaigh.[116]

Set to John oig mc ean vc innish ye sds lands of Marhwig & all Scalpay fro qch he payes yearely ane hundred & fourscore merks money rent & twenty merks of tythes.[117]

Martin Martin also tells us that:

John Campbell, Forrester of Harries, makes use of the singular Remedy for the Cold, he walks in to the Sea up to his middle with his Cloths on, and immediately after goes to bed in his wet Cloths, and then laying the bed Cloths over him, procures a Sweat, which removes the Distemper, and this he told is his only Remedy for all manner of Colds.[118]

Martin also records that John Campbell did not only have his own remedies, but was prepared to assist others:

One of the said John Campbel's Servants having his Cheek swell'd, and there being no Physitian near, he asked his Master's advice; he knew nothing proper for him but however, bid him apply a Plaister of warm Barley Dough to the place affected, this asswaged the swelling, and drew out of the Flesh a little Worm, about half an Inch in length, and about the bigness of a Goose-quill, having a pointed Head, and many little Feet on each side, this Worm they call Fillan, and it hath been found in the Head and Neck of Several Persons that I have seen in the Isle of Skie.[119]

Maraig continued to be held with Scalpaigh until about 1754,[120] when we find ¾ of Scalpay let to Donald Campbell and ¼ 'called Renigidile & Marick' to John Campbell. A side note to a rental, undated but of this period,[121] refers to 'Campbells, uncle and nephew'. A song made for the tacksmen of Harris, after the boat in which they were travelling was thought to have been lost, refers to 'Iain mac Aonghais a Marrig', so the John Campbell in Maraig must have been a son of Angus, another son of John the Forester.

It was to Maraig that Coinneach na h-Uidhe – Kenneth Campbell of the Uidh in Taransay – came when he left Tarasaigh. His only son, Domhnall Bodhar – Deaf Donald – had been killed in a brawl in Dunvegan Castle, and his only daughter was Peigi – Peigi na h-Uidhe. They had the farm of Maraig for a time, and Peigi married Norman MacLeod, a son of the farmer at Huisinis, but they lost the farm and had to take a croft across the loch at Eilean Anabuich. One of their family became the baker in An Tairbeart, and his granddaughter still has a silver ring with Peigi na h-Uidhe's initials on it.

MacIain wrote a fascinating story in the *Celtic Magazine* in 1878[122] about how the Campbells came first to Harris. Archie Campbell, a son of the duke of Argyll, had killed another man in a duel and had to flee Argyll. He came to Harris as a seaman on a boat, and captured the heart of the daughter of MacLeod of Maraig. MacLeod would not let her marry a common sailor, so he sailed away again, made his fortune and came back to claim his bride.

Unfortunately, the story does not appear to be true. There is no record of such a son of a duke of Argyll, and, even if there had been, Argyll was quite strong enough to safeguard any son of his own, especially in such a matter as a duel, which was looked on as almost legal in these days. Also, Archie was never a name in use among the Campbells in Harris, and in any case, we know that the Campbells came to Harris in the time of Mary, heiress of Dunvegan, in the mid-1500s.

Oddly enough, there may be a different basis for the story. The MacArthurs in Lewis very often are to be found under the name of Campbell, and they do use the name Archie, and they do seem to have arrived in Lewis at Ath Linne, just across the boundary from Harris. Could it be that a story of the MacArthurs has been mis-remembered, and attached to the Campbells?

Maraig was another of the villages broken into crofts in 1885, according to the evidence to the 1892 Royal Commission from Robert Finlayson Matheson, the then factor of the North Harris Estate.

52. Loch Maraig

Maruig, adjoining the east boundary of the forest, was, until 1885, let as a sheep farm, but on that year possession was resumed by Lady Scott, and the land given to six tenants, five of whom were taken from the Island of Scalpay, along with another four families from that island who were settled on new crofts at Ardvourlie in the forest.

Of the six tenants who got the farm of Maruig, one was a shepherd on the ground with stock, one was a crofter from Scalpay who also had stock, and the other four were cottars from Scalpay, whom Lady Scott supplied with a cow each, or money to purchase one.[123]

Eilean Anabuich

Eilean Anabuich – the Unripe Island – is an odd name for a village, and refers properly to a shoal which used to be off the mouth of the river there. It kept confusing the old census takers, and usually appears in their reports as an island off the coast of Harris.

There was a family of MacSweens here, who seem to have been no connection to the MacSweens of Stocinis and later Scalpaigh. The boundary dispute of 1850 mentions a family of 'MacSwedes' in this area, who may well be this family.

There were the Munros too, who lived at Ceann an t-Saile – the Head of the Bay – for a time. They had been shepherds and had moved around all over that area, between North Harris and the Pairc area in the south-east of Lewis. They had even been over on na h-Eileanan Mora, the Shiant Isles, and Murdo was born there, who later moved to Liurbost in Lewis. Out of six sons, only one – Hugh – stayed in Harris, and the Munros in An Tairbeart are all descended from him.

Reinigeadal and Molinginis (Rhenigidale and Molinginish)

Reinigeadal and Molinginis are on either side of Loch Trollamaraig, which used to divide the two parts of the Scalpaigh Farm, and the first people in both villages were no doubt boundary shepherds. When the forest was cleared in the early 1800s, both villages were receiving areas for families evicted from the forest, and especially from Teilisnis.

Until recently the only way to either village was by sea from Scalpaigh or Caolas Scalpaigh, or on foot across a path starting at Urgha, near An Tairbeart, and climbing almost a thousand feet over a saddle of Beinn a' Chaolais. From the top there was a straight path running down to Moliniginis, but to get to Reinigeadal you had to zig-zag down a cliff face to sea-level at the head of Loch Trollamaraig, only to have to climb up again on the other side for the last mile or so to the village. For any reasonably fit walker, it must be one of the most enjoyable walks in the whole of Harris – the views are spectacular, and there are beautiful cold streams and waterfalls.

Across the bay from Reinigeadal is Molinginis, and they say that Fionnlagh Og Campbell, the first tenant there, had so many sheep coming from Teilisnis that the first of them was in the village before the last one started up from Urgha! One branch of the family went out as shepherds to the Shiant Isles for a time, and their descendants are still known as 'muinntir an Eilein' – 'the people of the island'.

There was another tenant of the same Campbells in Reinigeadal, and his daughter went to Steornabhagh and married the captain of a tea-clipper sailing to China. She used to go there with him, and they say that she walked with a sailor's roll when she came back to Harris – and what else did they call her but 'Cailleach Hong Kong'?

One of the tenants there in the 1850s was Duncan – Donnchadh Dhomhnaill Thormoid – who was courting Marion (Mor Dhomhnaill) from Cuidhtinis, but her family had decided to emigrate to Australia, and she would have to go with them. Her whole family were gathered on the ship in An Tairbeart, ready to go out to the emigrant ship, and it looked as though Duncan was never going to see Mor again. He met a friend on the pier, who asked him what was wrong with him. 'Oh,' said the friend, 'I'll soon sort that,' and off he went on to the boat, and got into conversation with the skipper of the emigrant ship. 'I'm surprised that you're taking that girl with you,' he said, pointing to Mor 'and her expecting a child in a few weeks.' It wasn't true, but the skipper was going to have enough trouble on the voyage without that, so he put poor Mor ashore – and what could she do after that except marry Duncan?

Urgha

Urgha is a village at the An Tairbeart end of the track to Reinigeadal, and was settled at the same time as the fishing stations in the Bays. There are unusual names in Urgha – MacPhee, MacQueen and Fraser – and it has been suggested that these families descend from

53. Urgha

the widows of soldiers in the French Wars of the late 1700s. It is in Urgha also that we find the descendants of John Martin, the servant who was with the Old Trojan of Berneray in hiding in the cave at Gob an Tobha at Taobh Tuath. An oddity with this family is that many of them have the name MacKinnon rather than Martin, yet were full brothers and sisters of the Martins. Many reasons are given for this, but the same confusion appears in other parts of the Islands, and it appears that early registrars etc. were unwilling to accept the apparent Christian name 'Martin' as a surname, and used MacKinnon as an alternative – though that does not explain why MacKinnon was chosen. To further confuse matters the original John Martin is remembered locally under the nickname of Dughall Mor – Big Dougall – presumably because his people had been working for Dougall MacAulay, tacksman of his home area of Breanais in Uig, Lewis.

Carraigrich

Among the families of Carraigrich are the Campbells, who claim to be unconnected to the other Campbells of Harris, but to have come to the area from Glendale in Skye, as shepherds on the farm of Scalpaigh. Other families came here as 'refugees' from the Clearances, among them Tormod Dhomhnaill Bhain – one of the Fidhleirean MacLeods from Tolmachan.

Another family there were MacLeods from Seilibost, and if you didn't know where they came from, the name Panny in the family would tell you. One of the family, Angus, was a tenant in Carraigrich in the 1840s, and one evening he was on a hill at the shore there, watching his son Panny and his daughter Kirsty fishing in their little boat off the shore of Stiughaigh, an island off Scalpaigh. Suddenly the boat capsized, and the two youngsters were drowned in front of their horrified father, who died of the shock. His wife and family later moved to Scadabhagh, where you will still find his descendants and the name Panny.

Carraigrich was also the site of one of the best attested 'ghost' stories in Harris. There was a house there – fairly recently, for it was a slated house – and the people in Direcleit and other places across the loch kept seeing the roof of the house on fire: so much so that the local fire brigade of the day was sent out to quell the blaze. Of course it may just have been a trick of the sunlight on a wet roof – but you can't tell now, for the house burned down.

Caolas Scalpaigh (Kyles Scalpay)

Caolas Scalpaigh is one of these places which always seems to get more than its fair share of sunshine – if there is sunshine anywhere in Harris it will almost certainly include Caolas Scalpaigh.

In a little overgrown graveyard on the North Shore of St Anns Bay in Cape Breton, Canada,[124] is a gravestone with this inscription: 'In memory of Angus Morrison, Born in Keylis Scalbay, Harris, Scotland 1830, died May 25 1913, aged 83 years Agus tha toradh na fireantachd air a chur ann an sith do luchd deanamh na sithe' – the Gaelic text translating as 'And the reward of truth is to give peace to the peacemakers' (James 3: 18).

Angus was a son of Peter Morrison, Padruig Iain, who had, with his brother John (Iain Og) left Caolas Scalpaigh in the 1840s. His nephew Murdo (Murchadh Iain Mhoir) tells the story.

> Perhaps it may be unpleasant to some present to hear of how South Harris was ruled in the past, but it was the oppression that prevailed there that has brought our place of North Harris into the impoverished condition in which it is now. Pabbay was cleared and put under sheep. The half of Berneray was cleared and put under sheep. The people that were there were sent along with us to North Harris and to Scalpay. The original inhabitants of the place were sent to America, and when Pabbay, Bernera and these places were cleared, the people were sent out upon us.
>
> Then the sea-ware rights that the North Harris people had at that time were taken from them and given to the Scalpay people when it was crofted out. The patches of land we have in North Harris are only peat, and will not yield any crop, unless they are manured with sea-ware year by year, so that we are obliged to go for the sea-ware to the Isle of Skye and to the Lewis. I go in the spring tides to the Isle of Skye for sea-ware in a small boat of twenty feet keel. When we load that boat with sea-ware in Skye I am filled with fear and hope – the hope of reaching the shore if the weather holds, the fear of being drowned when it breaks. Whenever I can land safely with cargo I feel as pleased as other people would who might come laden with a cargo of gold, not because of the cargo and the sea-ware, but because I have saved my life.

When I arrive home at dusk, probably I may commence unloading the boat and putting the sea-ware up upon the land without waiting for shifting my clothes, or even taking a particle of food. There is no other way for it, and live.

I am that way during the week of the spring-tide. During the week of the neap-tide I carry up on my back from the sea-shore where I laid it, the sea-ware that I brought home during the previous week, up the hill to the land. Our practice is to cultivate the ground every second week; the other week we gather sea-ware.[125]

Murdo Morrison's own family scattered over the world, as far as British Columbia and the Falkland Isles, and only one son, Finlay, stayed at home, and you can recognise his house in Caolas Scalpaigh by the cabbage palms growing in the front garden.

John MacKay (Iain mac Choinnich Bhuachaille) – John, son of Kenneth the Herd – is given the credit in Harris for the eventual capture of Mac an t-Sronaich the outlaw. Iain had been working on the mainland and had earned a bit of money there. He had spent the night in an inn on his way from Lairg to the packet-boat at Strome Ferry, and they had warned him there that there was a suspicious character about who might well attack a single traveller. So Iain hid his money about his clothing, and filled his purse with bits of broken metal. Sure enough, he was stopped by Mac an t-Sronaich, who demanded his purse. 'Well, it took me long enough to fill it,' said Iain, 'so you can at least have the trouble of picking it up.' He threw the purse on the ground, where it clinked suggestively. Mac an t-Sronaich bent down to pick it up, and Iain gave him such a blow that he knocked him unconscious – and that, they say, is how Mac an t-Sronaich was caught, though some say that he managed to get away and hid in the meal-chest in a house, only to be given away by the blood trickling out from the bottom of the chest. But there is a story of him hiding in a meal-chest in the manse in Ceos in Lewis, where his aunt was the wife of the minister, so perhaps the two stories have become confused.

There was a family of MacDermids in Caolas Scalpaigh also, very much connected with the army. Domhnall mac Fhearguis (Donald, son of Fergus) was a soldier and so was his son James, who went to Canada. Could this be another of the families settled in the area after the Napoleonic Wars?

There is a sad little story too of the girl who had a boyfriend, and they were going to get married, but her boy went away to earn money, and promised to write to her regularly, but she heard no more from him. So after a year or two, she gave him up and got married to another suitor, the local postman. Years afterwards her first boyfriend came back to Caolas Scalpaigh on a visit, and asked why she had never answered any of his letters – the postman hadn't delivered them, to leave the field open for himself.

On the shore near the bridge to Scalpaigh is Mol na h-Atha, the beach of the kilns, and the ruins of the house where Alex MacLeod – Ailig na h-Atha – lived before he went with many other Harris families to Port nan Long in Skye, in the settlement there after the First World War. The kilns were the trenches for the slow burning of seaweed to provide the kelp ash when the kelp industry was at its peak in the early 1800s, and they used to say that the whole shores would be hidden in the acrid, biting smoke from the kilns. Many lost their sight through working at the kelp, and many another left the island, looking elsewhere for a livelihood away from the toil of cutting the weed and the smoke of the kilns.

It was to Caolas Scalpaigh that Mrs MacNab, daughter of Donald Campbell of Scalpaigh, came after leaving Tarasaigh, and Tobhta mhic an Abba is still shown above the shore there. Later the croft passed to Donald MacDougall, who had been grieve, or farm manager, for Alexander Stewart when he had the farm of Scalpaigh. Alexander was a son of Donald Stewart of Losgaintir. These Stewarts had come originally from Fortingall in Perthshire, and both Donald MacDougall and his wife had come from that area also, and both were related to the Stewarts. Their daughter Anna was famous in her day, and many of the more unusual surnames in the area, such as Fenton, Trotter and MacLachlan, come from her children.

There were lots of MacAskills in Caloas Scalpaigh, of two quite different families. The older group came from Aird Asaig, among them was Coinneach Mor, who was six feet eight inches in height, and was married to Jane Cunningham, who was six foot three, while the other group are descended from Niall Mor, one of the crofters evicted from Bearnaraigh in 1850.

It was in Caolas Scalpaigh too that Donald MacInnes from

Branndarsaig finally settled, after returning to Harris from Cape Breton.

Sceotasaigh

Sceotasaigh is a little island in East Loch Tairbeart, near the larger island of Scalpaigh. Although no one lives there now, there have been three occasions when it was inhabited. The first was in 1853, when two crofts were made on the island for families cleared from elsewhere in Harris. One of these was Tormod mac Ruairidh Thormoid Oig, Norman MacLeod of the family we noted in Leacli, cleared from na Buirgh, and the other Ruairidh Ghilleasbuig Gobha, Roderick son of Archie the blacksmith from Borgh on Bearnaraigh – but better known as am Bodach, meaning the Old Boy. They struggled on there until 1870, when they gave up the island in return for crofts elsewhere, Ruairidh to Becrabhig and Tormod to Urgha. The island then lay empty until 1887 when the two crofts were let again, to cottars from Scalpaigh: Donnchadh Dhomhnaill Alasdair (Duncan MacKay) and Iain Chaluim Iain (John MacSween) better known as Iain na Banndraich – the Widow's John – for his father was drowned coming from Wick to Steornabhagh with a cargo of flagstones, when Iain was only young. Life on such a small island was not easy, and the families eventually came ashore, the MacSweens to An Tairbeart and the MacKays back to Scalpaigh.

Then the island was bought by a Mr Taylor, who later bought Scalpaigh also; he built a holiday house there, and established a plantation of trees, though I believe the crofters retained their crofting and peat-cutting rights on the island, and perhaps still do.

Scalpaigh (Scalpay)

Martin Martin mentions Scalpaigh in his description of Harris in 1703.

> Next to Loch Seafort, which for some Miles divides the Lewis from Harries, is the notable Harbour within the Island, by Sea-faring Men call'd Glass, and by the natives Scalpa; it is a Mile and a half long from South to North and a Mile in breadth. There is an Entrance on the South and North ends of this Isle, and several good Harbours in each, well known to the generality of Seamen.[126]

54. Harbour at Scalpaigh

The earliest rental we have for Harris, in 1680, shows Scalpaigh shared by two tenants.

> Set to donald mc urchie voir the two pairts of ye pennie for wch he payes fourtie six merks eight shillings eight pennice.
>
> Donald baine payes for ye third part yrof twentie three merks four shills eight pence.[127]

Unfortunately we have been unable to identify either Donald mc urchie vor (Donald, son of big Murdo) or Donald Baine (Fair Donald). By 1684 Donald Baine had gone and by 1688 the whole island was let, along with Maraig, to John Campbell, the forester.

John Campbell was the subject of an *Oran Luaidh*, a song for waulking tweed, which must date from about 300 years ago, but has again become popular recently.

> Ceud soraidh bhuam
> Huthil horo
> Dha na Hearadh
> Ho hi ibho
> Gu Iain Caimbeul
> Huthil horo
> Donn, mo leannan
> Och oirinn o[128]

A hundred blessings from me / over to Harris / to John Campbell /
my brown haired gallant

John Campbell was famous in his day, but much more famous was
his son Donald. At the time of the '45 rebellion, Donald was in
general a government supporter, though he took no active part on
either side, until in 1746, a stranger arrived at his house, looking
for shelter for himself and his son. Donald MacLeod of Gualtergill,
who was also of the party, gave details to Bishop Forbes, for his
Lyon in Mourning.

> In the evening they set sail from Benbecula on board the same
> eight-oar'd boat for the Island Scalpay, commonly called the Island
> Glass, where they landed safely about two hours before daylight next
> day, the Prince and O'Sullivan going under the name of Sinclair,
> the latter passing for the father and the former for the son . . .
> In this island Donald MacLeod had an acquaintance, Donald
> Campbell, to whose house he brought the Prince and his small
> retinue before break of day, April 30th. Being all cold and hungry,
> Donald MacLeod desired immediately to have a good fire, which
> was instantly got for them. Donald MacLeod was here only one
> night, but the Prince remained four nights, and was most kindly
> entertained by his hospitable landlord, Donald Campbell, whose
> civility and compassion the Prince entertained a most grateful
> sense of.[129]

Donald Campbell was married to a sister of Hugh MacDonald of
Baile Sear in North Uist, and Baile Sear gave information to Bishop
Forbes also.

> As I'm writing this there coms to my hous a sister of mine marryed
> to one Donald Campbell in Scalpy, alias among sailors Island Glass.
> She says as he (the Prince) was going to Storniva after his first
> coming to the Long Isle, in order to get aboard, he was five nights in
> her hous in said isle . . . He'd be on foot every morning before man
> or woman stirred in the hous, woud go to the landlady's closet and
> ask what he'd have for brakefast the day. Once this was told, he'd
> then ask what was for his neighbours. Be what it will, he was still
> pleased. One morning as he got up he goes in to the kitchin, where
> in a cask of seeds he found a cuple of new laid eggs, with which he
> coms to the landlady's closet, and begg'd the favour she 'd allow him
> the eggs, which was done and prepared for brakefast. After brakefast
> he and one Kenneth Campbell, a young boy, the landlord's son, goes

a fishing. The Prince catches a small coad, which he pouch'd and immediately went hom, stood by till it was dresst for supper . . . But now, as the boy and the fisher were returning home, there meets them a cow of Mr Campbell's bogg'd. The boy attempted to drive her out, but would not do for him. The fisher seeing this threw off his upper coat, into the ditch with Kenneth Campbell he gets and trails the cow out of the bog; got his britches and white stockiness all dirtied.[130]

While the 'Sinclairs' were there, Revd Aulay MacAulay from Scarasta arrived on Scalpaigh with some soldiers, in order to arrest the prince and collect the £30 000 reward offered for him, but Campbell drove him away – he might not be a Jacobite himself, but the Prince had obtained shelter under his roof and the dues of hospitality were far stronger than those of politics.

The prince left Scalpaigh for Steornabhagh to try to get a ship there, but had to return to Scalpaigh, only to find that Campbell had had to go into hiding himself, so the prince and party had to head back from Uist.

There was a sequel to the story. Sometime in the 1880s, Robert Hornsby, who had the hotel in An Tairbeart, bought a Jacobite relic from a crofter – a piece of tartan, which it was claimed had been worn by the prince – a tartan which proved to be of the sett of MacDonald of Borrodale in Ardnamurchan. Now the prince had been kitted out in Borrodale before he came to Scalpaigh, and we know from Mrs Campbell's story that he got in a mess shifting the cow. Would she not have given him a change of clothing, and would that not have meant that he would have left Borrodale tartan in Scalpaigh? The original tartan is now in Stoneyhurst College in England, but there is a replica in *Seallam!* visitor centre in Taobh Tuath in Harris.

Later in his life Donald Campbell was persuaded by his son Kenneth that the increased rents being asked for farms like Scalpaigh were far too high, and he joined the other Highland tacksmen who went to Carolina. His will, made there in 1784 gives a list of his surviving family.

> I give and devise to Katherine McDonald, my lawfull and well-beloved spouse all and wholly my free estate in case she is the longest liver and afterwards to her disposal, to grant it to whom

she pleases. I also doth give and devise to my daughters Barbara, Christian, Margaret and Isobel, and my grandchildren also, John and Alexander, natural lawful children to the deceased John Campbell, my son, the payment of a bill due me, the said Donald Campbell, by Ranald MacDonald of Clan Ranald, North Britain, to the amount of One Hundred Pounds sterling money. Further I give and devise my son Malcolm the payment of a certain bill left in the hands of my son Kenneth, due by Donald MacKenzie of Skinidin, North Britain, for the sum of Twenty odd Pounds sterling. As for William MacLeod of Ose's Bill that I had for sixty pound sterling and the Laird of MacLeod, late of Harris's bond that I had for eight hundred marks, my son at home must be the best judge how much is due me of the said bill and bond . . .[131]

There is no mention of Kenneth, for Kenneth, having persuaded his father not to take a new lease of Scalpaigh, had turned back from the emigration ship at Liverpool, and taken the lease himself. All that 'my son at home' was left was the right to obtain payment of a long-outstanding debt – if he could get it.

Another reason for Donald's leaving Harris was no doubt the loss of his daughter Anna, whose story is one of the classic stories of the island.

The year was 1768. Anna Campbell was engaged to Allan Morrison (Ailean Donn) a son of a merchant in Steornabhagh and he was coming to Scalpaigh for the reiteach or betrothal. Anna and her father were on the headland watching the incoming ship under sail. A squall was seen on the Caolas – the narrows between Scalpaigh and the mainland – obscuring the view for a minute; when it cleared, there was no sign of Allan's ship, for it had foundered in the squall. They searched for survivors and eventually Allan's body was found, on na h-Eileanan Mora – the Shiant Isles – out in the Minch. Anna made a lament for Allan:

Ailein Duinn o-hi, shiubhlainn leat
Ach stoirm nan sianta 's meud na gaillinn
Dh'fhuadaicheadh na fir o 'n chala
Ailein Duinn o-hi, shiubhlainn leat[132]

Brown Allan o-hi, I would follow you / The storm, the gale, the sweep of the waves / Kept the men away from safe harbour / Brown Allan o-hi, I would follow you

Heartbroken, she died, and her body was taken by boat for burial at Roghadal. Another storm arose, and the boat containing the chief mourners and the coffin was driven far out into the Minch. Eventually they decided to put out the coffin to lighten the boat, and immediately the storm abated. They say Anna's ghost had raised the storm so that she would not be buried on land, but could join Allan once more, and that her body eventually came ashore on the Shiant Isles also.

The boat with the mourners eventually came ashore on Skye, but the people at home in Harris had given them up for lost. Two bards made songs on *Di-Sathuirn' an Fhuadaich* – The Saturday of the Loss – and that by Donald MacLeod refers to some of the tacksmen who were the chief mourners in the *Bata Caol Channach,* the narrow boat made in Canna:

> A Choinnich Chaimbeul a Sgalpaidh,
> Bu tu fear macanta smearail
> O, bu mhaith am fear iuil thu,
> Agus stiuir na do ghlacaibh.
>
> 'S iomadh loch agus curaidh
> San deachaidh cunnart air t-anam;
> Ach a nis chaidh do bhathadh
> Anns s' a Bhata Chaol Channach
>
> 'S iomadh long le cruinn arda,
> Thig air airin do bhaile,
> 'S theid a dh'ionnsuidh do Roide
> 'S bhios a foighneachd do thalla,
>
> Nuair a cluinn iad nach beo thu,
> Fhir nach sorach a ceannach –
> Gu 'm bi bratach gun solas
> Ac' a seoladh o t'fhearann.[133]

Kenneth Campbell from Scalpaigh / You were so gentle but strong / You were a good steersman / With the rudder in your grasp / In many a loch and boat / Your life was in danger / But now you have been drowned. / In the Bata Caol Cannach / Many a ship with high masts / Came to your village / And to your Campbell's badge of bog-myrtle / And asks after your halls / When they hear that you are not living / A man so scrupulous in business / Their flags will be dipped / As they sail from your land.

John Lane Buchanan gives a rather different picture of Kenneth Campbell

> There lives, at present, at Scalpa, in the Isle of Harris, a tacksman of a large district, who instead of six days work paid by the subtenants to his predecessor in the lease, has raised the predial service to fifty-two days in the year at once; besides many other services to be performed at different though regular and stated times; as tanning leather for brogues, making heather ropes for thatch, digging and drying peats for fewel; one pannier of charcoal to be be carried to the smith; so many days for gathering and shearing sheep and lambs; for ferrying cattle from island to island and other distant places; and several days for going on distant errands; so many pounds of wool to be spun into yarn. And over and above all this, they must lend their aid, upon any unforeseen occurrence, whenever they are called on. The constant service of two months at once is performed, at the proper season, in the making of kelp. On the whole, this gentleman's subtenants may be computed to devote to his service full three days in the week.
>
> This man was bred, like many of his countrymen, for the sea-service, and underwent many vicissitudes of fortune both by sea and land. He was shipwrecked, taken prisoner by the French, escaped almost naked, struggled with many difficulties for years in America, and afterwards came home to the isles, and dealt in spirits, sugar, tea, coffee and the kelp trade, by all of which means he amassed a considerable fortune. Thus rich and independent, this man, it is said, took his father's lease over his head. The old man and his wife, stung with vexation and grief, rather than live in some adjoining hut at the mercy of such a son, went with the rest of their family to America, where the aged parents of this unnatural child died soon after in wretched poverty. He afterwards turned out of his large and fine farm, the whole of his relations, who held little possessions on it, and who fell soon into great want.[134]

Kenneth Campbell was tacksman of Scalpaigh for many years after swindling his father out of the lease, and it was he who was the contractor for the first lighthouse on Scalpaigh. John Knox, reporting to the British Fisheries Society in 1786 recommended the building of a lighthouse there.

> For this purpose we landed on the island of Scalpay, or as it is sometimes called, Elen Glass, and staid the night with Mr Campbell,

a tacksman under Captain Macleod. As this island lies immediately
in the course of ships that pass through the outer channel to and
from the Baltic, and being near several clusters of rocks, it was
judged a proper station for a lighthouse; and in 1786, a bill was
passed for that purpose.[135]

Work on the lighthouse was commenced by Campbell in 1787, and
completed by Thomas Smith in 1789, and the light was lit for the
first time on 10 October 1789, with Alexander Reid, a seaman from
Fraserburgh, as the first lightkeeper.

According to MacIain, Kenneth himself came to a sticky end,
being killed by French pirates.

John MacDiarmid, Iain Ban na Faoilinn, told of the later history
of Scalpaigh to the Napier Commission in 1883.

> The island was formerly occupied by two or three tacksmen in
> succession, before it was crofted out, but these had to throw it up.
> When the factor found out that the tacksmen could not live there,
> he settled upon it twenty crofters. When the twenty were there they
> were pretty nigh contented, and able to make somewhat of a living
> out of it. Now Lord Dunmore's Commissioner, at that time, who
> had authority over the local factors, was a Captain Sitwell. This man,
> finding that this island was accessible by sea, thought it might be
> advisable to make it a fishing community, and so he added another
> twenty families upon the twenty who were there. By this time the
> families of the original settlers were growing up and having families
> of their own. Their families were sharing their own small plots of
> land with them. The practice grew apace, so that, to make a long
> story short, there are now, if not a full hundred, at least close upon
> a hundred families in the place.
>
> Of these forty who have land the utmost that can be said of their
> crops is that they would support them about two months of the
> year. The whole of the population – cottars and crofters – have to
> pursue the fishing, chiefly lobster fishing, and they have to be out
> summer, spring and winter, at least eleven months in the year. They
> have to go often from home, and live in bothies, and sometimes as
> far as Uist. Then everyone that can go to the east-coast fishing goes
> there – to Wick. Immediately after their return from the east-coast
> fishing they take to the home fishing. Some take to the long-line
> fishing, and others of them, at the fall of the year, to the lobster
> fishing. And then times are very hard.[136]

The first crofters were sent to Scalpaigh in 1842, and the second group in 1846. Most of the twenty extra crofters that were put in Scalpaigh were from Pabaigh. The Pabaich had never been fishermen – how could they be with no proper harbour on Pabaigh? – and there was for a time a tension between the Scalpaigh fishermen and the Pabaigh crofters. One of the Pabaich – Iain mac Chaluim (John Morrison) – became maor, or assistant factor, on Scalpaigh, and he used his position to try and consolidate all the crofts on Aird an Aiseag for his own family, which is why the numbers there run out of sequence. The only croft he could not get was that of Domhnall mac Uilleim (Donald MacLeod) from Pabaigh, for Donald's wife Anna was from Uist, and had been a nurse in her youth for the MacDonalds of Baile Raghaill, including Baillidh Domhnallach, the factor in Roghadal. Anna walked to Roghadal to ask the Baillidh to tell Iain mac Chaluim to leave her husband be, and that is how they managed to retain the croft on Aird an Aiseag.

One of the original setters in Scalpaigh in 1842 was Ruairidh Thormoid Oig (Roderick MacLeod) who had come from Leacli with his brother Iain to settle on Aird Teaganais. When the crofts were subdivided, Iain would not be content with half a croft, and returned to Leacli, but Ruairidh stayed on in Scalpaigh. His great-grandson Noraidh was a well-known bard, and a great source of local stories – many a night Noraidh and I spent yarning about families, while Mairi-Ceit fed us with scones and pancakes and wished we had something more interesting to talk about than eachdraidh (history). Here is one of Noraidh's songs in praise of the Gaidhealtachd – the Gaelic-speaking Highlands – and in dispraise of the game laws.

O, 's toigh leam fhein a' Ghaidhealtachd
Is toigh leam fhein bhith tamh innte
Is toigh leam fhein bhith 'n tir an fhraoich
'S e tir nan laoch 's nan armann i.

'S e tir gun eis a' Ghaidhealtachd,
'S gach ni chum feum tha fas innte
'S i tir an eisg, 's i tir an fheidh
'S i tir na spreidh, 's mo ghradh oirre.

Mo dhiombadh aig na baillidhean
'S gach oighr' 's gach Diuc tha fasachadh,

Le geamair gleusd' air fair 'n eisg,
'S air faire 'n fheidh mun tar sinn iad.

Ged leag iad cis is cain oirnn,
Is priosan mura paigh sinn iad
Gu marbh sinn fiadh is breac le lion
Mar chleachd sinn riamh, 's cha mheairlich sinn.[137]

O I like the Highlands / I like to be living there / I like to be in the land of heather / The land of heroes and warriors / The Highlands are a land without lack / Everything you need grows there / Land of fish, land of deer / Land of cattle, my love to you / My hatred to each factor / Each estate and clearing Duke / With keen keepers watching the fish / and watching the deer lest we get any / Though they put taxes and fines on us / And prison if we do not pay / To kill a deer or net a fish, / As we do, is no theft.

Scalpaigh with its excellent natural harbours and its skilled fishermen became the most prosperous part of Harris. The Cunninghams were at the forefront of the fishing industry, and Seonachan Ruairidh Alasdair (John Cunningham) and I made a video for schools a few years ago, in which he tells us how the family began to be involved in fishing.[138]

My grandfather, Alasdair Cunningham, was the first of the family to be born on Scalpaigh, and he brought the first smack to the island, a sailing ship by the name of *Jane*. Before he could get this smack he had to get a loan from the estate to buy it, and he built a house because of this and he was going to pay for the house and the smack by bringing coal up from Greenock – that was bringing coal to the Outer Isles and as far away as Gairloch and Ullapool. They were sturdy lads and it was with their own hands that they handled the cargo. They fared well, and they linked up with a broker in Glasgow, and he gave them help, giving them cargo, and doing work for them, office work and so on.

Now when Alasdair gave up work, his son Johnnie took his place, and he and Donald Morrison went down to Yarmouth, and they got a smack there – a bigger one with two masts – by the name of *Sybil*. They began the same work with her as Alasdair, my grandfather, used to do, and they started taking coal to the lighthouses.

As time went on the work became more plentiful and they were going as far as Runcorn, getting salt at Runcorn, and bringing it to the ports where they were curing the herring, in the islands. Then

55. *Hercules* at Scalpaigh

they had an unusual trade with the *Sybil* in the wintertime – she was anchored in the north anchorage in Scalpaigh, and the girls and the women gutted herring in her. Scalpaigh was really busy at that time with the herring, and the Cunninghams had a part in that as well.

I have been connected with fishing most of my life. The first job I had, I went with my father as a cook on a wooden boat that he had then. *Maggie Lockhart* was her name, and I'll never forget the first morning when we were going out by the Rudha Dhorchanach and my job was to make the breakfast. I was making bacon and eggs and there was a bad sea, and I was starting to get sea-sick – as sick as a dog – and I was wanting to get my head down. My father appeared in the galley and what did he do but grab my ear and he lifted me off the seat and he took me through the galley and then to the stove, with the frying pan, and I was still being sick, and after that I got used to it. You might think that my father was hard on me doing that, but that was not his intention, but to make sure that he got rid of my sea-sickness right at the start, in order to make me a fisherman.

And that's what I did, I kept on with the fishing, and many a year I was fishing, and I saw plenty of changes in the fishing. I was first

56. Pier at Scalpaigh

of all on the *Golden Eagle*. That was the first job I had as a skipper.
She did not have a wheelhouse – the wheel was in the stern and
uncovered, and it was the drift net that we were working with then,
hauling the drift nets.

In 1948 my father went to the East Coast, to Banff, and he
ordered a boat there and she was to be a ring-netter. This was the
first ring-netter to be built in the yard at Banff and a fortnight before
she was ready, I was sent out for the fitting out and she was fitted
out with all that was necessary.

Now I was for years on *A' Mhaighdean Hearach*, and we got on
really well and I was as contented there as I have ever been in any job.
But I had to go on to the coasters, and we went everywhere around
the coasts of Britain and down to France, Ireland and Holland.

Between the fishing and freight, Scalpaigh was as busy then as
I have ever seen it, and I think that the Cunninghams had a lot to
do with it.

Today, the young men do not have the same love for the sea
and the fishing as we had. I do not think that it is in their blood in
the way that it was in our blood. The Cunninghams are spreading
away from the island, some in teaching, taking up all sorts of other
trades.

We have not lost our connection with the sea yet. We still have a boat or two rented out to people and, who knows but you may be crewing one of them some time. And I know this for sure – you could probably cook bacon and eggs better than me!

Alasdair Cunningham, Seonachan's grandfather, was the proud owner of Am Bata Beag – the wee boat.

Tha'm bata beag cho boidheach beag
Tha'm bata beag cho boidheach
Tha'm bata beag cho boidheach beag
'S gu bheil i deis gu seoladh.[139]

The boat is so wee and bonny / The wee boat is so bonny / The boat is so wee and bonny / And she is ready to sail

Unfortunately he hit bad weather and rough seas, but the wee boat finally took him back to home and harbour.

Dol a-steach tron chaolas leinn
Bu chaonnagach i seoladh
'N sin lub i steach a h-iotadh
Don Bhagh Chuilce chun na morag

An t-eathar ur aig Alasdair
Mo bheannachd-s' aig a bordan
Cha robh gin sa bhail againn
A thigeadh as cho doigheil[139]

Coming in the Kyles with us / She battled her way / then turned in to the shallows / to Bagh Cuilce and the mooring / The new boat that Alasdair has / My blessing on her planks / There wasn't another in our village / Would have come back so happily

Until the start of the car ferry, Scalpaigh felt itself to be separate from the rest of Harris and developed a fierce loyalty among its own. They say that the schoolmaster asked the children one day to write an essay about Harris, and they started off: 'Harris is an island off the coast of Scalpaigh' – and no doubt that is how many of the Scalpaich feel still, though how this will change now that the island is connected to Harris by a bridge is hard to say.

PART SIX – HIORT (ST KILDA)

Village Bay

The first time I went to Hiort was with the late Andy Millar-Mundy, on his fishing boat the *Golden Chance* – and indeed I was very glad to see Hiort, for we had been lost en route. We had sailed from West Loch Tairbeart, and just as we were about to leave, a young couple on a motorbike had come up and pleaded to be allowed to join us, as they were on their honeymoon, and it would just make their honeymoon to get to St Kilda. They came aboard, and the young lad started being seasick before we left the pier, and continued till we reached the island, so I do not think that their honeymoon was quite so memorable after all.

Anyway we set off, and Andy's radar broke down, which would not have mattered too much had we not hit a thick fog-bank at the back of Gasgeir. We carried on, hoping that the fog would clear, but it only got thicker. Andy reckoned we were on course, but we started to see gannets, heading home after their day's fishing to their roosts on the Stacs, two massive fangs of rock sticking up out of the sea behind Boirearaigh, the island four miles to the north of the main Island of Hiort – and the gannets were going the wrong way. So Andy radioed the army base which was then on the island, and they picked us up on their radar and gave us instructions to bring us in to Village Bay.

Unfortunately, the gannets continued to go the wrong way, and we realised that something was far wrong; we learned later that we had been in the radar shadow cast by Boirearaigh, and that the boat they had been seeing and instructing was a different one altogether, to the south of Hiort. From Andy's reckoning, and the birds, we reckoned that we had overshot to the north of Boirearaigh, and were headed into the full Atlantic. But in a fog and in the dark, it is a comfort to know that, wherever the rocks and cliffs of Hiort are, they at least are somewhere behind you, so we lay to until dawn, when the fog cleared enough to let us get a bearing on the Flannan Isles, many miles to the north of our course. We turned then, and finally made it into Village Bay.

It is from our landing there that I derived one of my prized possessions: a paperback copy of Tom Steel's *The Life and Death of*

St Kilda[140] – still about the best general book about Hiort, although I think that my copy is probably unique in having been dropped into Village Bay and fished out again reasonably intact!

There is a tradition of rival crews of MacLeods from Harris and MacDonalds from Uist racing to Village Bay to claim Hiort. Colla MacLeod, the captain of the Harris boat, realising that the Uist boat was going to get there first, cut off his hand and threw it ashore, so claiming the island, as his had been the first hand to touch it. But the same story is told of other parts of Scotland too, so its authenticity must be doubtful.

Less dramatically, a manuscript history of the MacDonalds, published by the Iona Club,[141] states that 'Godfrey MacDonald had from his father a large portion of land, as North Uist, Benbicula, one half of South Uist, Boysdale, Canna, Slate and Knoydart. It was he gave Boysdale to MacNeill of Barra and gifted Hirta or St. Kilda to the Laird of Harris.'

The first documentary reference to the island is in 1346 in a charter of John of Isla to his son Reginald 'de insula de Egge, de insula de Rume, de insula de Huwyste cum castro de Uynvawle, de insula de Barre et de insula de Hert'[142] – of the island of Eigg, the island of Rum, the island of Uist with the Castle of Benbecula, of the island of Barra and the island of Hirta.

The Norsemen must have visited Hiort, for they left place-names there: Oisebhal, or East Hill, and Ruiabhal, or Red Hill, as well as Soaigh or Sheep Island, and Boirearaigh or Fort Island, but little else is left of their period there. It is little wonder that it was known to such seafarers, both as a danger point in the Atlantic, and as a source of fresh water on a voyage.

Even before that, Hiort was known to the Bronze and Iron Age peoples, who left buildings and burial sites to attest to their presence. These sites have been exhaustively surveyed and investigated by Dr Mary Harman, whose book *An Isle called Hirte*[143] is the definitive modern text on the island.

The Old Village

The village street runs in a crescent behind Village Bay, along the base of Conachair, the highest hill on the island, and the ruins of the houses deserted in 1930 are in a line along the street, but the original village was further behind these, in the scree-slope at the bottom of Conachair. It was this older village which was described by Martin Martin, the first visitor to write in detail about Hiort, after his visit there in 1697.

> This Isle belongs in Property to the Laird of Mack-Leod, Head of one of the Ancientest Families of Scotland; it is never Farmed, but most commonly bestowed upon some Favourite, one of his Friends or followers, who is called Steward of the Isle. The present Steward's name is Alexander Mack-Leod. The number of People inhabiting this Isle at present, is about One hundred and eighty, who in the Steward's absence are governed by one Donald Mack-Gill-Colm, as their Meijre, which imports an Officer.[144]

> The inhabitants live together in a small village, carrying all the signs of extreme poverty; the houses are of a low form, and the doors are all to the north-east, to secure them from the shocks of the tempestuous south-west winds. The walls are rudely built of stone, the short couples joining at the ends of the roof, upon whose sides small ribs of wood are laid, and these are covered with straw; the whole secured with ropes made of twisted heath, the extremity of which on each side is poised with stone to preserve the thatch from being blown away.[145]

Nearer to the shore were three old churches: Christ Church, nearest to the village, St Columba's to the west, and St Brianan's to the south, on the slope of Ruiabhal. It may seem strange that there was no church dedicated to St Kilda, but there is a good reason – there never was such a saint. The name, like Iona and Hebrides, is a spelling mistake. It appears that the name Skildar appeared on an old map –some say that it was meant for a different island group anyway – but it was misread as 'S. Kilda', and so the name arose. It is only in the 1600s that we find the name St Kilda coming into general use, and earlier documents refer to the islands by their Gaelic name Hiort. Strictly speaking Hiort refers to the main island of the group, but that was the only one inhabited in historic times, neither Boirearaigh nor Soaigh ever having had permanent populations.

Martin describes the people of Hiort.

> Both Men and Women are well Proportioned, nothing differing from those of the Isles and Continent; such as are not fair are

57. The old village at St Kilda, by Sir Thomas Dyke Acland

natives only for an Age or two; but their Off-spring proves fairer than themselves. The present Generation comes short of the last in Strength and Longevity. They shew'd us huge big Stones carried by the Fathers of some of the Inhabitants now living; any of which is a burthen too heavy for any two of the present Inhabitants to raise from the ground; and this change is all within the compass of Forty Years. But notwithstanding this, any one inhabiting St Kilda is always reputed stronger than two of the Inhabitants belonging to the Isle of Harris or the adjacent Isles.'[146]

He paints a picture of happiness and plenty on Hiort; indeed he went so far as to say that 'There is only this wanting to make them the Happiest People in this habitable Globe – that they themselves do not know how Happy they are.'[147]

Martin was the first to write of the idyllic life of Hiort, but many were to follow him, right up to the present day; but his view, and theirs, is that of a short-term visitor, arriving necessarily in reasonable weather. What life was like there in bad weather must have been a very different matter.

Martin had gone to Hiort as one of the party of the steward along with the minister of Harris, who had gone there to deal with 'Roderick the Impostor', one of the Hiortaich who had set himself up as a prophet and religious leader on the island. The Hiortaich had to feed the steward's party, which could be quite a strain on the economy of the island.

The steward in 1725 was Alexander MacLeod of Pabaigh, and the rent he paid to MacLeod of Dunvegan for Hiort was £85 Scots (about £7 sterling) and he would have recouped at least as much from the Hiortaich. There was no cash on the island at this date, so the rent would have been paid in kind, mainly mutton and sea-birds, and in addition the steward had the right to all the island's milk and dairy products from May to Michaelmas.

Alexander Buchan, who was the schoolteacher on Hiort in the early 1700s, has a rather different view from Martin.

> They are in a manner Prisoners, yea worse, all Things considered; Prisoners in other places have the advantage of Visits from Friends and converse with them, which that Poor People have not fore the Greatest Part of the Year, except when the Steward and his followers come among them to demand his rents, viz. Down, Wool, Butter, Cheese, Cows, Sheep, Fowls, Oil etc. and they look upon that Visit as no great Advantage to them, seeing that they are kept in continual Trouble while the Steward is among them, and they very much grudge what he carries away with him, and that they must all the Year be toiling for others.
>
> The Baillie or Steward at present is one called John Mack-Leod, and lives all winter in another Isle called Pabba. And he with his retinue that come along with him are a heavy Burden upon the poor People, who are sometimes 50, sometimes 60 or 100, sometimes fewer and sometimes more, they as t'were forcing their maintenance from them above their Ability, all the Time of his and their abode in the Place; he carrying off with him, almost, all they should live upon thro' the year.[148]

Martin was seeing the island economy from the point of view of the visitor, while Buchan saw it from the point of view of those left after the visitors had departed. Buchan had come to the island as a teacher and catechist to the Hiortaich:

> It is certain, that about the year 1704, they knew little of Christianity; the General Assembly of that year did refer it to their commission to send one thither privately to instruct the people in the Grounds of the Christian Religion, going from House to House, as appears

by the Index of the imprinted Acts of that Assembly, and in July that year, Alexander Buchan came to the Commission and offered to go to that place, and having produced ample testimonials, he was examined by a Committee, and having given then satisfaction, application was made to the then Laird of McLeod and his friends, about Mr Buchan's going to that place, and upon the 1st day of August the said year, he got his commission and instructions to go to Hirta as a Catechist, with 200 merks to carry his charges. And thereupon he went to that place the following year.[149]

The funding for the school failed in 1709 and Buchan paid a visit to Edinburgh to try to find new financial support:

bringing with him two native boys, whom he had taught Reading and the Principles of Religion; And they having learned to speak English, it gave such satisfaction to Ministers, and People at Edinburgh, that they were much encouraged.[150]

Responsibility for the school was assumed by the Society in Scotland for Propagating Christian Knowledge; Buchan was ordained a minister and returned to Hiort with the boys, whose names are given as Murdo Campbell and Finlay MacDonald. It must have been an incredible experience for them to have gone from Hiort to the city of Edinburgh, but we are not told what use they made of their English after returning to Hiort.

One of the intriguing statements made by Martin Martin was about the facial appearance of the Hiortach men.

Those of St. Kilda have generally but very Thin Beards and these too do not appear until they arrive at the Age of Thirty, and in some not till after Thirty five; they have all but a few Hairs upon the upper Lip, and point of the Chin.[151]

This hardly agrees with the later photographs of the 'St Kilda Parliament'. It looks as though there had been a complete change in the population of the island – and this is in fact what had happened.

In 1727 Donald MacDonald from Hiort died of smallpox during a visit to Harris. His clothes were taken back to Hiort – and so of course was the infection. In August a party of three men and eight boys had been put ashore on Stac an Armuinn, one of the off-shore stacs of the island of Boireraigh, four miles to the north of Hiort itself, to gather young gannets and feathers. By the time that the boat was due to come back for them, there were not enough fit people on Hiort to man it. The party was marooned on the stac until May of the following year, when they were picked up by the factor's boat, and when they got back to Hiort, they found only one old man and eighteen children – all the others had died of smallpox.[152]

Some of the survivors may have stayed on to start a new community, but others will have left, and it was by bringing in new settlers that the community of Hiort was re-established. Most of the newcomers were from Skye, with at least one family each from Uist and Bearnaraigh. It is said sometimes that they were sent to Hiort as a penal colony, but this appears to be too strong a statement, though there does seem at least some suggestion that the Skye settlers were those who were glad to get away from their proximity to Dunvegan, and that Dunvegan shared this sentiment.

However that may be, it was the new families – Fergusons, Gillieses, MacCrimmons, MacDonalds, MacKinnons and MacQueens – who brought their characteristics to the island, and produced the beards.

The Village Street

In 1812 Thomas Dyke Acland visited Hiort, and his sketches are the earliest visual record we have of the island. He was horrified by the squalor of the old village, and on another visit in 1834 left a gift of £20 to encourage the building of new houses. The Hiortaich were fortunate at this time to have a minister, the Revd Neil MacKenzie, who was interested in the physical as well as the spiritual welfare of the islanders. He encouraged the building of a new Village Street, closer to the shore than the old village, with new houses end-on to the Street. The arable land of the area was parcelled out into crofts, each running in a long narrow strip from the new head-dyke below Conachair to the shore. The new houses were still thatched, but they had windows and doors to the east, away from the wind, and at least elementary drainage.

A hurricane in 1860 damaged many of the new houses, and John MacPherson MacLeod, whose father had bought the island from the MacLeods of Dunvegan in 1804, decided to have new houses

58. The Village Street, St Kilda

built in a row facing the street, bringing in masons from Skye to build them and purchasing zinc sheets for roofing. The old houses were left standing in the gaps between the new houses, and were used for housing the cattle, which until then had shared the houses with the people. The new houses looked well, in a line facing the shore, but unfortunately they also faced into the wind, and many of the new zinc roofs blew away and had to be replaced with felt, held down with timber straps and ropes, usually anchored with gannets' beak as nails.

When the Hiortaich were evacuated in 1930, their sheep were sold to defray expenses, but after a few years, wild sheep were brought on to the island from Soaigh, the island to the west of the main island of Hiort. Soaigh means Sheep Island in Norse, and it held a flock of wild sheep, smaller than the domestic sheep, and ranging in colour from light ginger to dark chocolate. These sheep have now the run of the island, wandering along the village street and grazing on the deserted croft-lands.

The other main inhabitant of the village is the field-mouse, a sub-species special to Hiort – bigger, darker and longer-tailed than its mainland cousins.

The houses have crumbled with neglect since then, although the National Trust has rebuilt some of these as accommodation for their work parties. At the east end of the street, an army base was built – an ugly single-storey block and flat-roofed buildings – but in a way I preferred their honest ugliness to the rebuilt houses on the Village Street, with their misleading impression of authenticity. With all the modern conveniences available today, life on the village street is very different from what it once was, even if the external shape of the house is the same.

The Church

We have already mentioned the three old churches of Hiort, but the later church was built to the east of the village, largely through the instrumentality of the Revd John MacDonald of Ferintosh, one of the leaders of the evangelical wing of the Church of Scotland. He first visited the island in 1822, when he preached thirteen sermons in as many days, but, though his hearers were obviously moved by his preaching, the Revd Neil MacKenzie comments: 'I soon found that they were only charmed by his eloquence and energy, and had not knowledge enough to follow or understand his argument.' [153]

The Revd Neil took the first detailed census of the island,[154] giving names and ages for the 108 people then living there, though some of his translations and spellings of the Gaelic names are rather odd.

Neil MacKenzie should be one of the heroes of the story of Hiort; we have already noted his leadership in the building of new houses and the enclosure of land. He also encouraged agricultural improvements and the enclosure of the graveyard but he found that the Hiortaich required a leader:

> I got them persuaded after a little to build themselves new houses on a more enlarged and better plan, but I could only get them to work when I wrought along with them. So long as I could be with them they would work quite eagerly, but whenever I had to leave, they soon got tired.[155]

In 1843 the Church of Scotland was split by the Disruption and the breaking away of the Free Church. The Revd MacKenzie left, and the Hiortaich were for some years without a leader. When a new minister was found by the Free Church, their choice was disastrous for the Hiortaich. John MacKay was ordained specially for St Kilda, and although he obviously cared deeply about the spiritual welfare of his congregation, his doctrine was of a pessimistic nature, and he insisted on an ever-increasing number of religious services, to the extent that they came to interfere with the agricultural management of the islands.

Unlike MacKenzie, MacKay turned his back on the practical needs of his congregation, to concentrate on his own view of their spiritual needs. Worse still, he appears to have been under the thumb of his housekeeper: 'a remarkable woman, standing about six feet high, and proportionately well built, who is the terror of the whole island – when this person opes her mouth, no dog, not even the poor minister, dare bark', according to Robert Connell, who visited the island in 1886.[156]

According to Connell the church itself was starting to show signs of neglect.

> The Church is a plain barn-like building standing north-east and south-west. You enter by a door in the north-east gable. A bit of very rough causeway leads up the centre to the pulpit and precentor's box at the remote end. Other than this causeway, which is only the breadth of a narrow pavement, there is no floor to cover the cold, damp, black earth. Nine heavy coarse wooden benches without backs are placed on each side of the causeway, and these give ample accommodation for all the worshippers. Above your head are the bare rafters, with numberless spiders performing profane somersaults in the air while divine service is going on. On the white-washed walls of the building, now green and yellow with mildew and damp, and with great patches of lime constantly crumbling away, slimy and gruesome insects crawl lazily and indifferently along, one of the crowd every now and then alighting upon the shoulder of some devout worshipper.[157]

A stove was sent to the island quite recently to be fitted up in the Church, but it gave rise to much anxious searching of hearts among the islanders. They asked themselves whether it would be a proper thing to introduce a stove into the sanctuary. At first nobody cared to give a deliberate answer; even the minister, who is nothing if not dogmatic, was silent. His good angel, the housekeeper, came to the rescue. She pronounced the stove to be equally godless with the organ, and declared that it therefore could not be admitted into the house of the Lord. The scales fell from the eyes of the minister and people in an instant. They backed up the housekeeper, and stove was sent home across the sea to the impious Sassenach.[158]

John MacKay was replaced as minister in 1889 by Angus Fiddes. He was a man of a different mould, as we will see in the next section. The church has been rebuilt now, and is used for occasional services, but somehow I doubt if Revd MacKay would have approved of their content!

The Graveyard

About the centre of the village street there is an opening which leads to a little circular graveyard, surrounded by the stone wall which Revd Neil helped to build. In the usual way of Island graveyards, there are few inscribed stones – they were unnecessary, as everyone knew who was buried where. There are two inscribed stones, one for a sister of the Revd John MacKay and the other for 'Finlay, the only son of Angus Gillies', who died in 1898 at the age of twenty. This is one of the saddest things on Hiort, for in fact Angus Gillies had had six other children, all of whom had died of tetanus in infancy – and they had not even been counted.

Martin Martin made a list of diseases he found on Hiort, but there is no mention in it of tetanus, which was to become a scourge in the island community: the majority of babies born on the island died of the 'eight-day sickness'. Of twenty-three born between 1856 and 1865 only ten survived, and of twenty-six born between 1865 and 1875, only six survived.

The Hiortaich were so used to losing children that they did not reckon them as being properly alive until they passed the danger period. Under the Revd MacKay's pessimistic teachings, the islanders had become fatalistic about tetanus – 'If it is God's will that babies should die, nothing you can do will save them' – and it was even claimed by one minister that the tetanus was 'a wise device of the Almighty for keeping the population within the resources of the Island'.[159]

It is not known how the tetanus came to Hiort; one would think that if it was there in Martin Martin's time, he would have mentioned it. Perhaps the re-settlers after the smallpox brought it – as well as facial hair – or perhaps they had not built up the immunity that the previous inhabitants had acquired. Many writers have written about tetanus as if it were a disease peculiar to Hiort, but it is clear from the Statistical Account of 1791–99 that it was endemic all over the western coast of Scotland; it was also to be found in Ireland and Iceland.

This is an example of what happened with much of the literature about Hiort: visitors went there who had never been anywhere else in the islands, and saw occurrences unknown to them which they reckoned were specific to Hiort only. Even the famous St Kilda Parliament was nothing more than a normal discussion of the day's work essential in any area where work was done communally, and its equivalent could be found on any small island; but nobody ever went to the likes of Scarp to photograph it. All sorts of arcane reasons were postulated for tetanus on Hiort, without realising that it was in no way specific to that island only and was endemic all over the western coast of Scotland, Ireland and even Iceland.

The Revd MacKay had looked on the infant deaths as being the will of God, but his successor, Angus Fiddes, was of a different opinion – if medical care could save the children, he would find that care. First he had a nurse sent to the island, but the island women were unwilling to be persuaded by her to use antiseptics, so the Revd Fiddes went to Glasgow and took classes in midwifery himself. On his return, he was able to persuade the women, and the death of Mary MacDonald in 1891 was the last on the island due to tetanus.

Arrivals and Departures

Even as early as the late 1700s, Hiort became a place to visit, and it became the done thing to write about 'My Visit to St Kilda'. If few of the vistors really understood what they saw there, that did not reduce the popularity of their books.

Some visitors were beneficial to the island community, like Acland who gave assistance in rebuilding the village, but in general the influence of the visitors was prejudicial, encouraging the Hiortaich to rely on the bounty of visitors, and even worse, encouraging them to play up to their expectations. One visitor commented on a Hiortach man, who visited a yacht, and seeing

59. An intrepid visitor – Miss Heathcote on Dun

a mirror, hunted for the man behind it, as if he had never seen a mirror before; yet he was one of the few Hiortaich of the day to be clean-shaven himself.

Colin MacDonald, in his *Highland Journey*[160] tells of going ashore on St Kilda along with a new district nurse:

> When it came to going ashore, the Gaelic-speaking quartette got into a small boat in charge of a white-whiskered native and a youth – both wearing cheese-cutter caps. Now there was nothing in our external appearance to suggest to the boatmen that we were anything but just four of the sassunach 'towrists', and we never said a revealing word. The nurse had a grand sense of humour and was

idolised by her patients, but it must be admitted that whatever Fate it is which confers beauty on mankind at birth must have been on vacation on her natal day. Not the most biased of fond parents could call her facially well-favoured: far, far from it! But no one knew that better than herself and little did it bother her! As we were being rowed ashore, the youth sized us up with a stealthy glance and then, gazing at the sky as if discussing the weather, said to the older man 'Ciod e chuiridh sinn orra, saoil sibh?' (What will we charge them, do you think?)

The ancient then had a look at the sky and said hopefully 'Fiachaidh sinn da thasdan' (We'll try two shillings) – and promptly placed his inverted cheese-cutter in front of the nurse, with the announcement 'Two shillings, mem'. 'Two shillings!' exclaimed the nurse in horror, and her best English accent – 'What for?' There followed heated protests on both sides, but the nurse was adamant; she would give a shilling and not a penny more! At last the mariner gave up the unfair contest (he was at a heavy disadvantage with the language) and speaking in his native tongue, gave vent to the cryptic soliloquy – 'A Dhia! Nach e an te ghrannd tha cruaidh!' (God! Isn't it the ugly one that is hard!). Retorted the ugly one: 'Ma tha mi grannd, a dhuine, tha mi onarach' (If I'm ugly, man, at least I'm honest). Never have I seen an island gentleman so distressed and embarrassed – and we got off for the shilling!

One visitor who caused havoc in a different way was Robert Campbell of Shawfield. He was of the party of Henry, Lord Brougham, who visited the island as part of a cruise in 1799. Brougham was much impressed by the island, but not by the Hiortaich.

> The view of this village is truly unique. Nothing in Captain Cook's voyages comes half so low. The natives are savage in due proportion; the air is infected by a stench almost insupportable – a compound of rotten fish, filth of all sorts and stinking sea-fowl . . . A total want of curiosity, a stupid gaze of wonder, an excessive eagerness for spirits and tobacco, a laziness to be conquered by the hope of the above-mentioned cordials, and a beastly degree of filth, the natural consequence of this, render the St Kildian character truly savage –[161]

We have no record of what the Hiortaich though of Lord Brougham. But we do know what one of the Hiortaich girls thought of Campbell:

Mo ghaol oigear a' chuil duinn
Air 'n ghabh mi loinn 's mi og,
Dhurichdhinn duit pog 'san anmoch
Ged robh cach ga sheanchas oirnn

Cha'n ioghnadh mise 'bhi uallach,
On a thainig an duin' uasal,
Tha do ribeanan mu'n cuairt domh,
'S cumaidh iad mo ghruag air doigh.

'S gu'n robh Iain MacGilliosa
Anns an fhoghar rium a' fidreach,
Ach o'n thainig an t-Iarl Ileach,
Cha 'n eisd mi ri 'bhriodal beoil.

Sguiridh mi 'shugradh nan gillean,
Cha 'n fhuiling mi rium am mireadh;
O'n tha 'n Caimbeulach ga m' shireadh
Cha teid mi tuilleadh 'nan coir.
Mo ghaol oigear a' chul duinn[162]

My love of the brown locks / That I fell in love with while I was
young / I wish to kiss you in the evening / Even if the others would
whisper about us / No wonder if I am proud / Since the gentleman
came / Your ribbons surround me / And hold my hair nicely / It
was John Gillies / Who was wooing me in the autumn / But since
the Lord from Islay came / I will not listen to his fond words / I
will stop courting the lads / I do not like their wooing / Because
Campbell is seeking me / I will not go with them any more / My
love of the brown locks.

There are many versions of this song; this one was published in the
Transactions of the Gaelic Society of Inverness for 1880. Let us hope
that Campbell did not turn her head permanently, and that she
returned to Iain MacGhilliosa.

In 1852 eight families left Hiort to join the *Priscilla* on their way to
settle in Australia. There were thirty-six in the party altogether, and
it appears that they were among the strongest families on the island,
or at least those whose children had shown the most resistance to
the infantile tetanus. They went to Australia as an advance party to
set up a base for the others. The reason for their planning to leave at
this time is not clear; some say it was because of the trouble in the

Church: the islanders had joined the Free Church, but the church buildings still belonged to the established Church of Scotland, but we have to remember also that Hiort, as the rest of Scotland, had been affected by potato blight, which had destroyed the basic food-source of so many communities.

Tetanus had not been the only disease to affect the Hiortach; even in Martin Martin's time they were liable to Cnatan nan Gall – the boat-cough. They told Martin that they were affected by it every time strangers came to the island, and although he does not seem to have believed them, its effect seems to have been real enough, and the boat-cough even appears as a cause of death in the early registers. Clearly, it was a case of an infection to which they were not accustomed, and to which they had no immunity.

The emigrants on the *Priscilla* succumbed to the same type of danger. Measles broke out on board, and none of them had ever been in contact with measles before. Less than half the party reached land in Australia, dying either on board or in quarantine off Melbourne from the after-effects of measles. When word of this disaster reached Hiort, all thoughts of emigration were understandably dropped.

There is another link with Australia, though less direct. Thomas Dyke Acland, whom we noticed already as encouraging the building of new houses in the village, had a yacht which he called the *Lady of St Kilda,* in which he made his visit to the island in 1834. In 1840 she was sold to an Australian merchant and taken there. On one occasion she was stranded off a beach near Melbourne, which was later called the St Kilda foreshore after her, and when the area was developed as a suburb of the city, the name St Kilda was retained; the Hiortach emigrants who came ashore in Melbourne thus found an area there named after their native island!

Conachair and An Gleann Mor

From the village there is a steep climb up to the valley of An Lag bho Thuath, the north valley. Here there is a series of stone-walled enclosures which the National Trust for Scotland insist are sheep pens although they quite certainly are not; the walls are built with the sheer face on the outside and the slope on the inside, and so must have been intended to keep sheep out, rather than in. It is likely that, as with most other considerable stone-work on Hiort, they belong to the time of the Revd Neil MacKenzie, perhaps as enclosures for growing early crops, since they face south and are built over old cultivation beds.

From An Lag you climb again, only to find that the slope suddenly ends in a sheer cliff of over 800 feet. It is difficult to appreciate the height from the top, but if you can take a boat trip along the base of the cliff you then realise the sheerness of the cliff, with black volcanic dykes running along its face, and caves at the waterline.

Once you have recovered your balance, you can walk along the cliff edge on to the slopes of the Aird Uachdarachd – the Upper Headland – where it is said that one of the cliff stacs was originally a natural arch, but a ship fleeing from the wreck of the Spanish Armada tried to shelter against the cliff, caught her mast on the bridge of the arch and brought it down in ruins, sinking the ship and leaving the remains of the arch as an isolated stac.

Another climb and you reach the top of Conachair, which, when I was last there, still held the propeller of a plane which had crashed on that spot. The visitor cannot but be impressed with the cliffs of Conachair, dropping 1400 feet to the sea; I remember being there on one occasion when there was a strong wind and a heavy sea running. We were lying on the short turf on the top of the cliff, looking over and down to the sea below – I would not recommend standing in that situation – and being vaguely aware that something was not right. After a time that we realised that despite the heavy seas we could see breaking white at the foot of the cliff, we were hearing no sound of them – the noise was being carried away by the wind before it could reach us!

Over the slopes of Mullach Mor you come to An Gleann Mor – the Great Glen. If you keep to the cliff edge you come to Gob na h-Airde, the point of the headland, which has a natural tunnel running right through the headland; I think this tunnel is one of the most frightening places I have ever been in. The rock underfoot is polished by the action of the waves, and when a swell crashes against the mouth of the tunnel and rushes through at your feet, there is nothing to cling to but the walls of the tunnel itself. The seals enjoy the swell, and often flash past you in the rushing stream, to turn

60. The Amazon's house

and 'bottle-up' when they reach Glen Bay, as if they were laughing at the intruder into their realm.

Like Sulaisgeir to the north of Lewis, where the Ness-men go to gather the gugas, it is a place that I am very glad to have been, but very glad not to have to go to again. It is strange that both places are connected with gannets, for the mouth of the tunnel at Gob na h-Airde has a beautiful view out to Boirearaigh and the stacs where the gannets nest – if you can take your eyes away from the rushing water at your feet.

At the far end of the tunnel you come to Tobar nam Buadh – the well of virtues – a stone-built well of beautiful cold water, and beyond it Taigh na Bana-Ghaisgich: the female warrior, or Amazon's, house. According to Martin Martin:

> This Amazon is famous in their Traditions; Her House or Dairy of Stone is yet extant; some of the Inhabitants dwell in it all Summer though it be some Hundred Years old; the Whole is built of stones, without any Wood, Lime, Earth or Mortar to cement it . . . The Body of this House contains not above Nine Persons sitting; there are three Beds or low Vaults at the side of the Wall, which contains five Men each and are separated by a Pillar; at the Entry to one of these low Vaults is a Stone standing on one end; upon this she is reported ordinarily to have laid her Helmet; there are two other

Stones on the other side, upon which she is said to have laid her Sword; they tell you she was much addicted to Hunting, and that in her Days all the space betwixt this Isle and that of Harries, was one continued Tract of Dry Land . . . 'Tis said of this Warrior, that she let loose her Grey-hounds after the Deer in St Kilda, making their Course towards the opposite Isles.[163]

We may scoff at such a tradition, but Martin also mentions that a pair of large antlers were found when digging on Oiseabhal.

Remnants of later martial times can also be seen in the Gleann Mor, where the peat-moss at the back of the glen still occasionally throws up parts of a Wellington bomber that was wrecked there during the Second World War.

Mullach Bi and Ruiabhal

West of An Gleann Mor rises the hill of Mullach Bi; here also the hills descend abruptly to the sea, but, unlike the other side of the island, here there are steep slopes, some littered with broken rock, and others with deceptive green slopes, on which one slip would spell disaster. Below Mullach Bi itself is Carn Mor, a scree slope jumbled with broken rocks of all sizes. In among these nest the manx shearwaters and storm petrels, and at night the air is full of the birds, changing shift on their nests, deep in burrows among the rocks. The night is full of their song too; that of the storm petrel is often described as a churring, but to me it is more like the sound of a demented sewing-machine, followed by a hiccup.

Not far from the top of Mullach Bi is the Lover's Stone, a finger of rock projecting from the cliff top, 800 feet above the sea, on which it is said that a lover had to demonstrate his nerve on the cliffs, before being allowed to marry.

Martin Martin describes the ceremony:

Every Batchelor Wooer is, by an antient Custom, obliged in Honour to give a Specimen of his Affection for the Love of his Mistress, and it is thus: He is to stand on his left Foot, having the one Half of it over the Rock, he then draws the right Foot toward the left, and in this Posture bowing, puts both his Fists further out to the right Foot; after he has performed this, he has acquired no small Reputation, being ever after accounted worthy [of] the finest Woman in the

61. On the Mistress Stone

World; They firmly believe the Atchievement is always attended
with the desired Success.[164]

In a community whose food supply depended on dexterity on the
cliff ledges, it may well be that some kind of test of nerve was
required before a man was allowed to marry and start a family; the
test on this Lover's Stone is not nearly as difficult as it sounds, for
it is possible to walk on to the stone from the cliff-face, although it
does require a good head for heights and an ability to avoid looking
down to the sea, far below.

Unfortunately the stone shown by the National Trust and marked
on the Ordnance Survey maps is the wrong one: Martin Martin
describes the correct stone exactly.

In the Face of the Rock, South from the Town, is the famous
Stone, known by the Name of the Mistress Stone; it resembles a
Door exactly, and is in the very Front of this Rock, which is twenty

or thirty Fathom perpendicular in height, the Figure of it being discernable about the Distance of a Mile.[165]

Martin's description makes it clear that the Mistress Stone is on Ruiabhal, the southernmost point of the island. Here a stone is balanced across the top of a gap in the rocks, forming, as Martin says, a lintel across a doorway – and the only way up to it is through the 'doorway into nothing'. It is not nearly as high as the stone on Mullach Bi, but I can assure you that it is much scarier, both to get to, and to be on.

The Pier

Our circuit of the island has brought us back to the landing place at Village Bay. But if it is a place of arrival, it is also a place of departure, and it was from here that the Hiortaich finally left in 1930. The population had never recovered from the loss of the families who went to Australia in 1852, for the incidence of tetanus meant that they were unable to raise enough children to make up the deficiency. Even in 1886 Connell reports that:

> The opinion in favour of emigration was almost unanimous, the only dissentients being one or two old men, whom it would be folly to ask to go to a new settlement at their time of life.[166]

As contact with the outside world became easier, there was more opportunity, and more inducement, for young people to leave. The shortage of working population led to a greater reliance on assistance from outside, and for many years the main source of income was the bounty of well-meaning but misguided visitors.

In 1922 Lord Leverhulme proposed to evacuate the Hiortaich to his new port of Leverburgh, but although they initially agreed to his plan, they were persuaded by Neil Ferguson, their leader and postmaster, to reject it. The Revd Finlay MacQueen, a descendant of one of the 1852 emigrants to Australia, visited the island in 1928 and tried to persuade the remaining Hiortaich to come to Australia, but they preferred to remain where they were.

Two years later, they had no choice. Only thirty-six people were left on the island, and of these ten belonged to the MacKinnon family, who had decided to leave, whatever the rest might do. It would clearly be impossible for the rest to survive on the island, and in 1930 they petitioned the government to take them off.

> We, the undersigned the natives of St Kilda, hereby respectfully pray and petition H. M. Government to assist us all to leave the island this year, and to find homes and occupations for us on the mainland. For some years the manpower has been decreasing, now the total population is reduced to thirty-six. Several men out of this number have definitely made up our minds to go away this year to seek employment on the mainland, this will really cause a crisis, as the present number are hardly sufficient to carry on the necessary work of the place. These men are the mainstay of the island at present, as they tend the sheep, do the weaving and look after the general welfare of the widows. Should they leave the conditions of the rest of the community would be such that it would be impossible for us to remain on the island another winter.
>
> The reason why assistance is necessary is, that for many years Saint Kilda has not been self supporting, and with no facilities to better our position, we are therefore without the means to pay for the costs of removing ourselves and furniture elsewhere.
>
> We do not ask to be settled together as a separate community, but in the meantime we would collectively be very grateful of assistance, and transference elsewhere, where there would be a better opportunity of securing our livelihood.[167]

The government responded, finding houses and work for most of the families near Lochaline in Argyll; others moved to near Inverness and to Kincardine-on-Forth. On 29 August 1930, the *Harebell* took the remaining Hiortaich away from the island, and its history as a community was at an end.

Visitors to the island now can marvel at the majesty of the cliffs and the huge colonies of birds, but we cannot appreciate what the islands were once like. I myself know the difference in visiting the island of Tarasaigh since the people left – and how much greater is the difference in Hiort. We can look and try to visualise, but we cannot understand.

EPILOGUE

So there is my selection of tales and old stories from Harris.

Are all the stories true? Well, the best I can do is to quote Tormod Alasdair in Beudarsaig. He was a good story-teller, and one night he was in full flood with a yarn. When he was finished, the local missionary, who was visiting also, asked him: 'Now, Thormoid, was that story true?' Tormod had a puff or two at his pipe while he thought about it: 'Well, yes. It was absolutely true – when it started!' As he said another time, 'A good story never was worse for getting better!'

My excuse has to be the old Gaelic saying 'Ma 's breug bhuam e, is breug h-ugam e' – If it is a lie coming from me, it was a lie coming to me!'

APPENDIX

Gaelic names

Gaelic placenames have been used throughout the main text of this book, partly because that is the natural language of the island, and partly because of the great variety of English versions of the names, as can be seen in the quotations throughout. The problem is of course that they are mainly Norse derivatives, pronounced in Gaelic, and then written down in English. In most places we have used the names as spelled on the Ordnance Survey maps, except where these differ materially from local usage.

Gaelic personal names have been used also, especially in patronymics, which are often untranslatable. Rather than burden the reader with continual attempts at translation throughout the text, we have added a list of the more common names and their equivalents.

The standard form of patronymic is 'A mac B mhic C' – A son of B son of C – but the later parts of the name are in the genitive case, which can involve a change of spelling in Gaelic, so this also is given. 'Mac' means 'son of' but 'mhic' (pronounced 'vic') means 'of the son of', and 'nic' or 'ni'n' means daughter of'. Where patronymics are quoted from old documents, the originals are frequently written in pidgin-Gaelic, that is Gaelic as written down in English by a non-Gaelic speaker.

Gaelic	Patronymic	English
Ailean	mac Ailein	Allan
Ailig	mac Ailig	Alec
Alasdair	mac Alasdair	Alexander
Aonghas	mac Aonghais	Angus
Cailean	mac Chailein	Colin
Calum	mac Chaluim	Malcolm
Crisdean	mac Chrisdein	Christopher
Coinneach	mac Choinnich	Kenneth
Domhnall	mac Dhomhnaill	Donald

Donnchadh	mac Dhonnchaidh	Duncan
Dughall	mac Dhughaill	Dugald
Eoghann	mac Eoghainn	Ewen
Fearchar	mac Fhearchair	Farquhar
Feargus	mac Fhearguis	Fergus
Fionnlagh	mac Fhionnlaigh	Finlay
Iain	mac Iain	John
Iomhar	mac Iomhair	Evander (Ivor)
Lachlan	mac Lachlainn	Lachlan
Manus	mac Mhanuis	Magnus
Murchadh	mac Mhurchaidh	Murdo(ch)
Niall	mac Neill	Neil
Padraig	mac Phadraig	Peter (Patrick)
Raonall	mac Raonaill	Ranald
Ruairidh	mac Ruairidh	Roderick
Seumas	mac Sheumais	James
Seocdhan	mac Sheocdhain	Jock
Seonaidh	mac Sheonaidh	Johnnie
Somhairle	mac Shomhairle	Sam(uel)
Tormod	mac Thormoid	Norman
Uilleam	mac Uilleim	William
Uisdean	mac Uisdein	Hugh
Anna	mac Anna	Ann
Bessa	mac Bessa	Bess
Cairistiona	mac Cairistiona	Christina
Catriona	mac Catriona	Catherine
Ceit	mac Ceit	Kate
Ciorstag	mac Ciorstag	Kirsty
Oighric	mac Oighric	Effie
Fannag	mac Fannag	Fanny
Lecsaidh	mac Lecsaidh	Lexy
Magaidh	mac Magaidh	Maggie
Mairead	mac Maireid	Margaret
Mairi	mac Mairi	Mary

REFERENCES

1   Robert Heron, *A General View of the Hebrides*, Edinburgh 1794, p. 18
2   Bill Lawson, *St Clement's Church at Rodel*, Northton 1991, p. 20
3   J. L. Buchanan *Travels in the Western Hebrides*, London 1793, p. 68
4   *The MacDonald Collection of Gaelic Poetry*, Inverness 1911, p. 180
5   Draft Lease of Luskinder, National Library of Scotland – Charter 413
6   Published in *Chi Mi'n Tir*, Bill Lawson Publications, Northton 1996, p. 23
7   Alexander Carmichael, Journal 1870, p9
8   Statistical Account of Scotland, Vol 10, Edinburgh 1794, p. 354
9   'Oran a Chianalas' in *Leabhar nan Gleann*, ed. G Henderson 1898, p. 52
10 *Leabhar nan Gleann*, ed. G Henderson 1898, p. 96
11 *Celtic Magazine*, Vol 4, 1879, p. 185
12 Quoted in *The Isle of Taransay* by Bill Lawson, Northton 1997, p. 12
13 Duncan Shaw to Select Committee on Emigration (Scotland) 1841
14 *Inverness Courier* July 1839, in Inverness Public Library
15 Duncan Shaw to Select Committee on Emigration (Scotland) 1841
16 Highlands and Islands Commission 1884, p1177
17 Highlands and Islands Commission 1884, p1187
18 Highlands and Islands Commission 1884, p1185 (summarised)
19 Published in *Chi Mi'n Tir*, Bill Lawson Publications, Northton 1996, p. 27
20 Finlay J. MacDonald, *Crowdie and Cream*, London 1982
21 New Statistical Account of Scotland, Vol 14, Edinburgh 1845, p. 156
22 New Statistical Account of Scotland, Vol 14, Edinburgh 1845, p. 158
23 *The MacDonald Collection of Gaelic Poetry*, Inverness 1911, p. 137
24 *The MacDonald Collection of Gaelic Poetry*, Inverness 1911, p. 141
25 *Leabhar nan Gleann*, ed. G Henderson 1898, p. 53
26 Donald Morrison, *Traditions of the Western Isles*, p. 325 (summarised)
27 Quoted in Magnus MacLean, *The Literature of the Celts*, London 1906, p. 105
28 *Inverness Courier* March 1846, in Inverness Public Library
29 Bill Lawson *St Clement's Church at Rodel*, Northton 1991, p. 22
30 William Bald's Map of Harris, 1804
31 Royal Commission (Highlands and Islands) 1892, Vol 2, p. 1025
32 William MacGillivray *A Hebridean Naturalist's Journal 1817–1818* ed R. Ralph, 1996
33 Martin Martin *Description of the Western Isles of Scotland* 1703, p. 49
34 Martin Martin *Description of the Western Isles of Scotland* 1703, p. 49
35 Alexander Carmichael, Journal 1870, p. 7
36 Alexander Carmichael, Journal 1870, p. 7

37 Harris Estate Rental, 1724, in Dunvegan Papers

38 A more full version of this story appears in *The Isle of Taransay*, Bill Lawson Northton, 1997

39 Alexander Carmichael, Journal 1870, p. 11

40 Highlands and Islands Commission 1884, p. 1196

41 *Reader's Digest*, November 1978, p. 203

42 Harris Estate accounts 1753, in Dunvegan Papers

43 Documents of Sale of Leverhulme Estate, Knight, Frank & Rutley, 1925

44 *I Crossed the Minch*, Louis MacNiece, 1938, p. 82

45 *Scottish Home Industries*, undated, p. 71

46 *Leabhar nan Gleann*, ed. G Henderson 1898, p. 92

47 Translation in *Celtic Law*, John Cameron, 1937, p. 225

48 *Celtic Magazine* Vol 2, 1887, p. 382

49 *Scottish Home Industries*, undated, p. 68

50 More full details in *Royal Commission for Ancient and Historic Monuments – Western Isles*, 1927, p. 34

51 *St Clement's Church at Rodel*, Bill Lawson, Northton, 1991

52 Martin Martin, *Desription of the Western Isles*, 1703, p. 37

53 John Knox *A Tour through the Highlands and Hebrides* in 1786, p. 158

54 Harris-North Uist Boundary Dispute, Session Papers Vol 161, 1770

55 Highlands and Islands Commission 1884, p. 1174

56 Highlands and Islands Commission 1884, p. 1201

57 Highlands and Islands Commission 1884, p. 1171

58 Highlands and Islands Commission 1884, p. 1187

59 *Gaelic Songs of Mary MacLeod*, J Carmichael Watson, 1965, p. 20

60 Harris-North Uist Boundary Dispute, Session Papers Vol 161, 1770, p. 123

61 Judicial Rental of Harris, 1724 Dunvegan Papers

62 Harris-North Uist Boundary Dispute, Session Papers Vol 161, 1770, p. 18

63 Harris-North Uist Boundary Dispute, Session Papers Vol 161, 1770, p. 191

64 Told by Iain Ruairidh (Ferguson), Bearnaraigh

65 Royal Commission (Highlands and Islands) 1892, p. 1002

66 Highlands and Islands Commission 1884, p. 1187

67 *Oran Fuinn is Cladaich*, Murdo Morrison, Cape Breton; Glasgow 1931, p. 20

68 Harris Estate Rental 1698, Dunvegan Papers

69 *Celtic Magazine* 1880, Vol 5, p. 457

70 *Leabhar nan Gleann*, ed. G Henderson 1898, p. 54

71 Harris-North Uist Boundary Dispute, Session Papers Vol 161, 1770, p. 210

72 *The Apostle of the North*, Rev John Kennedy, 1978, p. 224

73 *The Teampull on the Isle of Pabbay*, Bill Lawson, Northton, 1994, p. 27

74 *Leabhar nan Gleann*, ed. G Henderson 1898, p. 54

75 Quote by W. Matheson in *Transactions of the Gaelic Society of Inverness*, Vol 46, 1969

76 *Our Journey to the Hebrides*, J & E Pennell, London 1890

77 *The Scottish Highlander*, 6th June 1889

78 *Lord of the Isles*, Nigel Nicolson, 1960, p. 214

79 John Knox *A Tour through the Highlands and Hebrides in 1786*, p. 170

80 Documents of Sale of Leverhulme Estate, Knight, Frank & Rutley, 1925

81 *I Crossed the Minch*, Louis MacNiece, 1938, p. 62

82 Draft Lease of Luskinder, National Library of Scotland – Charter 413

83 J L Buchanan *Travels in the Western Hebrides*, London 1793, p. 61

84 Donald Morrison, *Traditions of the Western Isles*, p. 95

85 Highlands and Islands Commission 1884, p. 1193

86 Report in *The Graphic*, London, 1883

87 Fourth Report of Congested Districts Board, 1902, p. xxi

88 Published in *Chi Mi'n Tir*, Bill Lawson Publications, Northton 1996, p. 9

89 Published in *Chi Mi'n Tir*, Bill Lawson Publications, Northton 1996, p. 5

90 Re-told in *The Isle of Taransay*, Bill Lawson, Northton, 1997, p. 13

91 Highlands and Islands Commission 1884, p. 852

92 Quoted by R. Balfour, *Highland and Island Emigration* in Transactions of the Gaelic Society of Inverness, Vol 57, 1993, p. 459

93 Report on Crofter Colonisation in Canada, 1890, p. 19

94 Report on Crofter Colonisation in Canada, 1891, pp. 8 & 11

95 Highlands and Islands Commission 1884, pp. 1021–1023 (Summarised)

96 *The Lyon in Mourning* Vol 1., Scottish History Society 1895, p. 193

97 Highlands and Islands Commission 1884, p. 1171

98 W. C. MacKenzie *History of the Outer Hebrides*, p. 599

99 Royal Commission (Highlands and Islands) 1892, p. 1032

100 Royal Commission (Highlands and Islands) 1892, p. 1036

101 Lewis-Harris Boundary Dispute, Scottish Record Office GD274/37/19 p. 33

102 Royal Commission (Highlands and Islands) 1892, p. 1036

103 Story from John Murdo Morrison, Harris Hotel, An Tairbeart

104 Highlands and Islands Commission 1884, p. 1166

105 Martin Martin, *Description of the Western Isles*, 1703, p. 33

106 Published in *Chi Mi'n Tir*, Bill Lawson Publications, Northton 1996, p4–0

107 Lewis-Harris Boundary Dispute, Scottish Record Office GD274/37/19 p. 49

108 Lewis-Harris Boundary Dispute, Scottish Record Office GD274/37/19 p. 14

109 Lewis-Harris Boundary Dispute, Scottish Record Office GD274/37/19 p. 18

110 Lewis-Harris Boundary Dispute, Scottish Record Office GD274/37/19 p. 25

111 Lewis-Harris Boundary Dispute, Scottish Record Office GD274/37/19 p. 74

112 Lewis-Harris Boundary Dispute, Scottish Record Office GD274/37/19 p. 72

113 Royal Commission (Highlands and Islands) 1892, p1035

114 Harris Estate Rental 1680 in Dunvegan Papers

115 Martin Martin, *Description of the Western Isles*, 1703, p. 35

116 Harris Estate Rental 1684 in Dunvegan Papers

117 Harris Estate Rental 1698 in Dunvegan Papers

118 Martin Martin, *Description of the Western Isles*, 1703, p. 40

119 Martin Martin, *Description of the Western Isles*, 1703, p. 40

120 Harris Estate Rental 1754 in Dunvegan Papers

121 Harris Esate Rental (Undated) in Dunvegan Papers

122 *Celtic Magazine* 1878, Vol 3, p. 222

123 Royal Commission (Highlands and Islands) 1892, p. 1036

124 Wreck Cove Graveyard, St Anns, Cape Breton

125 Highlands and Islands Commission 1884, p. 1176

126 Martin Martin, *Description of the Western Isles*, 1703, p. 31

127 Harris Estate Rental 1680 in Dunvegan Papers

128 The *MacDonald Collection of Gaelic Poetry*, Inverness 1911, p. 258

129 The *Lyon in Mourning* Vol 1, Scottish History Society 1895, p. 166

130 The *Lyon in Mourning* Vol 2, Scottish History Society 1895, p. 100

131 Will of Donald Campbell

132 Version from *Naigheachdan Firinneach*, Vol 2, by 'Fionn' 1907 p. 33

133 *Celtic Magazine* Vol 2, 1877, p. 382

134 J. L. Buchanan *Travels in the Western Hebrides*, London 1793, p. 55

135 John Knox *A Tour through the Highlands and Hebrides in 1786*, p. 167

136 Highlands and Islands Commission 1884, p. 1174

137 Published in *Chi Mi'n Tir*, Bill Lawson Publications, Northton 1996, p. 413

138 *Sloinneadh* le Aonad Bhidio Haldane, Steornabhagh

139 Published in *Chi Mi'n Tir*, Bill Lawson Publications, Northton 1996, p. 24

140 *The Life and Death of St Kilda* Tom Steele 1975 (paperback edition)

141 *Manuscript History of the MacDonalds* Iona Club, 1839 p. 297

142 Charter by John of Isla 1346/1372 Acts of the Lords of the Isles, SHS1986

143 Mary Harman *An Isle called Hirte* 1997

144 Martin Martin *A Late Voyage to St Kilda*, 1698, p. 91

145 Martin Martin *A Late Voyage to St Kilda*, 1698, p. 13

146 Martin Martin *A Late Voyage to St Kilda*, 1698, p. 71

147 Martin Martin *A Late Voyage to St Kilda*, 1698, p. 132

148 A Buchan *A Description of St Kilda*, 1727, p. 24

149 A Buchan *A Description of St Kilda*, 1727, p. 40

150 A Buchan *A Description of St Kilda*, 1727, p. 40

151 Martin Martin *A Late Voyage to St Kilda*, 1698, p. 155

152 *St Kilda and its Church*, Bill Lawson Publications, Northton 1993 p. 15

153 *Life of Rev Neil MacKenzie at St Kilda*, 1911, p. 31

154 *The Apostle of the North*, Revd J Kennedy 1978, p. 239

155 *Life of Rev Neil MacKenzie at St Kilda*, 1911, p. 31

156 *St Kilda and the St Kildians*, Robert Connell 1887, p. 36

157 *St Kilda and the St Kildians*, Robert Connell 1887, p. 84

158 *St Kilda and the St Kildians*, Robert Connell 1887, p. 90
159 *St Kilda and the St Kildians*, Robert Connell 1887, p. 100
160 *Highland Journey*, Colin MacDonald 1943, p. 85
161 *Life and Times*, Lord Brougham, p. 105
162 Transactions of the Gaelic Society of Inverness, Vol 9, 1881, p. 22
163 Martin Martin *A Late Voyage to St Kilda*, 1698, p. 22
164 Martin Martin *A Late Voyage to St Kilda*, 1698, p. 119
165 Martin Martin *A Late Voyage to St Kilda*, 1698, p. 118
166 *St Kilda and the St Kildians*, Robert Connell 1887, p. 162
167 Quoted in *St Kilda and its Church*, Bill Lawson Publications 1993, p. 37

PICTURE CREDITS

The illustrations in the book are taken mainly from slides taken by the author in the late 1960s and early 1970s, and from the collection of old post-cards gathered by the late Bob Charnley. Details of these and the other illustrations are shown below.

1. Clach MhicLeoid
   Bill Lawson

2. Nightfall at Losgaintir
   from *Searching the Hebrides with a Camera*, by A. A. MacGregor, London 1923

3. Seilibost and Beinn Losgaintir
   Bob Charnley Collection

4. Horgabost
   Bill Lawson

5. The old farm-house at Sgarasta Bheag
   from *Searching the Hebrides with a Camera*, by A. A. MacGregor, London 1923

6. Clach Steineagaidh
   Bill Lawson

7. Ceapabhal
   Bill Lawson

8. Bronze Age site and pottery at Taobh Tuath
   from *The Archaeology of Skye and the Western Isles,* by Ian Armit, Edinburgh, 1996

9. Teampall na h-Uidhe
   Bill Lawson

10. Taobh Tuath
    Bill Lawson

11. Drying tweed and fleece at an Taigh Sgoile, Taobh Tuath
    Bob Charnley Collection

12. *Seallam!* Visitor Centre
    Bill Lawson

13. Cladh Che on Tarasaigh
    Bill Lawson

14. Diagram of corn-mill
    Bill Lawson

15. Taking the peats home on Tarasaigh
     Bill Lawson

16. Caol na Hearadh
     from *Searching the Hebrides with a Camera*, by A. A. MacGregor,
     London 1923

17. The Old Smiddy at An t-Ob
     Bob Charnley Collection

18. An Clachan an An t-Ob
     Bob Charnley Collection

19. St Clement's at Roghadal
     from *Afoot in Wild Places*, by Seton Gordon, London 1937

20. Tomb of Alasdair Crotach MacLeod in Roghadal
     from *The Proceedings of the Society of Antiquaries of Scotland,* Vol 7
     1884

21. View of St Clement's, Roghadal
     as above

22. Rodel Hotel
     Bob Charnley Collection

23. The Gunnery of MacLeod of Bearnaraigh
     from *Searching the Hebrides with a Camera*, by A. A. MacGregor,
     London 1923

24. Landing Peats at Bearnaraigh
     from *Afoot in Wild Places,* by Seton Gordon, London 1937

25. At Bay Lochs, Bearnaraigh
     from *Afoot in Wild Places*, by Seton Gordon, London 1937

26. Teampall Mhoire, on Pabaigh
     Bill Lawson

27. Ruins of house on Pabaigh
     Bill Lawson

28. An Tairbeart
     from *West-Over-Sea*, by D. D. Pochin Mould, Edinburgh 1953

29. An Tairbeart
     Bob Charnley Collection

30. West Loch, An Tairbeart
     Bob Charnley Collection

31. Harris Hotel
     Bob Charnley Collection

32. Duncan MacAskill's shop in An Tairbeart
     Bob Charnley Collection

33. Pier Road, An Tairbeart
    Bob Charnley Collection

34. Peat-cutting at Stiocleit
    from *The Islands of Scotland*, by Hugh MacDiarmid, London 1939

35. Mol Ban at Cliubhair
    Bill Lawson

36. The rocky landscape of the Bays – Loch Stocinis
    Bill Lawson

37. Taking home the peats
    from *The Isle of Lewis and Harris*, by A Geddes, Edinburgh 1955

38. Geocrab
    Bill Lawson

39. 'Finsbay Lodge'
    Bob Charnley Collection

40. Collecting the mail at Fionnsbhagh
    from *The Islands of Scotland*, by Hugh MacDiarmid, London 1939

41. The emigrant ship HMS *Hercules*

42. The hills of North Harris
    Bob Charnley Collection

43. The bridge at Ceann an Ora
    from *Behold the Hebrides*, by A A MacGregor, Edinburgh 1925

44. Spinning wool at Aird Asaig
    Bob Charnley Collection

45. Dyeing wool at Aird Asaig
    Bob Charnley Collection

46. Bunabhainneadar
    Bill Lawson

47. Whaling station at Bunabhainneadar
    Bob Charnley Collection

48. Abhainnsuidhe Castle
    Bob Charnley Collection

49. The village of Scarp
    from *The Isle of Lewis and Harris,* by A Geddes, Edinburgh 1955

50. Taking the peats home to Scarp
    from *The Islands of Scotland*, by Hugh MacDiarmid, London 1939

51. Loch Siophort, from the Lewis border
    Bob Charnley Collection

52. Loch Maraig
    Bill Lawson

53. Urgha
   Bill Lawson

54. Harbour at Scalpaigh
   Bill Lawson

55. *Hercules* at Scalpaigh
   Bill Lawson

56. Pier at Scalpaigh
   Bill Lawson

57. The old village at St Kilda by Sir Thomas Dyke Acland
   from *St Kilda Portraits*, by David Quine, 1988

58. The Village Street, St Kilda
   Bob Charnley Collection

59. An intrepid visitor – Miss Heathcote on Dun
   from *St Kilda*, by Norman Heathcote, London 1900

60. The Amazon's house
   Bill Lawson

61. On the Mistress Stone
   Bill Lawson

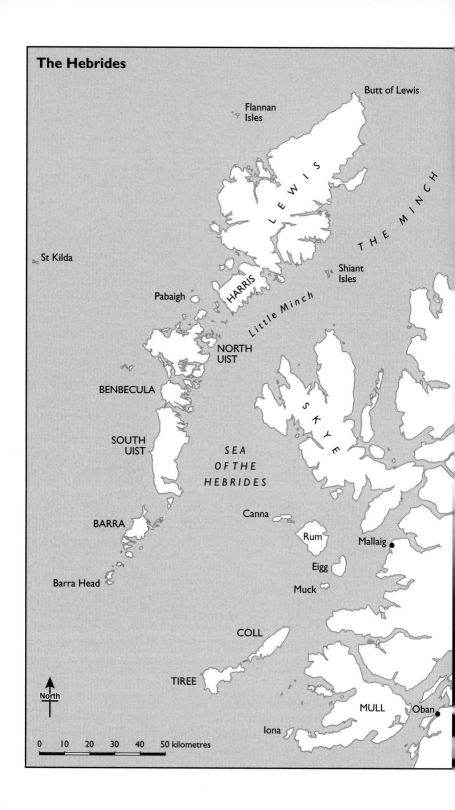

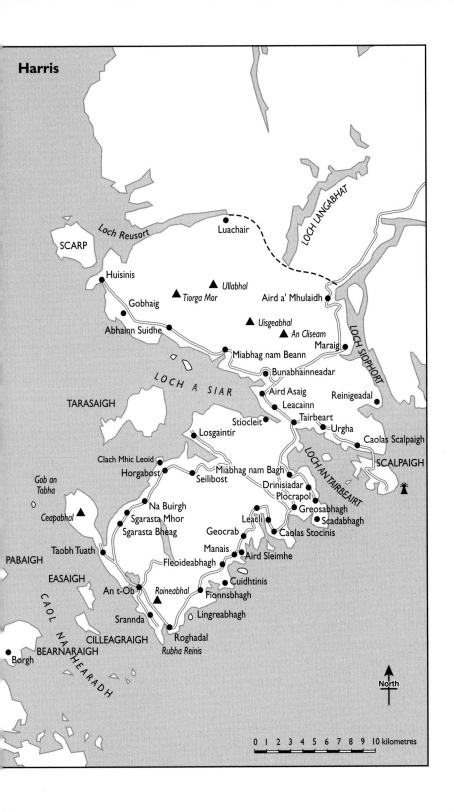

INDEX OF PERSONS

Barlow, Captain 143–145
Buchan, Alexander 190–191
Buchanan, John Lane 3–4, 105

Campbell, Anna of Scalpaigh 52, 177
Campbell, Donald of Scalpaigh 40, 174–177
Campbell, John, forester 163–164, 174
Campbell, Kenneth of Scalpaigh 150–151, 177–180
Campbell, Kenneth of Tarasaigh 19, 41, 43, 147
Carmichael, Alexander 8, 39, 40, 43
Connell, Robert 195–196, 206

Dunmore, Earl and Countess of 61–63, 149

Hogg, James 4, 150

Knox, John 68, 101

Leverhulme, Lord 54–55, 100, 124, 145, 206

Mac an t-Sronaich 119–120, 157, 162–163, 171
MacAskill, Angus of Cape Breton 79, 129–130
MacAulay, Revd Aulay 18
MacDonald, Finlay J 20, 24
MacDonald, Revd John Norman 22
MacDonald, Revd John of Ferintosh 87–88, 194
MacDonald, John, Factor 72
MacDonald, John of Tarasaigh 46, 47, 92
MacDonald, Kenneth of Sgarasta Mhor 16, 73
MacDonald, Revd Roderick 21
MacDonald, Mrs Sarah 53, 56, 62–64
MacGillivray, William 31, 32, 56
MacIver, Revd John 20
MacKenzie, Dougal & Donald of Manitoba 135–136
MacKenzie, Revd Neil 194
MacKinnon, Alexander of Cape Breton 89–90

MacKinnon, Malcolm of Leacli 119
MacLeod, Alasdair Crotach 28, 29, 64–65, 155
MacLeod, Alexander of Pabaigh 86, 87
MacLeod, Alexander of the Philippines 99–100
MacLeod, Captain Alexander x, 67–70
MacLeod, Donald, The Old Trojan 30, 66, 77–78, 157
MacLeod, Revd John of Harris 9
MacLeod, John of Aird Asaig 17, 72–73, 142
MacLeod Mary, Bardess 62–64
MacLeod, Sir Norman 60, 66, 74–77
MacLeod, Norman of An Tairbeart 95–98, 140
MacLeod, Chief William 65, 86
MacNab, Mrs Peggy 42, 172
MacNeil, Major of Pabaigh 88
MacNiece, Louis 55, 102
MacRa, Alexander, Fear Huisinis 32, 53
Martin John 30, 168
Martin, Martin 38, 67–68, 157, 163, 173, 188–191, 203–206
Matheson, Robert, factor 146, 152, 165
Morrison, Donald, An Sgoilear Ban 23, 111, 150
Morrison, Ewen of Ness 13–14
Morrison, John, Gobha na Hearadh 24, 95, 118–119, 126
Morrison, Murdo of Caolas Scalpaigh 16, 170
Morrison, Murdo of Cape Breton 82–83
Morrison, Neil, Bard Pabach 10, 11, 22, 85, 90–91
Mowat, Farley 49

Pennell, Joseph 93–94

Stewart, Prince Charles Edward 138, 174–176
Stewart, Donald xi, 5, 6, 14, 20

Torrie, Alexander 13

INDEX OF MAIN TOPICS

Agriculture 2, 7, 9, 33, 41

Battles 13, 23, 84–85, 92
Boundary dispute with Lewis 147, 160–162
Boundary dispute with North Uist 70, 76–78, 86

Churches viii, 18, 20–21, 27, 29, 40, 64–67, 85–86, 92–94, 155, 163, 188
Clearance xi, 8, 10, 13, 14–17, 20, 31, 71, 72, 80–82, 89–90, 106, 127, 137, 146, 147
Crofting tenure 7

Deer forest 6, 140, 146–147, 156, 163

Emigration xii, 14, 79, 83, 89–90, 99, 106, 123, 132–137, 167, 200–201

Fisheries x, 54, 68–70, 100, 182–184

Graveyards 3, 8, 18, 38, 66, 85–86, 153, 163, 194

Harris Tweed 61–64, 111, 112
Harris Walkway 107, 114
Hotels 74, 95, 101–103, 129

Jacobite Rebellion 30, 77, 87, 138, 174–176

Kelp xi, 10, 70, 131, 172

Machair 1, 18, 33
Mills 43–44, 110, 124

Napier Commission xii, 45, 70–73, 112, 122, 142, 154, 180

Norsemen viii, 12, 26, 28, 54, 64, 74, 92, 185

Peat 86–87, 108, 116
Prehistoric Sites vii, 12, 19, 26, 27, 40

Resettlement 5, 12, 24, 33, 82–83, 115, 163, 165

Schools 34, 43, 55–56, 148, 191

Tacksmen 2, 46, 53, 61, 81, 96, 105, 190

INDEX OF PLACES

Abhainnsuidhe 148–149
Aird Asaig 140–142
Aird Sleimhe 124–126
An t-Ob 54–60
An Tairbeart 92–105

Bearnaraigh 74–83
Beudarsaig 151–152
Bunabhainneadar 143–146

Caolas Scalpaigh 169–172
Caolas Stocinis 116–117
Ceanndibig 105–107
Cliasamol 147–148
Cliubhair and Collam 115–116
Cuidhtinis 127–130

Direcleit 105–107
Drinisiadar 110–111

Fionnsbhagh 130–136
Fleoideabhagh 127

Geocrab 122–124
Gobhaig 150–151
Greosabhagh 114–115

Horgabost 12–14
Huisinis 152–153

Leacli 117–122
Lingreabhagh 137–139
Losgaintir 1–6
Luachair 156–160

Maraig 163–166
Manais 126
Miabhag nam Bagh 109–110
Miabhag nam Beann 146–147

Na Buirgh 14–17

Pabaigh 83–91
Plocrapol 112

Reinigeadal 167–168
Roghadal 64–74

Scadabhagh 113–114
Scalpaigh 173–185
Scarp 153–156
Sgarasta 18–24
Seilibost 6–11
Srannda 60–64

Taobh Tuath 25–37

Urgha 168–169